Beautiful
WAR

For the soldiers of D Troop, Seventeenth Cavalry,
199th Light Infantry Brigade

Beautiful WAR

Studies in a Dreadful Fascination

Philip D. Beidler

The University of Alabama Press
Tuscaloosa

The University of Alabama Press
Tuscaloosa, Alabama 35487-0380
uapress.ua.edu

Hardcover edition published 2016.
Paperback edition published 2019.
eBook edition published 2016.

Typeface: Adobe Garamond

Cover image: Illustration of the Siberian War, No. 4, *The Japanese Army Defeated the German-Austrian Army Near Usri*, Japanese print illustration, Tokyo: Shobido & Co. [ca. 1919]; Library of Congress Prints and Photographs Division
Cover design: Michele Myatt Quinn

Paperback ISBN: 978-0-8173-5961-4

A previous edition of this book has been catalogued by the Library of Congress as follows:

Library of Congress Cataloging-in-Publication Data
Names: Beidler, Philip D., author.
Title: Beautiful war : studies in a dreadful fascination / Philip D. Beidler.
Description: Tuscaloosa, AL : The University of Alabama Press, [2016] | Includes bibliographical references and index.
Identifiers: LCCN 2016017206 | ISBN 9780817319304 (cloth : alk. paper) | ISBN 9780817390464 (e book)
Subjects: LCSH: War. | War in art. | War in literature. | Collective memory—United States. | Popular culture—United States.
Classification: LCC U21.2 .B386 2016 | DDC 355.02—dc23
LC record available at https://lccn.loc.gov/2016017206

Contents

Figures

Acknowledgments

Many people helped me with the research for and writing of this book, including Donald Anderson, Carmen Burkhalter, Chip Cooper, Catherine Davies, Deng Hongfeng, Melinda Fields, Louel Gibbons, Laurence Goldstein, Luoheng Han, Bob Olin, Mike Robbins, Steven Trout, Bill Ulmer, Pepe Vasquez, Dan Waterman, and the late Staige Blackford. As always, I am, moreover, grateful for the love and support of Ellen and Kat Beidler.

Acknowledgment is made for materials published in *Dalhousie Review*, *Michigan Quarterly Review*, *Military History Magazine*, *Virginia Quarterly Review*, and *War, Literature and the Arts*.

Beautiful WAR

Introduction

A Dreadful Fascination

This book is a study of war and some of its myriad representations in art, history, and memory from the early modern era to the present. Like much of my related work over the years, it has its origins in both personal remembrance and cultural reflection.

In the personal dimension, this work derives from my own experience of combat, now almost fifty years ago, as an armored cavalry platoon leader in the Vietnam War. But beyond that it stems from my deep sense of being a cultural legatee of the history of modern American wars. Indeed, some of my most vivid childhood memories are of small-town Pennsylvania Memorial Days in the late 1940s and early 1950s: of a parade led by the local World War I shell shock victim, followed by an American Legion color guard of younger veterans of the great 1941–1945 conflict; a political worthy invited to make a patriotic speech, a local boy or girl selected to recite "In Flanders Fields." Or of Sundays at the Presbyterian Church in Gettysburg, with President Dwight Eisenhower sometimes in attendance, sitting a few rows back from the pew where Abraham Lincoln had stopped for a moment of prayer on his way to speak the imperishable words of November 17, 1863. Of climbing Little Round Top on the great battlefield itself, or of hiding in the Devil's Den. Or, up in Quaker Valley, of exploring the old stone springhouse my ancestors had helped maintain as a stop on the Underground Railroad.

In the cultural domain, the reflections on the various topics addressed here are the product of ongoing decades of university teaching and writing, with a specialization in American literature that has involved the constant examination of myths of national exceptionalism, of geopolitical mission and providential destiny. As part of coming to terms with my own military experiences, such work led eventually to the contemplation of these themes in their relation to the literature emerging out of the Vietnam War. In this, I should note, I was guided by the example and encouragement of Paul Fussell, author of *The Great War and Modern Memory* and himself a World War II infantry combat veteran, who showed definitively how the literary representations of twentieth-century wars had done much to create the habit of mind we now call modernism. Pursuing my own research and writing on the subject, I wrote book-length studies of war and American cultural mythmaking on topics ranging from World War II to the recent military conflicts in Afghanistan and Iraq.

Here I choose an extended range of cultural examples to address some larger questions about war in its relations to art, history, and memory. They are questions that probably have no answers but are still worth asking. Why do people make art out of war? What is the human fascination with war as a subject of popular culture myth? For all of its sheer irredeemable hideousness and monstrosity, what strange imperatives of instinct and/or imagination provoke us to keep going back to war in history or memory?

I should note some related questions I do not ask. I do not address the origins of war; I indirectly address its biological or cultural imperatives and its political, historical, and technological evolutions. Other authors, such as the late Sir John Keegan and his American counterparts Donald Kagan and Victor Davis Hanson, as well as writers as diverse as Robert O'Connell, Gwynne Dyer, and Barbara Ehrenreich have done this magisterially. Nor do I delve into the philosophical arguments for and against wars or the distinctions between just and unjust wars, although I sometimes comment on the moral complexities of historical and geopolitical motives related to warmaking. Rather, I defer respectfully to a vast historical literature that extends from Augustine and Aquinas through Erasmus, Thoreau, Tolstoy, and Gandhi to the distinguished work in our own time of Michael Walzer, Richard Norman, and others.

Then there is that reflexive, even oxymoronic title. This too, I should explain from the outset, comes from my own evolving attempt—again both as a former combatant and as a professional scholar-critic—to come to terms with the strange, almost perversely "aesthetic" hold of war on memory and imagination. Are there soldiers who have said war is beautiful? Some famous ones—professional warriors, generally—have come close. Robert E. Lee is alleged to have said, while watching the unfolding slaughter of repeated Union charges against his entrenched Confederates at Fredericksburg, "It is well that war is so terrible, lest we should come to love it so much." Similarly, George Patton is famously supposed to have remarked during the dash of his Third Army across France, "Compared to war, all other human actions shrink to insignificance." Douglas MacArthur, in his valedictory speech to the cadet corps at West Point, turned to his own recollections of combat. "Their memory," he said, "is one of wondrous beauty, watered by tears and coaxed and caressed by the smiles of yesterday. I listen vainly, but with thirsty ears, for the witching melody of faint bugles blowing reveille, of far drums beating the long roll. In my dreams," he went on, "I hear again the crash of guns, the rattle of musketry, the strange, mournful mutter of the battlefield."

Winston Churchill wrote to a friend from battalion command in France during 1916: "I think a curse should rest on me—because I love this war. I know it's smashing and shattering the lives of thousands every moment—and yet—I can't help it—I enjoy every second of it." Going back to the American Civil War, we may recall the much-quoted reflections of Supreme Court Justice and decorated Union officer veteran Oliver Wendell Holmes. "The generation that carried on the war," he claimed, "has been set apart by its experience. Through our great good fortune, in our youth our hearts were touched with fire. It was given to us to learn at the outset that life is a profound and passionate thing."

Among the most frequently quoted lines from Ernest Hemingway, the renowned literary chronicler of twentieth-century wars, may be those from *A Farewell to Arms* proclaiming the end of old illusions of military manhood and heroic sacrifice. For those who have truly experienced battle, thinks the chastened hero of the novel, Frederick Henry, "abstract words such as glory, honor, courage, or hallow were obscene beside the concrete names of villages, the numbers of roads, the names of rivers, the numbers of regiments and the dates." Yet in life and literature alike the celebrity-author could not stop traveling to the fronts of the seemingly endless wars of the age and bearing witness to their commingled horror and dreadful allure. So even the austere George Orwell, badly wounded in the Spanish Civil War, could watch, from his place on a trainload of convalescents the stirring view of another train filled with new volunteers and their weaponry going forward toward combat. "It was like an allegorical picture of war," he wrote, "the trainload of fresh men gliding proudly up the line, the maimed men sliding slowly down, and all the while the guns on the open trucks making one's heart leap as guns always do, and reviving that pernicious feeling, so difficult to get rid of, that war *is* glorious after all."

The average soldier of modern wars, to be sure, has frequently taken a less aesthetic and exalted view. The World War II novels that remain preferred reading for most of us run to the decidedly unheroic: Norman Mailer's *The Naked and the Dead*, Joseph Heller's *Catch-22*, Kurt Vonnegut's *Slaughterhouse Five*. We respect the somber reflections of combatants such as William Manchester and Eugene Sledge in the Pacific and Charles McDonald and Paul Fussell in Europe. Our authorities on the Great War are the trench ironists of the western front: from the British experience, Robert Graves, Siegfried Sassoon, and Wilfred Owen; from the US, William March; from Germany, Erich Maria Remarque; from France, Henri Barbusse. Yet, it is also a notable fact that many such authors who lived to a reflective age often later expressed more harmonious memories of quiet pride of service, unit loyalty, and comradeship in battle. Similarly, the popular American television series *Band of Brothers*—based on Steven Ambrose's World War II chronicle of Easy Company, 101st Airborne Division—intersperses combat drama with such elements of personal reflection from many of the characters portrayed. Even Ernest Hemingway's testament of post–World War I malaise, *The Sun Also Rises*, contains a crucial scene featuring a British minor character that Jake Barnes and Bill Gorton have picked up as a fishing companion in Spain. Like the Americans, he has served in combat. "Really you don't know how much it means," he says in farewell. "I've not had so much fun since the war." Everyone knows what he means.

In my own generation of Vietnam War combat veterans normally regarded as the closest inheritors of post 1914–1918 disillusionment, one frequently encounters a similar sense of mixed remembrance. A US infantryman in an oral history collection puts it simply: "There was no bullshit. You get in a firefight and you find out exactly who's who. There wasn't anything phony. It was all very real, the realest thing I've ever done. Everything since seems totally superfluous. It's horseshit." Similarly, Philip Caputo writes in his celebrated memoir *A Rumor of War*, "I could not deny the grip the war had on me, nor the fact that it had been an experience as fascinating as it was repulsive, as exhilarating as it was sad, as tender as it was cruel." Then there are the words of award-winning veteran-novelist Tim O'Brien, as close to a fictional laureate of Vietnam War combat as we will have, "War is hell," he writes, in *The Things They Carried*:

> but that's not the half of it, because war is also mystery and terror and adventure and courage and discovery and holiness and pity and despair and longing and love. War is nasty; war is fun. War is thrilling; war is drudgery. War makes you a man; war makes you dead. . . . You admire the fluid symmetries of troops on the move, the harmonies of sound and shape and proportion, the great sheets of metal-fire streaming down from a gunship, the illumination of rounds, the white phosphorus, the purply orange glow of napalm, the rocket's red glare. . . . You hate it, yes, but your eyes do not. . . . Any battle or bombing or raid or artillery barrage has the aesthetic purity of absolute moral indifference—a powerful, implacable beauty—and a true war story will tell the truth about this, though the truth is ugly.

Marine veteran William Broyles, in a famous article titled "Why Men Love War," goes even further in remarking on the allure of the thing—the sheer intensity of the experience, the black-and-white clarity of the issues, the deep and moving comradeships with fellow soldiers; and, yes, the strange beauty, the weaponry, the spectacle, the noise, the totality of physical sensation. "The seduction of war," he concludes, "is in its offering such intense beauty—divorced from all civilized values, but beauty still."

In my own work over the decades as an academic specialist on war in its aestheticized representations, one sees both the frequently terrible beauty of the relevant art and—in myth, history, and popular memory—the never-ending recurrence, for veteran and outside observer alike, of the dreadful fascination. So, for instance the critic John Limon poses the crucial question directly in *Writing After War*, a study of the strange variety and plenitude of American literary responses to the nation's military adventures, a genre that embraces everything from the escapist fabulation of Washington Irving's "Rip Van Winkle" to the twentieth-century sports novel. "Is war beautiful?" he asks in his opening sentences. The answer is "of course not." Still, I know what he, the professional academic critic, is talking about, that strange, guilty, aesthetic pull between "a mode of beauty"—in Limon's definition, the idea of literature—and what he calls "the perfection of squalid disarray." Like John Keegan in the corresponding genre of military history, Limon admits forthrightly that he has never experienced combat or even military service. Still, he might find his most supportive company in many figures of the modern era who themselves have been soldiers and who have gone on to explore the peculiar relationship between aesthetics and warfare: from the Great War, Robert Graves, Edmund Blunden, Ernst Junger, and Sir Herbert Read; from World War II, Louis Simpson, Farley Mowat, Norman Mailer, Kurt Vonnegut, Paul Fussell, and Samuel Hynes; from the Vietnam War, Tim O'Brien, Philip Caputo, Michael Herr, and others. One might as easily go on to these authors' noncombatant literary counterparts: Stephen Crane, Ezra Pound, Virginia Woolf, Rebecca West, Graham Greene, Thomas Pynchon, Sebastian Faulks, and Pat Barker. In the visual arts, beyond the millennia of classical and medieval representation, there is also the modernist inheritance of works by Benjamin West, Theodore Gericault, Francisco Goya, Eugene Delacroix, J. M. W. Turner, Winslow Homer, Lady Butler, John Singer Sargent, Pablo Picasso, and Otto Dix. On a shortlist of classical music, we have Haydn, Beethoven, Lizst, Tchaikovsky, Verdi, Prokofiev, Vaughan Williams, Britten, and Shostakovich.

On the question of war and its inspiration of authorship more generally, the historically grounded analyst of the subject would have to go all the way back to the beginnings of literature itself: the Hebrew Bible; the Koran; *The Epic of Gilgamesh*; the *Iliad*; the *Aeneid*; the *Ramayana*; the *Mahabhatara*; the *Song of Roland*, the *Nibelungenlied*, the *Lay of the Cid*, *Beowulf*, the *Volsungsaga*, *Tristan and Iseult*, *Jerusalem Delivered*, *Le Morte D'Arthur*, *Orlando Furioso*, the *Faerie Queene*, and *Paradise Lost* comprise a list that brings us at least up to the Enlightenment. Then there is the visual dimension: cave drawing, carving, sculpture, ceramic decoration, clay tablet, hieroglyphic, frieze, bas relief, tapestry, painting, engraving, printing, illustration, not to mention the arts of military attire, armor, heraldry, weapons design, and decoration.

The most written about and represented historical figure in classical and early medieval literature is Alexander the Great. The corresponding early modern icon of military representation in the arts is Napoleon. Over the history of the West it must strike us as nearly astonishing that the iconic figure called the Prince of Peace should supply the major inspiration for the nearly continuous Christian warrior violence of the Middle Ages and early modern eras, paralleled from the late first millennium onward in the East by the rise of militant Islam. Meanwhile, analogous representations in Asian art, history, and philosophy point to the cultural centrality of war in the Chinese and Indian classics.

In the realm of general human understanding, much of the cultural representation of war derives from the impulse we call myth, featuring religious deities, figures of historical legend, and larger-than-life archetypes of epic and romance. As stories that may or may not be true in any literal sense but that still contain meaning, such representations of war most often depict it as a natural extension of the basic values of a civilization—its heroic verities and virtues. The rationalizing of armed military conflict, the rise of war as military science (a human technology) comes only with the Renaissance and Reformation and the development of the modern nation state. In this regard, the definition of modern war—what Clausewitz famously calls the continuation of politics by other means—is practically a neologism. The most widely accepted standard definition—a state of armed conflict between different nations or states or different groups within a nation or state, practiced as an instrumentality of ideological or geopolitical power relations—is one that the world has spent most of modernity getting used to.

It is at the moment of this fundamental shift in mentalities concerning war and its representations in art, history, and memory, that I begin—the moment, that is, where we see war emerging from myth in the traditional sense to become a rationalized instrument of state power, and where new definitions of human individuality are reconfigured against the ideological backdrop of the militarized modern nation state. To be specific, I start where this turn becomes evident in English literary culture, in the plays of William Shakespeare. Of Shakespeare's many guises, I propose that one of the most important is that of the great poet of the early modern wars of the English nation. Moving forward chronologically toward the present, I then expand the exploration of this "aestheticization" process beyond literature to include painting, music, photography, film, historical preservation, battlefield curatorship, memorial art and architecture, museum culture, and popular media iconography. The historical treatment of warfare moves accordingly from the Wars of US Indian Removal and the American Civil War through the Age of Western Asian Colonialism, the British Wars of Empire, World War I, World War II, the American War in Vietnam, and the Cuban Revolution to the latest wars of American Empire in the Middle East.

The resulting chapters trace out a disturbing but fundamental truth: that modern war, as with the ancients and premoderns, continues to give aesthetic inspiration; and that representations of war in art, history, and memory continue to do what they have done traditionally for millennia, albeit under increasingly troubled and problematic circumstances—to provide aesthetic experience while serving ends as various and complex as ideological or geopolitical history, the production of popular memory, and even mass-culture entertainment. To put this more directly, it seems clear that war and the mythic imagination—as for the ancients and pre-moderns—continue to have an assumed conjunction. As warrior cultures have moved from creation narratives and myths of supernatural conflicts through accounts of great corresponding human actions, so they have continued to celebrate and admire their representations in evolving forms of art, history, and memory. Today, we need only consult the offerings at the Cineplex or the familiar glimpse of one of our own children playing World of Warcraft on the latest iPhone to see that we are not so different in this respect after all. We live now in a world where increasingly the function of the nation state seems to be its capacity to make war. Accordingly, it must now seem ubiquitously clear that the endless new unfoldings of its representations will likely, if anything, continue ever more relentlessly to inscribe themselves upon our own visions of daily life.

I present this at once as a theoretical assertion and, I hope, as a strand of evolutionary argument linking the series of historical essays that follow. The point is explicitly rejoined in my brief conclusion, which one might see also as a set of notes toward the definition of new postmillennial cultural myth. It is called "The Forever Wars." But first, on the subject at hand, there is the great span of modernity to be navigated.

I

Arms and the Bard

Soldiering in Shakespeare

For all the prodigality of Shakespeare's godlike capacity to create what Harold Bloom calls the intensely "vitalizing" force of the Shakespearean imagination, it is startling to realize how often the historical world of the plays is prodigal in its organized human capacity to destroy. In play after play, the world presented is frequently either itself one of war or is somehow significantly connected with a world of war. In the broadest sense, Shakespeare's drama often becomes the staging of a world of politics and history in a form we recognize all too well: in which the state exists for the purpose of making war. Nor should it be surprising, as will be shown here, that it is Shakespeare who remains the laureate of war for the English-speaking peoples.

In this, as in many other respects, Shakespeare comes to us as the last ancient and the first modern. For Elizabethan and Jacobean audiences, still responding to classical and medieval codes of heroism, there would have been the appeal of older forms of warfare, ranging from epic adventure to blood feud and tribal curse. It is in this latter sense that, as asserted by Jonathan Bate, "In both plot and metaphor, Shakespeare's plays are stuffed with what Othello calls 'the pride, pomp and circumstance of glorious war'"—the great affairs, that is, of kings, princes, nobles, masters and commanders, all of them celebrations of the historical tradition of the Warrior Hero.

As familiarly, such audiences would have also been beginning to attend to wider and more pervasive imagings of war in some version of the form which we ourselves have come to know—that is, of organized, state-sponsored military violence or what Clausewitz described as the continuation of politics by other means (*"Krieg isl eine blojie Fortsetzung der Politik mit anderen Mitteln"*). In Shakespeare these are frequently the wars of early modern nationhood, emerging out of struggles of dynastic inheritance into newer designs of empire.

According to Bate and Thornton, "This was a militarized society, in which Shakespeare was a war poet: there was a war in the Netherlands in the 1580s, war with Spain through the 1590s and rebellion in Ireland." To this may be added the grand spectacle of conquest and imperial military rivalry in the New World. As to newer images of heroism, this world of war was also that of the first great age of secular individualism, echoing with the cultural renown accorded to the Renaissance adventurer hero in figures as diverse as Sidney and Spenser and Raleigh and Essex. Here, in history and literature, could be found a celebratory Elizabethan and Jacobean spectacle of national consolidation and imperial conquest. The great event of course was the repulse of the Armada, heralded in the exploits of Drake and Hawkins. These military seafaring heroes were joined in New World explorations and conquests by figures ranging from courtiers such as Sir Humphrey Gilbert to such upstart adventurers as Myles Standish and John Smith (the real-life avatars of what Stephen Greenblatt has so memorably called Renaissance self-fashioning). Most directly in the domestic mind throughout the era were the land wars of the Isles, Wales, Scotland, Ireland, as well as conflicts across the Channel.

Sidney is killed fighting in the Netherlands. In Ireland, Spenser writes the *Faerie Queene* while serving as embattled Lord Proprietor. In a later unfolding of the Ireland drama, the fallen and resentful Essex, fresh from his military adventuring there, actually brings Shakespeare and the King's Men in suspicion of treason with his command staging of *Richard II* amid his own fatal plot.

Such dramas of power and the quest for worldly reputation frequently find something of a rough, jostling replication in the early modern English theater. Indeed, with its rival companies, its political and financial intrigues, its relentless courtship of patronage in circles of power, the literary world of the celebrity promoters, playwrights, and players was itself a precinct of passionate, violent, not to mention grandly histrionic men. Shakespeare's fellow dramatists, like their sponsors and supporters, were a swaggering, hotheaded lot, quick to take offense and act with fell intent, perpetrators and victims of military and political bloodlust. Ben Jonson, having served in the Low Countries as a young soldier, was more than once imprisoned for his mixings of political and literary intrigue and was nearly executed for killing a fellow player in a duel.

Christopher Marlowe, likely a government agent in the employ of spymaster Francis Walsingham and indicted by royal warrant as a "blasphemer" and a "heretic," suffered a fatal stab wound to the head in a tavern brawl. Thomas Kyd, author of *The Spanish Tragedy*, was almost certainly the political betrayer of Marlowe, a quondam companion and housemate, while facing torture and imprisonment for his own alleged crimes as a libeler and an atheist. The very terms of organized, commercial playwriting employed military language. The War of the Theaters became the *Poetomachia*.

In all these connections, we might do well to remember that Shakespeare the player/playwright makes his authorial appearance on the stage as a chronicler of war. His formal career as a dramatist begins in the set of plays now known as the *Histories*, mainly devoted to the rise of the English nation. Specifically—in alleged response to the influence of Marlowe's epic drama of war and conquest, *Tamburlaine*—he begins with the first of two cycles of military struggle and triumph, corporately known as the *Henriad*, each now understood to comprise a major tetralogy on the related themes of war and kingship. The first, now largely unread save for the fourth installment, consists of *Henry VI* (parts *I*, *II*, and *III*) and *Richard III*. The second, far better known, delves back into earlier proto-Tudor history, beginning with *Richard II* and then moving on to *Henry IV* (parts *I* and *II*) and *Henry V*. Here alone are eight plays. If one adds *King John* (interpolated in mid-career), and *Henry VIII* (added on at the end), and perhaps even *The Merry Wives of Windsor* (in which the roistering soldier-knight Sir John Falstaff makes a comic return), we then have among the histories alone fully eleven—nearly a third—of the extant plays, all on the matter of the military rise of England and almost all relating to wars and rumors of wars: the Anglo-French wars of the late Middle Ages, the wars of the Yorks and Lancasters, the great spectacle, in sum, of the relentlessly militarized rise of the Tudors.

Beyond this, of course, stand the frequently military protagonists of the other plays. In the great tragedies, Othello, Macbeth, and Lear are all modeled on warrior figures. Warrior women of comparable stature include Cleopatra and Lady Macbeth. Hamlet attempts to right the personal and political crisis of monarchy in Denmark in the face of the Fortinbras invasion. For most of *Henry IV*, accorded comparable canonical status as the greatest of the histories, it is the tragic Hotspur who contends directly for our sympathies against the callow and heedless Prince Hal. We have the Trojan War to thank for *Troilus and Cressida*. All four of the Roman plays are centered on warrior figures: Julius Caesar, Mark Antony, Coriolanus, and Titus Andronicus. (It is in this vein that Harold Bloom groups *Coriolanus* with *Julius Caesar* and *Henry V* as Shakespeare's most "political" plays.) Along with *Othello, Macbeth*, and *King Lear*, the plots of the Roman cycle all turn on the failure of military heroes to adapt to situations in which warrior virtues are not applicable. A parallel strain may even be noted in the great comedies. In *Much Ado About Nothing* we see Benedick and Claudio, recently returned from the wars, soldier figures out of their depth in the world of politics and sexual, marital, and familial relationships. In *As You Like It*, Jaques's famous "All the world's a stage" speech places the military man dead center in life:

> Then, a soldier,
> Full of strange oaths and bearded like the pard,
> Jealous in honour, sudden, and quick in quarrel,

Seeking the bubble reputation
Even in the cannon's mouth. (2.7.148–52)

War is thus repeatedly thematic in Shakespeare. But in the larger sense of historical consciousness that concerns us here—the standing on the bridge between antiquity and modernity—one should also note that war in these plays is in the fullest sense structural, and again in the same twofold dimension. It is frequently an underlying visionary structure first in the sense we find throughout the classical and medieval inheritance of literary art—from Homer and Virgil to Chrétien de Troyes, Ariosto, and Malory, among others—where writing war is the fundamental task of the authorial imagination; war, that is, defined as traditional military combat but also a matter of playing out one's appointed role against some grand drama of the fates, design of the gods, or some other overarching creation plot. It involves heroic military aspiration in its abutment against the very fabric of the universe—what D. H. Lawrence, describing the work of the thoroughly Shakespearean Herman Melville, called "the great slidings and collidings of matter." For the models of Shakespeare's noble and kingly warriors in this dimension, the correct places to look are classical and medieval legend, Plutarch's *Lives*, the chronicles of Froissart and Holinshed.

But war is also as often structural in the more familiar modern political sense of what it means to be an individual human person living in the world of history. It is in this dimension that we most frequently contemplate such distinctive figures as Lear, Macbeth, Hamlet, or the elevated characters of the *Histories*. A key transitional figure here is Othello, at once the warrior and the mercenary, the master and commander and the soldier of fortune. Here the Renaissance adventurer hero could not be more the creature of the historical world, the Christianized Muslim Mauretanian of Venice enlisted in defending Venetian Cyprus, formerly a Byzantine possession, against the Ottoman Turks.

Of most importance to us here, pertaining particularly to Shakespeare's legacy among Anglophone cultures as a poet of war, is his portrayal in the *Histories* of a host of similarly transitional warrior figures—kings, princes, and nobles joined together with various depictions of the generic English man-at-arms. The former include Henry VI, Richard II and III, John of Gaunt, Hotspur, but most prominently Prince Hal of *Henry IV*, and his subsequent manifestation as the warrior king of *Henry V*. The figure of the man-at-arms, of course, has come down to us immortalized at its most vivid and most human in the second *Henriad* in the character of Sir John Falstaff—to such a degree that, according to Harold Bloom, the cycle should really be called the Falstaffiad. But also vividly given here, as in no other Shakespearean play or in the general literary art of the era, are also deeply human portraits of the various common English fighting men of the day. Some few, like Falstaff, sport knighthoods earned on the battlefield. Others carry the early commissioned-commoner officer ranks of captain, lieutenant, ensign, or their noncommissioned counterparts of serjeant or corporal. We also meet the private soldiers, the English yeomen of legend here brought humanly to the stage—frequently along with their equally colorful wives, lovers, and sundry other consorts—to speak a prose of war that has vied with the poetry of "pride, pomp, and circumstance" in providing the most memorable and cherished passages of thought and expression in the Anglo-American literary inheritance.

As noted, when the image and utterance of the professional man-at-arms are invoked in the military plays, it is invariably Sir John Falstaff who is allowed to dominate the stage as the archetype or epitome of early modern English military professional, if only for his vivid, rollicking, omnivorousness for life. Yet here, what almost always follows is the too easy compartmentalization of even a figure so expansive as Fat Jack into a late medieval or early modern English *miles gloriosus*—a national type of the classical braggart soldier originating in Greek and Roman low comedy—with localized cultural additions, according to E. Wilson Knight, of the figure of Vice from the morality plays. Often there follow after-the-fact attributions to the rising tradition of the comic knight-errant, as in the figure of Don Quixote, *el hidalgo ingenioso* mixed with the *picaro*, the low-life rapscallion, the rogue. (*The Adventures of Don Quixote*, parts *I* and *II*, were first published in Spain in 1605 and 1615 respectively, with the earliest translation of *Part I* in English, that of Thomas Shelton, available in 1612; on the other hand, the classic *Lazarillo de Tormes*, establishing the prototypical image of the *picaro*, had been published in 1554.)

In any such discussion, virtually all text commentary on Falstaff, as well as on the extensive array of companion figures in the second *Henriad* in particular, ignores the emergence of the man-at-arms as a historical and literary archetype both in early modern England and in Europe. Here, we speak initially of the figure called the knight, the central cultural and literary embodiment of military manhood in Anglo-European warfare of late Middle Ages: a mounted soldier in full, closely crafted armor, with state-of-the-art weaponry including a lance or spear, as well as possibly a mace, battle-axe, or truncheon, but always featuring the broadsword. With a warhorse itself frequently outfitted with armor and decorative bearings, such a knight and his cohorts would represent what we would now call heavy cavalry. Alone or in a group, the mounted warrior would always be differentiated from the common foot soldier, with the latter likely to be a conscripted or "pressed" fighter serving as a pikeman or archer.

Initially such distinctions of soldierly function would have been almost exclusively those of feudal class. The expense and prestige of knightly outfitting, the rigorous training required, the commitment to and understanding of complex codes of honor, would all have distinguished the knight as a member of the nobility or extremely rich gentry. Chivalry and cavalier, derived of *cheval* and *caballo*, the French and Spanish words for horse, were the original signature terms. But then, at some point, the language began to change along with the function. Increasingly, among medieval rulers with their disparate armies, frequently assembled in ad hoc alliances across rapidly shifting borders, there came the awarding of knighthoods for military performance.

In turn, the rise of the knightly mercenary may be traced through a number of identifiable points. In the German regions, the figure became the *landsknecht*, literally the "land knight." In Italian-dominated armies arose the *condottiere*, literally "contract soldier" but also hired leader. The current French word *gendarme* derives from the era, as gentleman at arms.

In English form, even down to the distinctive phrasing, the man-at-arms figure seems to have its own parallel deroulement. The differences from continental developments involved the rise of the Tudors and, under the twinned pressures of Renaissance and Reformation, the distinctive concept of the English nation. The attendant advance of secularization and general literacy also led to conditions of political, economic, and social mobility that outstripped other European cultures as far as both political position and social mobility were concerned. Particularly under Elizabeth I, fame and fortune were the rewards of the swaggering court favorite, the sea dog, the adventurer-hero. (Almost all the trade and colonization enterprises of the era, it is well to remember, conjoined the soldier of fortune with secondary nobles and rich gentry. "Adventurers" were now what we would call "investors.") In high literature, it was the age of Sidney and Spenser. In the literature of exploration, adventure, and conquest, it was the age of Hakluyt and Purchas. In drama, it could elevate to celebrity status an upstart crow named Shakespeare.

In all this, Falstaff remains to be sure sui generis, a complete creation. But the basis of his character is that of the man-at-arms. He has made a life of soldiering, at some point having earned a knighthood on the battlefield; along the way he has mastered the attendant career attractions of eating, drinking, whoring, robbing, and various other acts of mild outlawry. By the time we encounter him, he has gone fat, dissolute, devious, and is a bloated blowhard living on his pretended laurels and friendship with a callow crown prince. He acts the soldier because he is alive to tell the soldier's tale. If called to soldiering again, the next time he may not be so lucky. He is a survivor, like most old soldiers a fugitive from the law of averages. Honor is a fig. He who survives the wars, as we shall see in the case of the fat knight, is truly he who fights and runs away and thereby lives to carouse and fornicate another day.

Traditional Shakespeare commentary rightly associates Falstaff with two historical figures usually taken to be direct historical models. Both, it turns out, were themselves men-at-arms. The first, named Sir John Oldcastle—as was the original Shakespeare character—was a Lollard heretic actually living in the time of Henry V. Like Falstaff, he was an early friend and companion of the king but wound up eventually a rebel against the crown and was executed for treason. The second, named Sir John Folstoff, was a medieval knight, also a Lollard, winning military renown during the French campaigns of Henry VI but indicted for cowardice after an English defeat at Patay and in consequence temporarily stripped of his knighthood. In his own dramatic role, he appears in *Henry VI, Part I* as a coward. Given the foundational man-at-arms concept undergirding the characterization of Falstaff, a third figure should now also be brought to light. This was Sir John Hawkwood, a famous fourteenth-century English mercenary warrior-leader, whose exploits were recorded by Froissart and Machiavelli in main service as leader of continental condottieri. He is said to have earned his spurs in France, however, under Edward III, perhaps fighting at Crécy and according to legend was knighted either by the King or the Black Prince. As to Shakespeare's likely knowledge of Hawkwood, the latter's rise to fame and fortune—along with that of other English figures of humble birth—had been chronicled in *Nine Worthies of London* by Richard Johnson. It was published 1592, just five years before the appearance of *Henry IV, Part I.*

Here, then is the particular English genealogy of this grand collocation of boastfulness, appetites, overbearing mental and fleshy presence that we meet at the Boar's Head in the play's opening scenes of earthy tavern badinage and almost slapstick Gad's Hill outlawries. (In just this, one might add, it is hard not to see as well a caricature of the roistering, wenching, eating and drinking, loving and betraying Henry VIII—in major moments as Falstaffian as it gets.) When matters take a serious military turn and Prince Hal commits himself to battle in support of his father the King against the rebel Percy and his son Henry, the renowned Hotspur, he secures a place for Falstaff as leader of a company of foot. Falstaff protests. He would prefer cavalry. While events of royalist and rebel plot and counterplot take their course, he spends his early war recruiting, cornering potential candidates for conscription who in some cases can buy him off. Although the extortion lines his pockets, it results in a motley command of hopeless of cannon fodder. At their parting before the climactic engagement against the Percy faction, Falstaff asks that Hal protect him should he fall wounded on the battlefield. Hal replies, anticipating the famous speech of Feeble in *Part II*, "Well, thou owest god a death" (5.1.126). This is soldier's code; Falstaff has been there and done that, he says, in a concluding soliloquy, and has replaced it with the new holy rule of staying alive.

> Can honour set to a leg? no: or an arm? no: or take away the grief of a wound? no.
> Honour hath no skill in surgery, then? no. What is
> honour? a word. What is in that word honour? What
> is that honour? air. A trim reckoning! Who hath it?
> he that died o' Wednesday. Doth he feel it? no.
> Doth he hear it? no. 'Tis insensible, then. Yea, to the dead. But will it not live with the living?
> no. Why? detraction will not suffer it. Therefore
> I'll none of it. Honour is a mere scutcheon: and so
> ends my catechism. (5.1.131–40)

Accordingly, at Shrewsbury, attacked by the rebel knight Douglas while Prince Hal fights and kills Hotspur, Falstaff fakes his own death in combat. He then concocts a claim of credit for killing Hotspur. As with Stephen Crane's Henry Fleming five centuries later, for the cagey Falstaff bravery and courage are matters of that which has been seen or unseen.

In *Henry IV, Part II*, the drama centers on a new war, another rebellion. Here are visibly twinned but largely discrete plots, a Henry plot and a Falstaff plot. It is a play on the one hand about Henry learning to become a king amid rebellions and family intrigues at court. It is on the other as much a play about Falstaff, if anything an enlargement on earlier depictions of his exuberance, his irrepressibility, carousing, cadging, wenching, his antics amid a band of "irregular humorist" hangers-on and the immortal bawds Mistress Quickly and Doll Tearsheet. As to military matters, among the most memorable of all the scenes in the play—mirroring *Part I* and outliving those of the court, the tavern, and the battlefield—is Falstaff's country journey to recruit. With his old friend Justice Shallow, he exchanges reminiscences of roistering youth while pursuing the usual dishonesties upon a crowd of available yokels, Bullcalf, Feeble, Mouldy, Shadow, and Wart. Two of them, Bullcalf and Mouldy, given extortionate guidance on what we would call claims of draft exempt status, are clever enough to buy themselves off. As they are allowed to stand aside, a third, named Francis Feeble of all things, comes forward with a fighting resoluteness expressed in words that will become immortal. "By my troth," he says, "I care not; a man can die but once; we owe God a death. I'll ne'er bear a base mind: an 't be my destiny, so; an 't be not, so. No man's too good to serve 's prince; and let it go which way it will, he that dies this year is quit for the next." Falstaff's henchman Bardolf replies, "Well said; thou'rt a good fellow." Feeble replies, "Faith, I'll bear no base mind" (3.2.232–38).

Shortly, the military action is done and the hurly burly is over, again with a Lancastrian victory. The two main trajectories of character building since the early scenes of *Henry IV, Part I* now climax in Hal—at his father's death now the new King Henry V—finally casting off Falstaff, the companion of his youth. An epilogue further predicts that Falstaff himself will probably not be long for this world.

Early on in *Henry V* we find the prediction coming true, in a set of scenes poignantly enacted with the old man offstage, namely, an account of the latter's likely mortal illness narrated by Mistress Quickly to former hangers-on—Lieutenant (formerly Captain) Bardolf, Ensign Pistol, and Corporal Nym—and a boy who has served the old man as a page. Shortly thereafter a final interlude in the larger action shows the group, joined by Doll Tearsheet, called to the bedside of the mortally ill Sir John, as he is reverently called. It is soon reported by Mistress Quickly that he is in Arthur's bosom, for an English immortal at least the equivalent of Abraham's. He has called out of sack, it is said. He has called out of women. He is dead. Pistol completes the memorial service: "Let us to France, like horseleeches, my boys,/To suck, to suck, the very blood to suck!" (2.3.51–52).

Falstaff has gone his way. Henry goes his as the central hero-protagonist of the play. Accordingly, until the concluding scenes of courtship between the victorious English king and the French princess, *Henry V* is a play about battle. After a choral apology for confining so legendary an instance as Agincourt to a playhouse, the opening scenes reveal the Archbishop of Canterbury and the Bishop of Ely urging Henry to royal warfare in the tradition of his "puissant" kingly forebears. In scene two, the chorus returns to describe war fever. Events quickly move to Southampton, amid the hubbub and bustle of invasion and the roiling, jostling soldiery. A royal roundup of domestic traitors is followed by kingly resolve to depart for France. "Once more into the breach, dear friends, once more," the young king famously intones, familiarly concluding,

> For there is none of you so mean and base
> That hath not noble luster in your eyes.
> I see you stand like greyhounds in the slips,
> Straining upon the start. The game's afoot.
> Follow your spirit, and upon this charge
> Cry "God for Harry, England, and Saint George!" (3.1. 29–34)

As has been variously noted, it is at such moments and beyond in *Henry V*—as if fulfilling the terms of the famous John of Gaunt "sceptered isle" speech in *Richard II*—that Shakespeare becomes not just the poet-dramatist of Britain but of England. What remains less noted—in a title to which has been attached cultural mythologization, if not enshrinement, as a drama of kingly combat—is also a play increasingly bringing into relief the historical importance of the English common soldier, becoming not just a military play but a soldier-play, and by being a soldier-play very much of a modern war play. We may note, for instance, on all of these accounts, a properly multinational colloquy on war aims that transpires at one point among officer men-at-arms such as Captain Gower, an Englishman, Captain Fluellen, an Englishman, Captain McMorris, an Irishman, and Captain Jamy, a Scot. Here, as is often the case, soldier talk is played for dialect humor. But there is also a clear intent to portray the army as a national microcosm. The point seems even more pronounced in Henry's famous incognito ramble on the eve of battle among the troops. He is also carrying the shade of Prince Hal. Again we encounter Gower and Fluellen. Pistol, married back in England to Mistress Quickly, has reappeared. Significantly, the scapegrace Bardolf is dead in an act of internal military discipline. He has been executed for looting a sacred object from a French church, a fate Henry dispenses without blinking an eye. There is also an interest now in figures of descending rank: serjeant, corporal, what we would now call noncommissioned officers, NCOs. We once again encounter the stoic Corporal Nym, who had earlier intoned, echoing his predecessor Feeble, "Faith, I will live so long as I may, that's the certain of it; and when I cannot live any longer, I will do as I may: that is my rest, that is the rendezvous of it" (2.1.15–16). But most arresting and interesting, one suspects, for an audience of the day is the late kingly encounter and exchange with the private soldiers Alexander Court, John Bates, and Michael Williams. Here one finds no playing of the spear-carriers for laughs. The subject is that of just and unjust wars, a soldier's personal responsibilities for his acts upon the battlefield.

Henry teases out the subtle politics. The no-nonsense Williams picks a bone and eventually a fight. A little touch of Harry in the night provokes a common-soldier voice forthrightly speaking the prose of war. The eloquent Michael Williams responds:

> But if the cause be not good, the King himself hath
> a heavy reckoning to make, when all those legs
> and arms and heads, chopp'd off in a battle, shall join
> together at the latter day and cry all "We died at
> such a place"; some swearing, some crying for a
> surgeon, some upon their wives left poor behind them. . . .
> I am afeard there are few die
> well that die in a battle; for how can they

charitably dispose of any thing, when blood is their
argument? Now if these men do not die well, it
will be a black matter for the king that led them to it. (4.1.133–40)

Only the next day—and in this distinctive context of the night before—come the most memorable lines in the Shakespearean inventory about English military valor, Henry's famous St. Crispin and St. Crispian's day speech before Agincourt, the famous Band of Brothers oration. Is the small army sufficient unto its great challenge?

No, faith, my coz, wish not a man from England:
God's peace! I would not lose so great an honour
As one man more, methinks, would share from me
For the best hope I have. O, do not wish one more!
Rather proclaim it, Westmoreland, through my host,
That he which hath no stomach to this fight,
Let him depart; his passport shall be made
And crowns for convoy put into his purse:
We would not die in that man's company
That fears his fellowship to die with us.
This day is called the feast of Crispian:
He that outlives this day, and comes safe home,
Will stand a tip-toe when the day is named,
And rouse him at the name of Crispian.
He that shall live this day, and see old age,
Will yearly on the vigil feast his neighbours,
And say "To-morrow is Saint Crispian:"
Then will he strip his sleeve and show his scars:
And say "These wounds I had on Crispin's day."
Old men forget: yet all shall be forgot,
But he'll remember with advantages
What feats he did that day: then shall our names.
Familiar in his mouth as household words
Harry the king, Bedford and Exeter,
Warwick and Talbot, Salisbury and Gloucester,
Be in their flowing cups freshly remember'd.
This story shall the good man teach his son;
And Crispin Crispian shall ne'er go by,
From this day to the ending of the world,
But we in it shall be remember'd;
We few, we happy few, we band of brothers;

For he to-day that sheds his blood with me
Shall be my brother; be he ne'er so vile,
This day shall gentle his condition:
And gentlemen in England now a-bed
Shall think themselves accursed they were not here,
And hold their manhoods cheap whiles any speaks
That fought with us upon Saint Crispin's day. (4.3.30–67)

On the day of battle, it is the poetry of a prince. One must note, however, how it has been dramatically and politically foregrounded by the words of forthright common men who have in their own way spoken on the eve of battle with forthright bravery. As things turn out, it is a battle in which they will also prove militarily brave in good English yeoman style. To be sure, there is more of the dread prose of war. A French attack on the English baggage trains results in the killing of English boys, including Falstaff's former page. Henry orders the reciprocal killing of French prisoners. This may be a war crime. It may, on the other hand, be a necessary deed of mass murder upon the remnants of an enemy formally refusing to cede the field. In act 5 comes the postmortem exchange of fighting soldiers on deeds and events. Fluellen, Gower, Pistol, another war behind them, contemplate what awaits at home.

News is received that Doll Tearsheet meanwhile has died of her own French malady. Dramatically interpolated is the distracting love comedy of Anglo-French reconciliations at court, Henry, Charles, the Princess Catherine. But our memory of the play remains with the army: the working officers: captains, lieutenants, ensigns; the troop handlers, serjeants, corporals; the common, private soldiers—henceforth English men-at-arms in their modem historical definition, the true national microcosm, those who will be called upon over the centuries to do yeoman service.

Thus we see the military and political progression of Shakespeare's *Henry IV* and *Henry V* cycle increasingly giving voice to the figure we know today as the private, the enlisted man, the conscript, the common soldier. The chorus at the conclusion provides a kind of voice-over with the further history of Henry, his son the future Henry VI, and the old wars of England and France, with which an earlier *Henriad* had dealt; but the larger history of arms and the Bard has now come to comprehend both the greatness of the great actors and the humanity of the common soldiers by whom they are attended.

The noun soldier seems to have appeared first as a French noun of the 1300s: *soudier, one who served in the army for pay*. The verb form, *to soldier*, seems to have arisen in the 1640s during the English Civil Wars. By then significant years had passed, with Shakespeare already acknowledged as the great poet of England and of English national heroism. When called upon on decades and centuries hence as the great poet-dramatist of war, he could unfailingly provide the requisite Shakespearean chestnuts:

> Once more unto the breach, dear friends, once more;
> Or close the wall up with our English dead. (*Henry V*, 3.1.1) Lay on, Macduff, And damn'd be him that first cries, "Hold, enough!" (*Macbeth*, 5.10.33–35)
> Cry "Havoc," and let slip the dogs of war. (*Julius Caesar*, 3.1.276)

He became apace the great war poet both of England and of the English-speaking peoples. He would serve on both sides in the great English political civil wars—Parliamentarians versus Royalists in England and Wales, Covenanters in Scotland, Catholics in Ireland—and in the Shakespearean names of legendary battles stretching beyond Shrewsbury, Agincourt, Crécy, and Bosworth to Edgehill, Marston Moor, Naseby. He would likewise be claimed by warring parties in the American Revolution and by such purveyors of Romantic fiction on both sides of the Atlantic as Scott and Cooper. In the American Civil War, the cherished "band of brothers" phrase figures in both "Hail, Columbia" and "The Bonnie Blue Flag." In late Victorian England, he is the great literary outrider of empire, with his Englishness elevated into the new religion of what G. B. Shaw called "Bardolatry."

As to World War I, if we are to judge from the works of poets Rupert Brooke, Edmund Blunden, Robert Graves, Siegfried Sassoon, David Jones, Edward Thomas, Isaac Rosenberg, Allen Seeger, and John Macrae, one will never know how many young Anglophone warriors went into the lines with pocket Shakespeares in their haversacks. Similar resonations appear in prose memoirs ranging from Blunden, Graves, and Sassoon to Vera Brittain. Graves begins *Good Bye to All That* with an elegiac remembrance of his parents' Shakespeare reading circle. In official England, as if some literary *missa in tempora belli*, the Bard received an official tercentenary tribute in *A Book of Homage to Shakespeare* edited by Israel Gollancz. Its 557 pages contain 166 tributes to Shakespeare by scholars, novelists, poets, literati, and public figures from both sides of the Atlantic and around the globe. According to Coppelia Kahn in *Shakespeare Quarterly*,

> By commemorating Shakespeare, the book aims to create an imaginary unified community in the face of the deep, increasingly bloody divisions of the Great War. It also aspires toward a sense of historical continuity, through a narrative of origin in which Shakespeare becomes the icon of a racial purity that lends itself to a sense of imperial mission. Eight tributes take the war as a central motif. Four of them, not surprisingly,

imagine Shakespeare as a transcendent figure imparting unity and firmness of purpose to English forces. Eight tributes take the war as a central motif. Four of them, not surprisingly, imagine Shakespeare as a transcendent figure imparting unity and firmness of purpose to English forces.

Roughly contemporary, and even more expressly devised for wartime purposes, was a compilation by Edward Thomas titled *This England,* although interestingly it does not include the John of Gaunt "Sceptered isle" speech. That of Henry V before Agincourt is there, to be sure, although again interestingly juxtaposed with the Prince Hal/Falstaff "Go thy ways, old Jack" valediction from the Boar's Head. Also, in a "vital commoners" section, there appears Michael Williams's bold riposte to Harry Le Roy, "if the cause be not good." Even less reverent in his homage was the Australian postwar novelist Robert Manning, in his fictive exposé of the squalor and brutality of the trenches. First titled *Her Privates We* and later toned down to *The Middle Parts of Fortune*, it took the Shakespearean *locus classicus* as Hamlet, but concentrated on the hapless Rosencrantz and Guildenstern. In contrast, with piercing sadness, Virginia Woolf's novel *Mrs. Dalloway*, in which the war-damaged veteran Septimius Smith plays a central role, invokes the titular heroine's yearning for a world before war in some faraway remembered lines: "Fear no more the heat o' the sun/Nor the furious winter's rages" (4.2.285–6). They are from the dirge of *Cymbeline.*

Interestingly, in musical England, barely a year before hostilities began, Sir Edward Elgar brought forth a 1913 symphonic study/long tone poem centered on *Henry IV Parts I* and *II* that was at the time compared favorably with comparable works by his German contemporary Richard Strauss. Between the wars, Ralph Vaughan Williams, himself a stretcher-bearer veteran of the front, would return to the subject with *Sir John in Love/The Fat Knight*, based on *The Merry Wives of Windsor* with additions from Sidney, Middleton, Beaumont, and Fletcher.

For embattled, isolated England, World War II (especially in the dark early days after the fall of France, as the country fought on alone against the Nazi scourge) became a new Shakespearean war, with *Henry V* beyond all others as the great Shakespeare play. Amid the gloom of 1941, Winston Churchill would intone, "These are not dark days, these are the greatest days our nation has ever lived; and we must thank God that we have been allowed, each of us according to our stations, to play a part in making these days memorable in the history of our race." And of course later, at the decisive moment of the air combat now called the Battle of Britain, would come the history-making "Never in the field of human conflict was so much owed by so many to so few." In 1944, a sparkling, inventive, Lawrence Olivier color film pro-

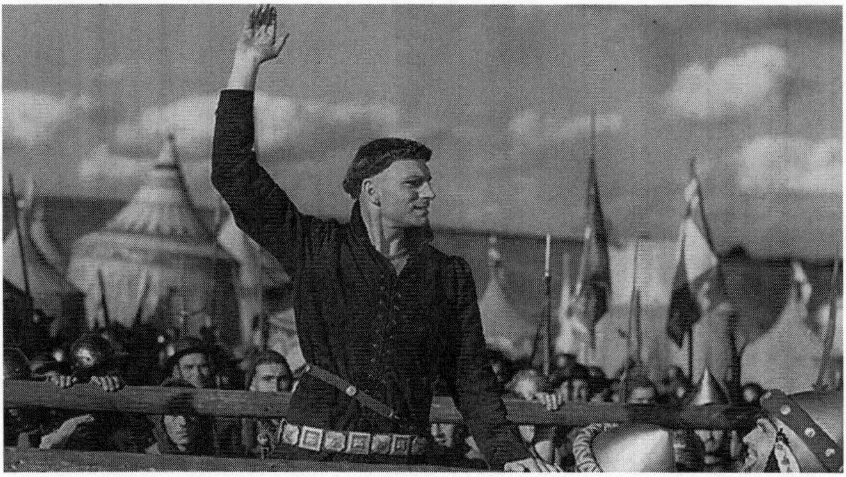

Figure 1.1 Sir Laurence Olivier, St. Crispin's Day Speech, in the 1944 production of *Henry V*. 1946, Two Cities Films.

duction of *Henry V*—unapologetic in its morale-building, propagandistic glorification of the English military tradition and culminating in the St. Crispin's and St. Crispian's Day oration—would gladden the nation's way toward victory. One may profitably compare the film, for instance, with the 1989 version by Kenneth Branagh, in which the kingly rhetoric is played repeatedly as a medium of psychological and political manipulation.

Incredibly, on the American side, not a single Shakespeare title would support the war effort in the extensive paperbound Armed Services Editions distributed to US servicemen around the globe. In something of an idiosyncratic flourish, on the other hand, Ernest Hemingway, in his introduction to the widely circulated *Men at War* anthology of the world's greatest combat writing, would highlight his own reverence for the no-nonsense common soldier wisdom of Feeble as expressed in the *Henry IV*, *Part II*, "we owe God a death" speech previously cited. In Hemingway's case, it had already been used by the British white hunter Williams in "The Short Life of Francis Macomber," where he attempts to restore the titular character, however briefly, to manhood after an act of cowardice in the field. In *Men at War*, Hemingway related his own parallel autobiographical version of the incident when, as a scared, badly wounded nineteen-year-old veteran of Red Cross service in Italy, he had gained "a permanent, protecting talisman when a young British officer I met when I was in the hospital first wrote out for me, so that I could remember them, these lines: 'By my troth I care not; a man can die but once, we owe God a death . . . and let it go which way it will, he that dies this year is quit for the next.'" The young officer—Eric Dorman Smith, to become a lifelong friend of Hemingway and eventually a World War II British general—is not named. Nor, interestingly, is Shakespeare identified in any way as the source of the passage. Nevertheless, Hemingway continues, "That is probably the best thing written in this book and, with nothing else, a man might get along all right with that." It is the Bard's single appearance. In the anthology, there are selections from the Bible, Virgil, and Hemingway himself, three times. No further word is heard of Shakespeare.

Today, as if in historical and literary reparation, a ubiquitous new American re-appropriation of Shakespeare, Henry V, and the St. Crispin's and St. Crispian's day oration has been used to celebrate World War II military heroics—albeit emphatically invested in the courage of the common infantry soldier—in perhaps the most widely seen drama of combat against the Nazis in Europe ever broadcast on the planet. Originally produced as an HBO series in collaboration with the popular historian Stephen Ambrose, the prominent movie actor Tom Hanks, and the legendary Hollywood filmmaker Steven Spielberg, it traces the brave, bloody, and finally triumphant odyssey across Europe of a single infantry unit of men in close combat: the officers, NCOs, and enlisted men of Easy Company, 101st Airborne Division. They are led bravely and find their own bravery exemplified by a young officer, Dick Winters, a citizen soldier who rises to become a leader of quiet but heroic manliness—played, one might observe, to enforce the point of long historical and cultural transmission, by Damien Hirst, a British actor and old Etonian. The series is titled, of course, *Band of Brothers.* The point is that common soldiers, many of them still alive in our times, have become characters of Shakespearean humanity and permanence.

To test the proposition about ubiquitous reference, one may Google the phrase "Band of Brothers." To the surprise of no one who knows late twentieth-century popular culture, the first four screens are devoted exclusively to the US television series and feature extensive references to Ambrose, Hanks, and/or Spielberg. Interspersed are advertisements for books, DVDs, and video games, accompanied by several dedicated fan websites. As screens progress, one notes the appropriation of the term by several evangelical Christian male fellowships. Along the way there is one mention of Shakespeare, having to do with a western Pennsylvania theater company featuring an African American ensemble. Another use of the title identifies an Ohio State University diversity initiative. A recent news story announces how the US army has become a band of brothers and sisters. At the tenth screen can be found a rock and roll group and an organization promoting solidarity among chiropractors. At

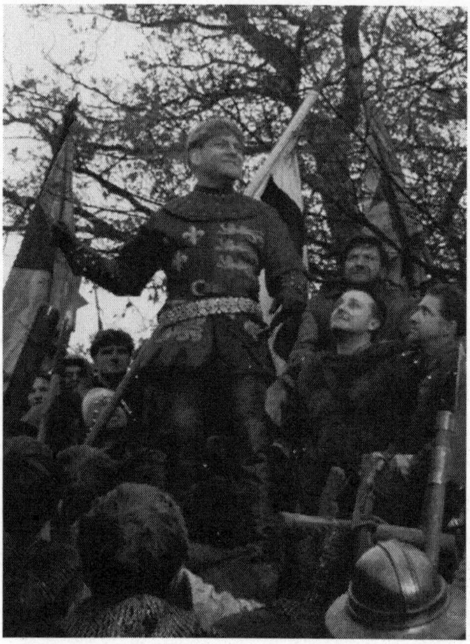

Figure 1.2 Kenneth Branagh, St. Crispin's Day Speech, in the 1989 production of *Henry V.* 1989, BBC Renaissance Films.

screen fourteen appears a phrase finder entry. On screen sixteen, one finally arrives at a movie clip of the St. Crispin's and St. Crispian's Day speech delivered by Kenneth Branagh.

New appropriations of the Shakespearean phraseology can be found frequently among veterans of the US wars in Vietnam and more lately Iraq and Afghanistan. By now, of course, the references themselves are more likely not to the drama of Shakespeare but to that of Hollywood's Ambrose, Hanks, and Spielberg. This is not to diminish the power of the concept or the phrasing. Shakespeare understood the power of war over the imagination of soldiers and nations. Above all, he somehow caught the strange pride of the veteran and the brotherhood of veteranship. "Back when it was history, I was there; I did that; we were there; we did that."

This is not to say Shakespeare predicted Waterloo, the Somme, the Normandy landings, or any of the great modern wars of mass armies of conscript soldiers. He is remembered rightly for his larger-than-life figures, noble souls, monarchs of the worlds they survey. At the same time, he understood that noble souls could reside in many places. For anyone who has undergone the experience of combat, he is a uniquely, if strangely "vitalizing" Shakespeare—a Shakespeare who, beyond his other many excellences, writes also wisely and humanely about one of the most elusive and strange of subjects, about soldiering. The fact is, he tells us, that anyone who has been in combat in a war, be that person a king or a commoner, knows somehow—oddly perhaps grimly, but abidingly—that it was the most exciting thing he ever did in his life, that he will always remember the people who were with him when he did it, and that they will always have something together no one else can know. It is sometimes objected that Shakespeare may have never traveled outside London, possessed little education, could not have known much about life at court. It is certain that he never fought in a war. As with so many other features of his writing, where the great Shakespearean heart and imagination were concerned, these are things of no matter. In the case of arms and the Bard, maybe Shakespeare was not a grunt. But he knew how to soldier.

2
Bury Their Hearts at Horseshoe Bend

Nearly any person who travels to the US Military Park at Horseshoe Bend, near the Georgia border in east central Alabama, goes there on purpose. Appearing out of the largely featureless rural landscape of small farms and crossroad towns, of cropped-out fields and second-growth forests and centered on a great oxbow of the Tallapoosa River, today it is a place utterly miles from nowhere. Meanwhile, the same figure of empty cartography may now be said in large degree to characterize its place in American historical consciousness and the larger human record of the continent. This is a decidedly unfortunate omission. For here was fought, two hundred years ago, the single most decisive nineteenth-century battle east of the Mississippi between US military forces and Native Americans. It was a battle that would simultaneously initiate the great Indian removals of the ensuing quarter century and the mass importation of enslaved Africans to replace them on newly claimed lands in the great antebellum cotton enterprise of the lower South, extending from west Georgia through Alabama, Mississippi, Louisiana, Arkansas, and eventually into Texas and the desert Southwest.

The opposing forces and their leaders comprise a historical panoply of the famous and the now-forgotten. US participants were largely made up of a territorial militia led by the ascendant Andrew Jackson, with troops from Tennessee, Georgia, and the present-day states of Alabama and Mississippi. An addition crucial to the Horseshoe Bend action would be one regiment of US regulars. As important would prove a force of five or six hundred Native American auxiliaries. The opposing force of Native Americans is usually estimated at around one thousand warriors from a tribe called the Muscogees—known to settlers as Creeks because of their life along the region's abundant streams and rivers, a tribal domain extending across enormous tracts of Georgia and Alabama. This group of fighters came from a breakaway Muscogee faction technically known as the Upper Creeks—as distinguished from Lower Creeks, who had a history of closer contact with whites, under the influence of Fed-

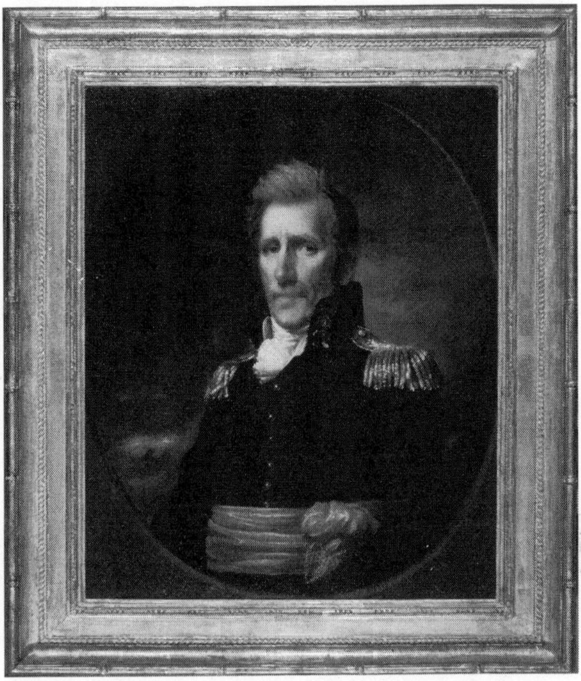

Figure 2.1 Oil portrait of General Andrew Jackson, ca 1814, by Samuel Lovett Waldo. The Historic New Orleans Collection, New Orleans, Louisiana.

eral Indian Agent Benjamin Hawkins. Familiarly called Red Sticks because of a distinctive style of war club, the Upper Creeks were led by the war chief William Weatherford, the son of a Scots father and Indian mother known as the Red Eagle. The loyalist Lower Creek faction also claimed a war chief of similar mixed-race pedigree, in this case William MacIntosh.

The primary Upper Creek grievance leading to the hostilities was the usual matter of relentless white encroachment over a period of years. One proximate cause was allegedly the building of the Federal Road, actually an aggregation of several routes, extending from west Georgia directly through the Creek lands to the regions of Mobile on the Gulf of Mexico. In its suspicion of such an avenue of white advance, the Red Stick faction was prescient. Initially a trade and postal route, and then, with the rise of tensions, a military road, it would become ultimately the superhighway of settlement known as "Alabama Fever." A second alleged cause was the supposed radicalization of the tribes of the lower South through the visit of the Shawnee Chief Tecumseh—who had earlier attempted to unite tribes of the upper Midwest against the

Americans during the Revolution—accompanied by his brother Tenskwatawa, a shadowy figure known as the Prophet. As context, parallel US pressures were being exerted to the north against the Shawnee, Ottawa, Potawatomi, Sauk, and Fox. In 1811 Tecumseh had traveled to the southern regions in the hope of rallying all the tribes east of the Mississippi in a last ditch effort against white pressure for removal.

As to the actual ignition of the military conflict that came to be known as the Creek War of 1813–14, various explanations continue to be offered. Some chroniclers cite an isolated incident involving a war party of Red Sticks returning from the Midwest through the Ohio Valley and robbing and murdering a settler family along the way. More often cited is the ambush of a Red Stick column, returning from Spanish-held Pensacola with supplies, by a militia force under one Colonel John Caller. The ill-disciplined Americans, having scattered a Creek party one-fourth their size, stopped to loot the pack train, in turn allowing the Creeks to reassemble and put them to rout. (The ignominy of the incident, and the ineptitude of the commanding officer, were sufficient to be memorialized by a provincial wag in a scurrilous mock-epic poem grandly titled *The Last Campaign of Sir John Falstaff the II; or The Hero of the Burnt-Corn Battle.*) Things proved hardly so skirmish-like, however, when Creek retribution led to a substantial massacre of at least 250 settlers—men, women, and children who had taken refuge at Fort Mims, an ill-defended sanctuary twenty miles above Mobile—in which Weatherford was said to have played an active but ambiguous role. A running military campaign conducted by forces under Jackson then began in earnest during November 1813, with a first battle at Tallusastchee and then a series of engagements at Creek strongholds, including Talledega, Hillabee, Autosee, and Tallassee. The year concluded on December 23 with a battle at a place called Holy Ground. On January 22, 1814, US campaigning began again at Emuckfaw. Then, on March 27, after much forest travel, US forces arrived at the Horseshoe Bend of the Tallapoosa, where the Creeks, in a last-ditch effort, had erected a massive rampart on the neck of the peninsula along with a village, in the bow of the river, called Tohopeka.

The action was initiated by a US cannonade, with Jackson's two artillery pieces firing against the formidable Creek barricade consisting of heavy logs. This was followed by an infantry assault on the ramparts, led by the US regulars. Of the one thousand Creeks defending, only a third are estimated to have been armed with firearms. The defenders were eventually pushed back to an elevation now called the High Ground, midway between the barricade and the village. Meanwhile, Colonel John Coffee maneuvered an attached force of five hundred Cherokees led by Gideon Morgan and one hundred Lower Creeks under the aforementioned William McIntosh onto the opposite banks of the river just across from the village. First swimming across the river and

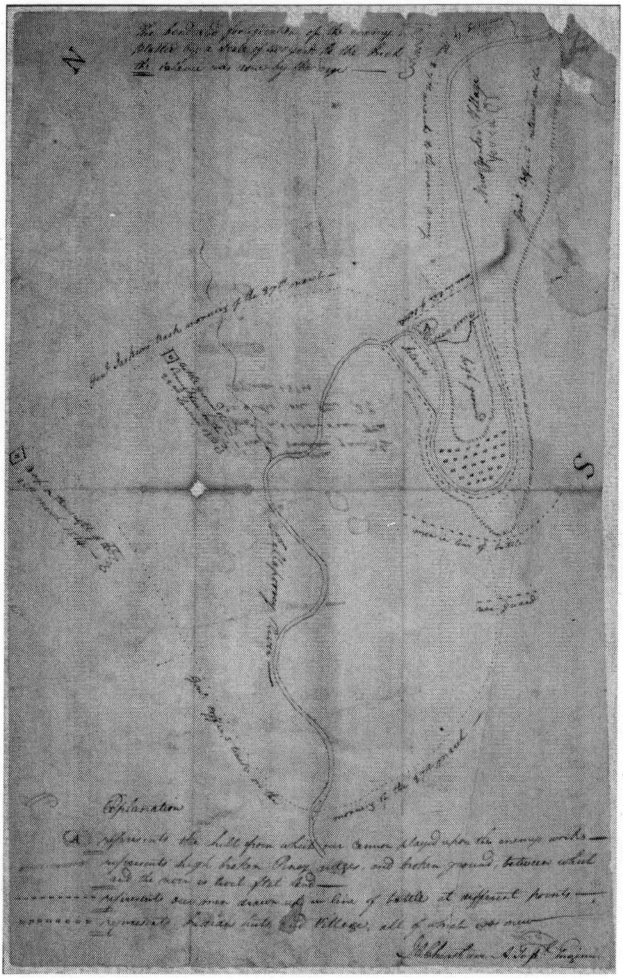

Figure 2.2 John Cheatham's Battle Map of Horseshoe Bend, March 27, 1814. President William H. Harrison Papers, Record Group 77, CWMF, Misc., 11–2, National Archives and Records Administration.

then making use of stolen canoes, this substantial force soon mounted a full attack on Tohopeka, which was occupied by three hundred fifty women and children. Attacked from both sides, the Creeks made a final defense on the High Ground. A vast majority fought to the death. The final casualty total was estimated at eight hundred Red Stick warriors killed. If US reports are to be believed, all three hundred fifty civilians were further taken alive, along with three warriors. US forces suffered forty-nine killed and one hundred fifty four

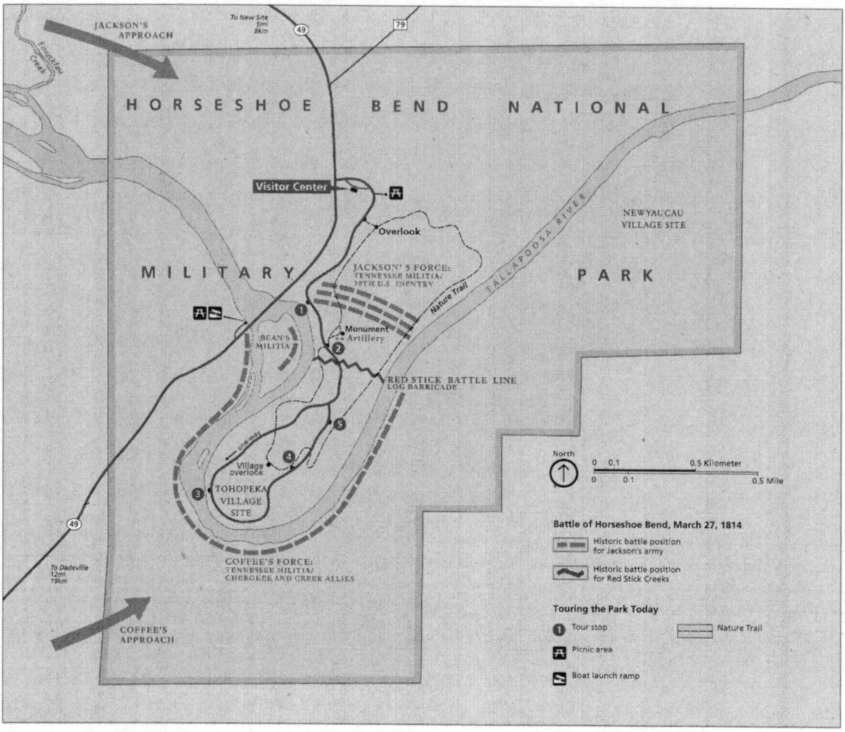

Figure 2.3 Opposing formations at the Battle of Horseshoe Bend, March 27, 1814. Horseshoe Bend National Military Park Map.

wounded. William Weatherford himself seems not to have been present. The actual commanding war chief Menawa—Weatherford's deputy—did manage to escape, though badly wounded.

Such tactical details seem to have quickly given way to the popular mythification of the two main war leaders. Horseshoe Bend became a legendary battle with a legendary outcome, fostering a heroic tale of the larger Jackson-Weatherford relationship that has been much romanticized in history and literature. In the basic story, Weatherford, ready to sacrifice his life for the preservation of his people, was said to have personally sought out Jackson in the aftermath of the battle and voluntarily surrendered. In turn Jackson is said to have been so impressed by the nobility of his former foe that he decided to spare Weatherford's life. Or so the event went as recorded in the mostly forgotten historical romance *The Lost Virgin of the South*, a vast, sprawling captivity narrative—much in the vein of James Fenimore Cooper, William Gilmore Simms, Catharine Maria Sedgwick, or Lydia Maria Child—in which fictional characters mixed with historical figures such as Jackson and Weather-

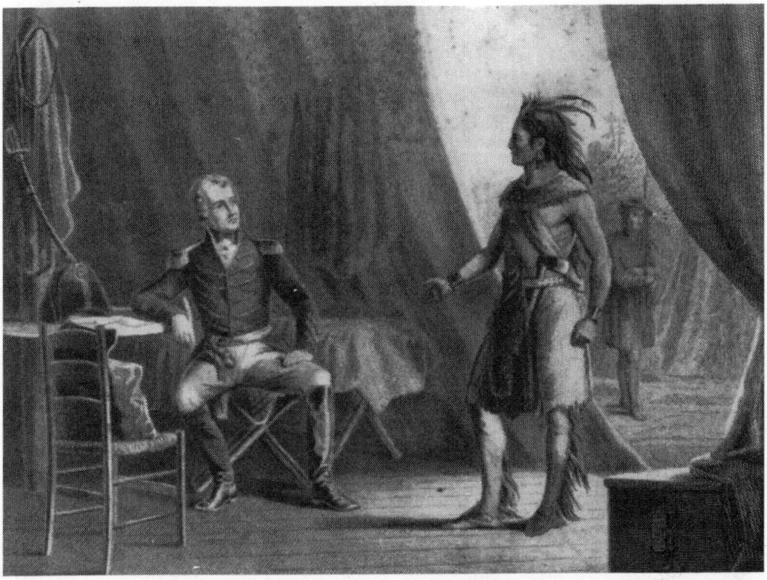

Figure 2.4 William Weatherford, "Red Eagle," surrenders to Andrew Jackson at the end of the Creek Indian War of 1813–1814. Alabama Department of Archives and History.

ford on a canvas of battle comprising depictions of both Horseshoe Bend and New Orleans. Within decades, the Weatherford-Jackson relationship was still further immortalized in Albert S. Pickett's *History of Alabama*, to this day reprinted as a parallel achievement to those of such great nineteenth- century practitioners of romantic art as Francis Parkman, William S. Prescott, and John Lothrop Motley. And then, just before the Civil War, Horseshoe Bend was once more celebrated as the focus of a truly Homeric literary enterprise, an epic poem by Alabamian Alexander Beaufort Meek titled *The Red Eagle*—which had the most impossibly bad fortune to be published in the same year as both Henry Wadsworth's *Song of Hiawatha* and Walt Whitman's first edition of *Leaves of Grass*.

As to the actual historical figures whose actions undergirded the heroic legend, Weatherford would settle on the land and live until 1824 as a slave-owning planter in nearby Monroe County. MacIntosh, his Lower Creek opposite number, became a US brigadier general, again fighting against his fellow Native Americans—and Muscogee kinsmen—in the ensuing Seminole war of 1816 and was ultimately shot and killed by dissident fellow tribesmen for signing the Treaty of Indian Springs. In larger American history and legend, of course, Jackson and his American force would make their way to New Or-

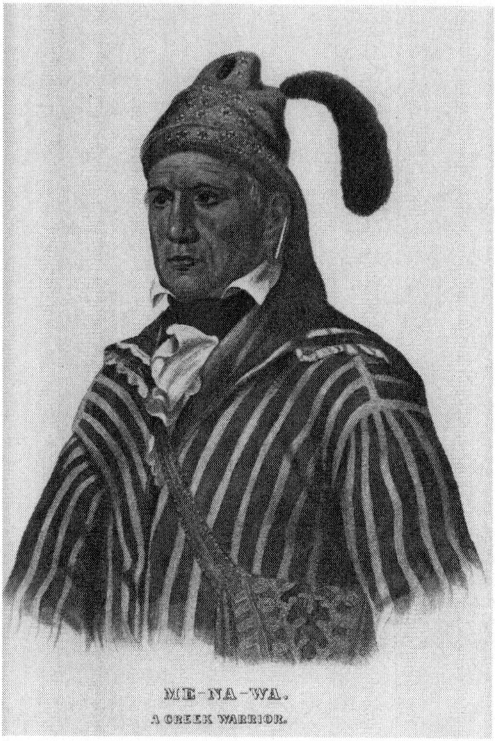

Figure 2.5 Menawa, the military leader of Red Stick forces at Horseshoe Bend. Thomas L. McKenney and James Hall, *History of the Indian Tribes of North America*, Volume 1 (Philadelphia: E. C. Biddle), 1836.

leans, where on January 8, 1815—redeeming the ignominy to the north of the British capture and burning of Washington, DC—they would defeat British regulars in the concluding battle of the War of 1812, an action no less heroic, it seems, for having been fought a full three weeks after the Treaty of Ghent had officially ended the war.

Less known than the metaphorical signature that Jackson put to the final conflict of the nascent United States with their former colonial rulers, but more germane to this account, were the events set in motion by his suppression of the internal uprisings by the great Native Peoples of the South. Those might be said to have begun with a signature as well—in this case a literal one—affixed to what became known as the Treaty of Fort Jackson, signed August 9, 1814, six months after the Battle of Horseshoe Bend near present day Wetumpka, Alabama. This was the first step in a process of mass cession of lands and ultimate removals that would within two decades involve all Native peoples of the Lower South, centering on what were termed the "Five Civilized Tribes"—the Creeks, Cherokees, Choctaws, Chickasaws, and Seminoles—but finally encompassing the remnants of all the other ancient Algonquians of the region. At Fort Jackson alone the business began with the cession by the Creeks of lands estimated at twenty-three million acres.

For the Creeks and associated Southern tribes, ensuing events would continue to mix further periods of open war against American military forces with an increasingly tragic fraternal history, largely US provoked and manipulated, of internecine conflict. Native peoples of the Gulf region, faced with the relentless advance of American settlement and the transformation of territories into new states—Louisiana in 1812, Mississippi in 1817, Alabama in 1819—were pressured into the forlorn hope of alliance with former occupiers such as the British or Spanish in east and west Florida for survival. Meanwhile, the US did its best to continue the policy of pitting tribe against tribe. Jackson at Horseshoe Bend, as noted, had already counted among his native auxiliaries six hundred warriors—five hundred Cherokees and one hundred Creeks. Also numbering among his forces at Holy Ground had been five hundred Choctaws under the legendary Chief Pushmataha. Native American auxiliaries continued to participate in three subsequent wars with the Seminoles. After continued betrayals of political and property rights through a series of treaties, a second Creek War flared in the 1830s. The Cherokees of northeast Georgia, having staked their claims to post-Revolution Americanness on decades of assimilation, got for their pains the Indian Removal Treaty of 1832 and their marching orders westward on what became known as the Trail of Tears. With the power of the tribes fragmented and compromised, no room was left even for domestic bargaining. The Choctaw, having ceded twelve million acres of land, were newly confronted in 1830 with the Treaty of Dancing Rabbit Creek. The Chickasaw held out long enough to settle for evacuation money, three million dollars that they were never paid. The treaties flaunted such phrasings as "where the wind blows and the grass grows." The once-great tribes got Oklahoma, from which they would eventually be removed once again. It was all a sorry business, aided, abetted, and finally ramrodded at every turn by Jackson himself, the Canebrake Napoleon. After Horseshoe Bend he was a made man, with the Battle of New Orleans supplying icing on the proverbial cake. Catapulted to prominence as an unapologetic, relentless Indian fighter and a world class military leader, scoring two legendary military victories in an otherwise utterly ignominious war for the Americans, he became within a decade the most powerful American of the antebellum era—King Andrew—and his word was law.

Added to his epithets must surely be, in the once-familiar nineteenth century phrasing, the Indian Hater, in his particular case the remorseless instigator of the great Native American removals of the 1820s and 1830s. Indeed, with the Jackson ascendancy, the lower South was wide open, stretching to Texas and the desert Southwest, and US power was there to stay. The Creeks, Choctaws, Cherokees, Chickasaws, and Seminoles had joined their already displaced Algonquian kinsmen originally east of the Mississippi, the Iroquois, Mohawk, Cayuga, Onandaga, Oneida, Seneca, Huron, Ojibway, Lenni Lenape, Chickahominy, Powhatan, Wampanoag, and countless others. To the north, the concurrent exercise of antebellum US power would add to the roster such tribes as the Shawnee, Ottawa, Potawatomi, Sauk, and Fox. The creation of the states Louisiana, Alabama, Mississippi, Arkansas, and Texas would be accompanied by the creation of Ohio, Indiana, Illinois, Minnesota, and Michigan. There would be flickers of rebellion, amid futile attempts to conciliate and domesticate. From the 1830s and 1840s onward, the great eastern drama was mostly over, leaving the final tragedy of the second half of the century to play itself out in the trans-Mississippi west.

What one feels now in the crucial place where this history made its fatal turn—a place, it must be said, of great haunting silence and natural beauty—is surely the great sadness of it all. Partly this is because Horseshoe Bend has become an official United States military park, one that like virtually all others in the system, particularly in the east, is immaculately preserved and maintained, like Valley Forge or Gettysburg. As a result, it now seems just perfect—enshrined, manicured, quietly signposted, with park rangers, museum, maps, glossy brochures, in short, the works. That is the irony of military preservation. Horseshoe Bend has now become one of those particular places—Antietam comes to mind—where one can stand there and see it all. The site of Jackson's battery looks down on the carefully marked expanse of the crucial barricade. Lying beyond, down in the river bend, is the village site, looking like some royal forest in England. Rising up in between is the high ground where things were finally decided.

A further irony of more general historic preservation is involved as well. It lies in the topographic symbolism of the view the place now gives—by being so perfectly restored to something like original appearance—of the natural richness of the original landscape and of why exactly it had to be cleared of native peoples and repeopled with enslaved Africans for cotton production. In its natural state., the rolling green expanse now itself proclaims the reason it was so valuable, the forests cleared, the fertile river bottoms planted, the region blessed with waterways going to the Gulf: the Chattahoochee, Coosa, Tallapoosa, Warrior, Tombigbee, Alabama.

Bury their hearts at Horseshoe Bend, one is tempted to say: the Native Americans and the US soldiers, but also those who died in the continued extensions of American territorial hunger culminating in the final occupations of the West. The lands taken from the Five Civilized Tribes, with the short staple cotton they grew in profligate abundance made profitable by the invention of Eli Whitney's cotton gin, gave slavery a completely new lease on life on the plantations of the lower South, west Georgia, Alabama, Mississippi, Louisiana, and Texas. And so we might ultimately pronounce the same epitaph for the great Native Peoples beyond the Mississippi in this eastern prefiguring of their eventual removals and exterminations. The final closing of the American frontier at large would be announced by Frederick Jackson toward the end of the century in his famous essay, based largely on 1890 census figures. As to original inhabitants, the "Turner Thesis," as it was called, would be confirmed and punctuated that census year by the Wounded Knee Massacre of February 17, 1890. Here the last-stand legends would involve a charismatic leader, Sitting Bull, a messiah movement inspired by Spotted Elk, and desperate Ghost Dance followers believing in magical protection from US soldiers' bullets. Precipitated by the attempts of the US Seventh Cavalry to disarm an encampment of Lakota at Pine Ridge, South Dakota, it resulted in totals of 150 Lakota killed and fifty wounded and US casualties of twenty-five killed and thirty-nine wounded.

Bury their hearts at Horseshoe Bend. As will have been noted by readers of late-twentieth-century Native American history, the phrasing of my title here is in fact taken from Dee Brown's groundbreaking book, *Bury My Heart at Wounded Knee*, the first comprehensive account of the American Indian West. Brown, in turn, borrowed his title from a popular post–World War I Stephen Vincent Benet poem titled "American Names." Here is the concluding stanza:

I shall not rest quiet in Montparnasse.
I shall not lie easy at Winchelsea.
You may bury my body in Sussex grass,
You may bury my tongue at Champmédy.
I shall not be there. I shall rise and pass.
Bury my heart at Wounded Knee.

As the poem makes clear, Winchelsea and Sussex are places in an ancestral England; Montparnasse and Champmédy are names of French locations near which Americans had recently died. The last phrasing, in contrast, seems to suggest the poet's understanding that some names in the national history may even go deeper than America. One of those now surely calls us back to the Old Southwest, to the original Indian territories, before the Trail of Tears, in the opening years of the century of the great removals and exterminations. With tragic prescience, as it turns out, the Creeks themselves had already added a new word to their own language for this terrible thing they saw coming to the native inhabitants. *Ecunnaunuxulgee*, they called it; "people grasping after all lands." Accordingly, Horseshoe Bend remains the name of the American place where a great part of it may be said to have begun.

3
Ted Turner et al. at Gettysburg; or, Reenactors in the Attic

Let me admit that I am no fan of the Civil War industry. For one thing, I was born in Gettysburg, Pennsylvania and spent the better part of the 1950s and 1960s watching the place fill up with everything from a gigantic commercial viewing tower to a Jesus wax museum. For another, as a former armored cavalry platoon leader in Vietnam, I recoil against any attempt to render war attractive—the Civil War, the Vietnamese war, any war. Particularly as regards the perverse spectacle called reenactment, I remain absolutely clueless as to why grown people, all their attestations about "living history" notwithstanding, would want to dress up in period uniforms and go out for weekends of mock-battle where, between bouts of sleeping in soggy bedrolls and consuming grim repasts of sowbelly and hardtack, they pretend to maim and slaughter each other. It is a perplexity hardly assuaged, I should add, by my recent reading in Tony Horwitz's 1998 *Confederates in the Attic* of a much-admired reenactor whose battlefield star turns include the ability to puff and blow himself into the semblance of a bloated corpse.

Still, I do not plan to spend an essay here arguing that Ted Turner made the movie *Gettysburg* just so he could dress up like a Confederate general and get killed leading a brigade during Pickett's Charge—although by all accounts his passion for Civil War history does seem to have had much to do with his decision to bankroll the project. Neither, despite my less than reverent title, do I wish to speak here merely of the current reenactment mania, whether played out—as with Turner—at the tip of the production pyramid or among the ranks of thousands of costumed hobbyists known to have provided his project and others like it with cinematic cannon fodder. What I do want to talk about is the packaging and marketing of the Civil War as part of a larger commodification of cultural desire in which the making of Turner's film and his participation in it become exemplary. I wish to speak, that is, of *Gettysburg* as a case study in the ongoing manufacture of the Civil War as the quintessential American item—a product not unlike its cousin the sport

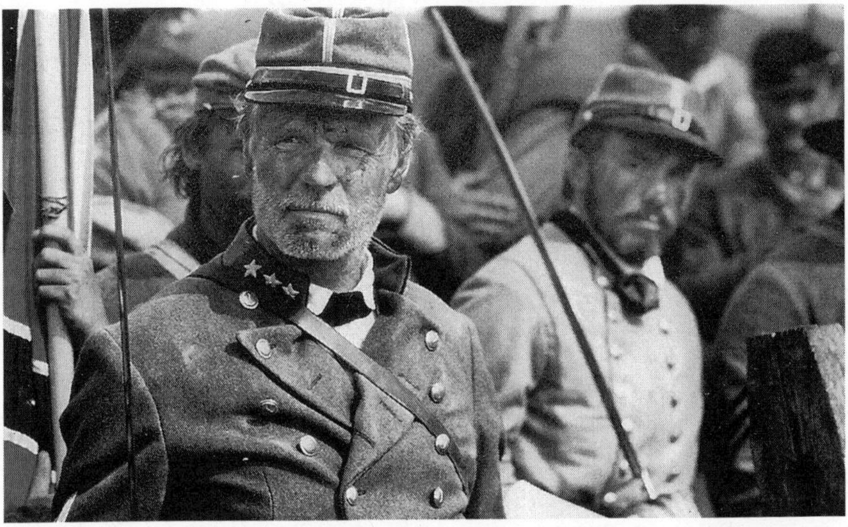

Figure 3.1 Ted Turner in the 1993 production of *Gettysburg*. Turner Pictures, 1993.

utility vehicle, as dangerous as it is big and handsome, a shining exterior fabricated around the killing power of the machine.

Here, the property that reached Turner was one with a production history stretching back nearly two decades, namely, to the publication of Michael Shaara's 1974 novel of the Battle of Gettysburg, *The Killer Angels*. Considered at the time something of a quirky anachronism—a historically compendious and wide-ranging account of most of the significant action during the three-day engagement, simultaneously re-created through the eyes of major participants on both the Union and Confederate sides—it had nonetheless won that year's Pulitzer Prize for fiction. Over the years, it gained the reputation of a cult classic among military history and historical fiction enthusiasts.

The big picture was contained in the novel's imposing overall structure. A foreword outlined Lee's 1863 plan to invade the North and, in the vein of the breathless *dramatis personae* technique made famous by Douglas Southall Freeman in *Lee's Lieutenants*, sketched out present-tense biographies of major figures soon to be involved in the slaughter of Gettysburg. After detailed scene-setting, separate battle chapters were devoted to the three days of major action: the Union rout of July 1 and withdrawal to fortified high ground; the furious Confederate attempts of July 2—at the Wheat Field and Peach Orchard, the Devil's Den, and finally Little Round Top—to destroy the Union left; and the powerful July 3 denouement of Pickett's Charge. A brief afterword detailed the later lives of surviving participants.

Shaara's novel found an ingenious expedient for conveying the human dimension of the battle by shifting back and forth between the points of view of selected, mainly well-known historical players. For the South, these tended to be major command figures, notably Lee and Longstreet, largely superintending Confederate decision-making during the battle. Also included more briefly were "Harrison," a Confederate spy in Longstreet's employ; General Lewis Armistead, shortly to die at the forefront of Pickett's Charge; and Colonel Arthur Fremantle, a British observer traveling with the Confederate command. For the North, focal figures were General John Buford, the cavalry commander largely responsible for the first day's holding action that allowed Meade's army to assume the commanding positions of the second and third; and Colonel Joshua Lawrence Chamberlain, who along with his regiment, the Twentieth Maine, became the hero of the afternoon of July 2 during the crucial Union defense of Little Round Top.

Looking back, one sees why the book so attracted the movie director Ron Maxwell, who saw the opportunity to make a faithful re-creation of historical spectacle while forming the human drama of the event around the development of a fascinating ensemble cast of major characters. According to C. Peter Jorgenson's account, Maxwell first read the book in 1978 and bought the film rights in 1980. He then spent most of the ensuing decade trying to market the enormous concept, completing coauthorship of a script with Shaara before the latter's death in 1988 and going so far as to sell his house to keep the project solvent. Fortunately, in 1990, amid the phenomenal success of Ken Burns's eleven-hour PBS series *The Civil War*, Maxwell met Burns, who averred that a reading of *The Killer Angels* had inspired his own efforts. Burns next ran into Turner at an awards ceremony and mentioned the novel in the same connection, lamenting that Turner did not have the rights to the property, which he thought would make a fine television series. Negotiations were begun between the independent production company holding the rights to the Maxwell project and executives at TNT, and with Turner already hospitable to the project on the basis of his discussion with Burns and his personal interest in the Civil War, corporate funding of $10 million was finally secured. Casting of major roles ensued, including Tom Berenger as Longstreet, Martin Sheen as Lee, Sam Elliott as Buford, and Jeff Daniels as Joshua Lawrence Chamberlain. The script was in the meantime thrice rewritten.

With the solution of what seemed Maxwell's biggest money, personnel, and script troubles, however, new problems in getting cinematic armies to fight again at Gettysburg arose in the rank-and-file. Here, his trump card, following on the success of Marshall Zwick in the 1990 film *Glory*, had been his belief that he could recruit hordes of reenactors. People with this kind of investment in the Civil War, he reasoned, authorized to reenact something *really* big with all the gaudy trimmings and given the additional promise of having their participation immortalized in a major movie, would flock to the project and perform with minimal compensation. The unforeseen difficulty was that by now large numbers of individual hobbyists and the larger reenactor units of which they were a part were veterans of a number of such movie wars, with sufficient previous action having occurred to support a small subindustry specializing in the brokerage of reenactor casts. This market in turn had been cornered by an enterprising couple named Massengill, whom Maxwell was now counting on to deliver for the new enterprise. Unfortunately, they had worn out their good standing among major reenactor constituencies, with new groups bearing such weighty titles as the Civil War Reenactors Liaison Committee, the Confederate Army of Northern Virginia, and the National Regiment demanding to be brought into complex negotiations. To make a Civil War analogy, the reenactors were no longer eager militia volunteers, willing to work for the typical offer of "a baseball cap, a T-shirt, a video, a booklet and a Civil War print, nominal mileage for infantry and double mileage plus twenty-five dollars for cannon and crews." Having served out earlier hitches, they now demanded reenlistment bounty. Event registration fees, devoted to battlefield preservation, would be paid by the studio; units mustering one hundred participants or more would get a special fee, with an additional bonus for each man over the minimum; an on-site historian acceptable to the negotiators would be engaged to insure historical "accuracy" and to take over "reenactor coordination" activities from the despised Massengills.

Meanwhile, disputes arose with the local Teamsters and the International Alliance of Theater and Stage Employees. Lawyers had to get an injunction against a low-flying plane with a banner reading "Union Yes" that disrupted filming for the day. The Civil War Reenactors Liaison Committee historian weighed in with forty single-spaced pages of script changes.

Then there was the battlefield. While preserving intact the sites of the major actions, Gettysburg was a forest of concrete memorials, many of them the size of buildings, not to mention the aforementioned viewing tower dominating the scene of the third day's action. These had to be covered with camouflage netting or edited out of the final print. Also, because of government safety regulations, combat sequences involving musketry and cannonry had to be moved off-location to nearby sites chosen or rebuilt to resemble their historical analogues.

Amid all this, it must have seemed minor to Maxwell that the president of TNT wanted to play a general. And so it turned out to be, as far as evolving dramatic chemistry was concerned, especially among the featured players. As Longstreet, Tom Berenger proved suitably underplayed, laconic, and grumpy. On the other side, as Chamberlain, Jeff Daniels took the mildly fuddled professorial type perfected in *Terms of Endearment* and elevated the same qualities into a sturdily convincing model of the heroism of the average man called to higher duty.

A source of critical dismay, on the other hand, was the casting of Martin Sheen as Robert E. Lee, who seemed too youthful in appearance and manner to be persuasive, even beneath the steel-grey beard and flowing silver hair. Equally negative was comment on Sam Elliott's over-acting in the role of John Buford, full of *Lonesome Dove* snarl and bark and diminishing the opportunity to create a neglected character of major historical import.

There were also more cheering by-blows of casting. Foremost was the performance of Richard Jordan, himself dying of a brain tumor, playing the doomed, romantic Confederate Brigadier Lewis Armistead, facing across the line an old beloved friend, Union General Winfield Scott Hancock. Indeed, as with the book, this was one of the production features that actually came closest to capturing the spirit of soldiering and of male comradeship in an age when men North and South did often talk about their feelings in windy, romantic phrasings out of Shakespeare and Walter Scott.

Similarly, Stephen Lang, as Pickett, played a better George Pickett than George Pickett himself probably ever was. Legendary for graduating last in his class at West Point, he is played by Lang with a kind of bully obtuseness, making a fool out of himself with blustering good humor in political discussions and reveling in the taunts of his fellows about his playing the perfumed dandy.

The reenactors, as noted particularly by observers with knowledge of Civil War combat, were commensurately good, especially in scenes involving complicated battlefield drill and maneuver, where their work far exceeded that which might have been expected of paid extras. The problem is that in many ways they were excessively good. Uniforms were authentic to a fault. The Union officers were replete with the requisite Second Empire goatees and moustachios. Southern officers and men alike became models of a studied idiosyncrasy. The former went for dashing decoration: the braided jacket, the sash, the colorful kepi. The latter, with their bedrolls, slouch hats, and jangling kit, became studies in unreconstructed rebel personality.

In their total authenticity, then, they could have hardly been surpassed as figures in a reenactment. Unfortunately, precisely the qualities that made them star reenactors—their highly choreographed drill and maneuver, for instance, however "authentic," and their tendency in costume and gesture to strike attitudes of the picturesque—were not so happily married to a movie, with its intense visual impressionism and its related qualities of sweeping movement and symbolic action. The result was a *tableau vivant* quality of overdetermined detail.

As shooting was completed, evolutions were taking place in marketing concept. Originally conceived of and filmed to meet the production format of a

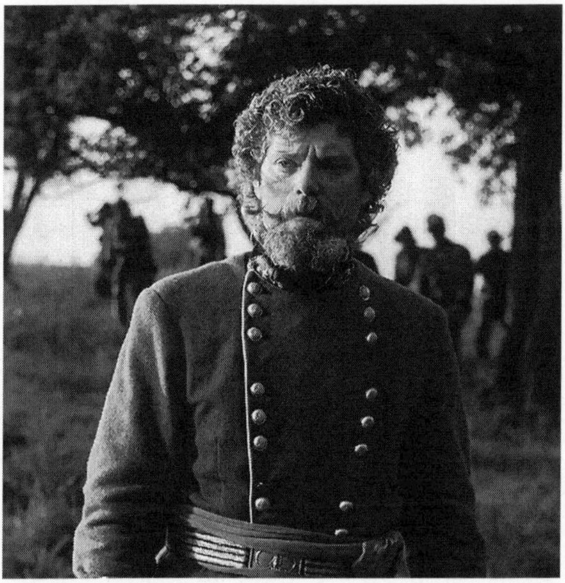

Figure 3.2 Stephen Lang as George E. Pickett in the 1993 production of *Gettysburg*. Turner Pictures, 1993.

TV miniseries, the resulting artifact persuaded its creators that it should also be offered as a theater release in carefully selected locations. This was done with considerable success, attracting largely favorable publicity which also continued to attach to multiple showings in spring of 1994 as a three-night TNT miniseries. It was then released in video. Meanwhile, spinoff properties from the filming began to be advertised in popular history publications. A video was offered on the making of the film. A companion promised costumed participants doing period music.

Elaborate advertising was also made of a coffee-table book, with art by Mort Kunstler (the dean of popular Civil War illustrators), parallel text by Pulitzer Prize-winning historian James McPherson, and a preface by Martin Sheen. Illustrations reproduced images of major characters, scenes, and incidents from battle. Some were recyclings of earlier Kunstler "classics"; others derived from the film, with many of the worthies depicted thus oscillating in resemblance between their historical originals and the actors who played them. Overall, the effect was something akin to visiting your lawyer's or dentist's office when your lawyer or dentist is a Civil War history buff—as opposed, say, to a collector of fox-hunting lithographs or limited edition college football prints. Both posed arrangements and "action" scenes look exactly like reenactments. The commanders exercise picturesque individual variations on uniform: some braid, a sash, a plume, a neck scarf. Men wear wire-rimmed glasses and jaunty little hats. Even the smears of sweat and gunpowder residue on the cheeks look painted on. A single figure in the entire book, picturesquely draped over a cannon amid furious action in "The High Water Mark," seems to have some blood on his uniform sleeve; there is not a disassembled body part in sight.

In the audio market, a soundtrack album appeared in record stores, reproducing the Randy Edelman score in dramatic vignettes and interspersing it with period music that was also part of the film. Individual sections were given titles ranging from the functional to the heavily atmospheric. "The Battle of Little Round Top" jostled with "From History to Legend"; "Over the Fence" with "March to Mortality." Interwoven were a tenor solo of "Kathleen Mavourneen" and a soulful reprise of "Dixie."

Meanwhile, Shaara's book also got new life in a handsome hardback reissue by Random House. A trade paperbound was issued by Ballantine, a leading publisher of popular war narrative. Visibly an upscale item in the Ballantine/Ivy lineup, it featured full-size pages and elaborate maps. The cover reproduced the depiction of the third day's climax at the Bloody Angle from the vast cyclorama painting by Paul Philoppoteaux. Heralding the text as "The Pulitzer Prize-winning Civil War novel," with "2.5 million copies in print," it also carried blurbs from James McPherson, Ken Burns, and Norman Schwarzkopf.

Further, in a compounding of familial and literary genealogies, *The Killer Angels* eventually came to spawn its own novelistic spinoffs, with Jeff Shaara, Michael Shaara's son, publishing a 1996 companion volume from Ballantine, *Gods and Generals*. He followed it in 1998 with another, *The Last Full Measure*. Both continued the formula of *The Killer Angels*. The first, known in the trade as a "prequel," attempted to elaborate the prior histories of many of the same figures Michael Shaara had depicted as meeting their fates at Gettysburg. Also included, however, were narrative segments from the perspective of such other worthies as Stonewall Jackson, killed six weeks before Gettysburg at Chancellorsville, and Winfield Scott Hancock, the Union commander responsible for the repulse of Pickett's Charge but not given much of a role in the original novel. The second, picking up amid Lee's retreat from Gettysburg, followed the deadly endgame of the Army of Northern Virginia and the Army of the Potomac that culminated in the Confederate surrender at Appomatox. Again, Joshua Chamberlain is a featured character, sharing point of view this time with Lee and Grant. But most eye-catching in both cases, from a design and marketing standpoint, was the degree to which the son's novels were in every way presented as companion pieces to that of the father, even down to title-author design and jacket art in Philoppoteaux-like period style. Inside, the sense of replication was reinforced in print format. Naturally, the collection was immediately dubbed a "trilogy." (Things did not end here. By now, indeed, the Jeff Shaara project may be said to have become a franchise

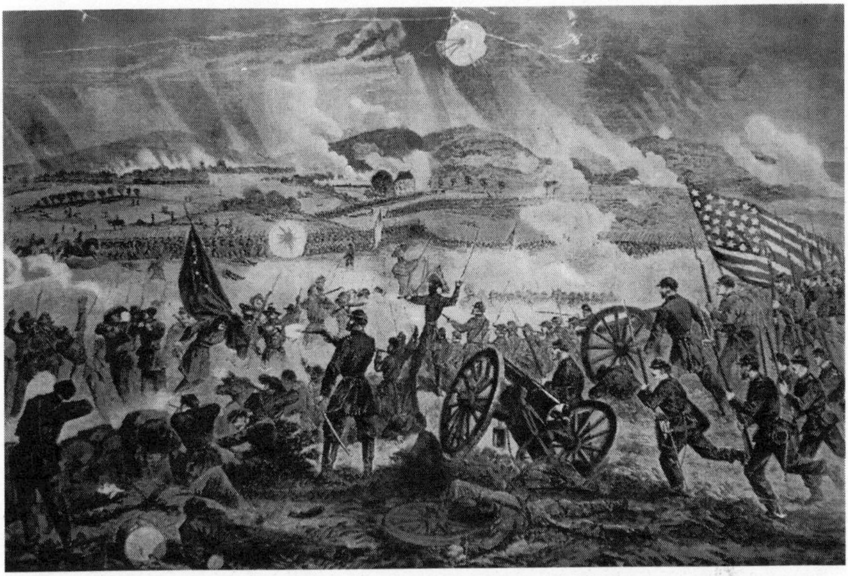

Figure 3.3 Pickett's Charge. *Harper's Weekly*, August 8, 1863. NPS History Collection.

unto itself, with thirteen titles in print, running from the Revolutionary and Mexican Wars to World Wars I and II.)

Thus did the business of *Gettysburg* come full circle. A Pulitzer Prize-winning novel became an epic film. The film appeared in theater release, then as a television miniseries, then in video. The film spawned a sound track album. It also inspired a coffee-table book of popular illustration, with text by a famous historian. The video inspired other videos. Meanwhile, the book that inspired the film came out in newly elaborate hardbound and paperback reissue. This in turn inspired new books by the author's son, artfully designed as companion volumes. What they call in Hollywood a "concept" had become a "property" beyond any marketer's dream.

Apace, along its entire production trajectory, the project had enacted with nearly seamless perfection the regnant popular culture aesthetic of Civil War memory. To appropriate the military argot of the era depicted, it is all handsomely done. Or, to enlarge the metaphor, war itself at every point has been made lovely and moving by being made handsome, with the handsomeness now exactly that of the glossy "enthusiast" magazine, the limited-edition print, the reenactor's impeccably authentic getup, the immaculately preserved and manicured battlefield. And it is through this same handsomeness that it conceals almost to perfection the brilliantly ironic secret of its success. It manages to arrive at a final product purporting to represent war by having virtually nothing to do with combat—with the killing and wounding, that is, the being on the giving or receiving end in the inflicting of death or disabling injury that supplies war's essential content. To be sure, in the movie, the most immediately lifelike of the representations, individual soldiers fall, they flop, they fold, and they fly. Indeed, substantial numbers of them do it over and over again. That is just the problem. As a *Commonweal* reviewer put it, the wounded "always seem to be taking the same forward dive or sideways crumple," a "grisly recycling effort" of "the same bodies going through the same deathly acrobatics over and over."

The bigger problem here is that they always do the deathly acrobatics so described with all major surfaces and parts of their bodies *intact*. They certainly don't disintegrate. They don't even explode a little, the way bodies do when a bullet hits them. Oh, to be sure, we see state-of-the-art Hollywood bullet wounds, those little electro-percussive things, along with a grunt; maybe a moan, a sinking to the dirt. And in fact, as Peter Svenson has reminded us in *Battlefield*, bullet wounds accounted for 90 percent of the war's casualties. A more compelling fact, however, was that, aside from grazes and flesh wounds, they were also notably big and notably ugly, doing a lot of damage coming and going. For the Minie Ball, as it is known to persons familiar with the history of infantry weapons, was anything but "mini-" and nothing like a ball. Rather it was a conical lead projectile, with three additional metal rings cast into its waist for rifling, of an extremely large .58 caliber, emerging from the barrel of the weapon that fired it as a solid ounce of deformed, unstable, flesh ripping, bone-shattering soft metal, big and heavy and slow. Like the slug from the .45 caliber pistol or submachine gun, which it really resembles more closely than the high-velocity round in the .20-.30 caliber range of the modern infantry rifle, it was a stopper if ever there was one. An astonishingly big round—comparable, for instance, to that fired from the modern heavy .50 caliber machine gun—it was also invariably a maimer. The first aid of choice in an arm or leg wound was frequently amputation simply because, as to bone, muscle, nerve, or artery and vein damage, there was not much really left to fix. Head wounds were frequently skull-penetrating, causing massive facial destruction or brain injury. And wounds to the chest and abdomen were comparably messy and invariably septic. All in all, bullet wounding almost made desirable injuries delivered from close quarters, things like saber cuts, bayonet punctures, blows to the head, neck, and body from huge, heavy rifles and muskets used as clubs, with their heavy metal butt plates.

But even more notable an avoidance here in the representation of wounds—particularly given the Technicolor scale of the noise and action and the astonishing special-effects ingenuities employed to ensure other forms of authenticity—is the film's lack of any serious attempt to represent the dismemberment and evisceration frequently resulting from the war's most appalling technological innovation, the advanced use of artillery, new and improved in maiming and killing power both at long and short range. In its more traditional role as a long-distance weapon, it now mixed traditional solid shot (already known as easily decapitating bodies and cutting them in half) with explosive shell that tore and cratered victims with huge, incredibly destructive shrapnel wounds, or, in the case of a direct hit, simply disintegrated them. At close range, improved grape shot and canister rounds—with the latter amounting to huge-bore shotgun ammunition—commanded astonishing new killing power, in repeated accounts simply vaporizing entire masses of charging men.

By contrast, amid all the action and spectacle of *Gettysburg*, not a single body part in sight is separated from its companions. There are no exploding skulls. Bodies do not instantly become headless, legless, armless torsos. And those are just the human packages. As visibly missing is the stuff that is on the inside: brains, lungs, hearts, livers, intestines. There is some blood spatter. But even that is nothing on the scale required, nothing like the astonishing volume that a human body contains, quarts and quarts of the stuff, flooding from veins, spurting from arteries, flying and splashing all over the place. There is no red mist of human disintegration, no sticky mess in the grass, no collecting on the ground in puddles and gouts.

Close up in *Gettysburg*, there is blood quietly pooling from the hole a sniper has just put behind John Reynolds's ear, dreamily incongruous and appropriate to the strangeness and suddenness of his death; a dying sergeant's white uniform shirt is literally sopping with it as it pours from wounds in the armpit and shoulder. And if you look closely during a scene at a field hospital, an orderly works on what looks like the stump of a knee, very red. What we don't see, even there, is the thing many veterans remembered, the piles and piles of amputated arms and legs, the blood all gone out of them, so incredibly pale and white.

Does one go for the standard reflex and blame the movies? Perhaps, although in terms of combat realism *Gettysburg* certainly takes us far beyond the ludicrous sanitizations of the guts and glory tradition—extending from *Sands of Iwo Jima* to *Patton*—that for so long has served as the standard of the American war film industry. It is surely at least as "realistic," for instance, as such widely applauded films about the Vietnam War as *Platoon* or *Full Metal Jacket*.

Blame the books? Certainly, likewise, there is no more sanitization in Shaara the novelist than in the long tradition of literary war in novel, history, memoir. If anything, here we find at least an advance on a long Civil War tradition of "handsome" history by Bruce Catton, Shelby Foote, and the like, where an engaging unit receives "a galling fire," is "roughly handled" or suffers "a sharp repulse."

Blame the material culture of reenactment, the hobby magazines. the marketing of memorabilia? Yes, to a certain extent. Why do they do Gettysburg or Antietam or Manassas, one begs to ask, and why don't they do Tarawa or Belleau Wood, the Chosin Reservoir or Hue City? The most obvious answer is probably the truest one: that the Civil War battle sites are American and they're there. And then there is also the point that participants on both sides at Gettysburg would have claimed they were trying to make: it is, after all, a free country. As one reenactor put it when questioned on his dedication to the hobby, "Why do people ski or collect coins?"

In all these respects, one might do as well, at the level of mythic symbology, to blame war itself as among the most highly evasionary of all "body" forms of cultural narrative. As Elaine Scarry writes, this has always been the case, with even so direct a medium as documentary evading any "acknowledgment that the purpose of the event described is to alter (to burn, to blast, to shell, to cut) human tissue, as well as to alter the surface, shape, and deep entirety of the objects that human beings recognize as extensions of themselves." Indeed, she goes on, as a kind of cultural "narrative," war "requires both the reciprocal infliction of massive injury and the eventual disowning of the injury so that its attributes can be transferred elsewhere, as they cannot if they are permitted to cling to the original site of the wound, the human body."

And surely in the present case we must blame this war—or at least our traditional understandings of it, both popular and official—for persistently inviting us to step outside of the obscene figurations of the mutilated and dying body. For it was, truly, the last pageant war, a war in which bravery and butchery actually coexisted in a way that the culture found psychologically manageable. This was the dreadful conjunction persistently expressed, for instance, in the words and understandings of the participants. In the personal dimension, high flown concepts of romantic chivalry and Victorian spiritual steadfastness fed themselves into military extensions of the ethos of embattled courage and comradeship that defined nineteenth-century male identity in word and deed. And in the political, participants on both sides testified with poignant eloquence at the time and long afterward to the perceived loftiness of their motivations.

It thus all truly does have the cachet of national tragedy, with the old clichés possessing the customary problem of clichés ("the crossroads of our being," "the war of brothers," etc.): that they begin by being true in the first place. More than one hundred years after Oliver Wendell Holmes's famous 1885 Decoration Day speech, whether in celebration of the glorious Union or in honored memory of the Lost Cause, the overwhelming sense of the war remains that of Holmes's sentiments: that it must have been an almost holy thing to have been in it.

The reenactors certainly make this point with their near religious devotion to authenticity, their frequent testimonies to have somehow actually visited for a moment in the past, in a world where uniforms weren't really uniforms, belief was really belief, and it was still actually possible to talk about giving one's last full measure of devotion. "The material appurtenances of reenacting," as Rory Turner has written, do actually "become deeply treasured emblems of identity" and drills and battles "extraordinary pieces of collective choreography," a kind of dance of hallowed celebration. But in the dance is also the danger, the mentalized reprise without the terrible body consequences: "bloodless battle," one commentator calls it. Another refers to it as patriotic "gore," with heavy emphasis on the quotation marks. "It is this feeling reenactors look for," remarks a third, "to revise history, bind up the wounds, and efface the scars of the great slaughter. It is, perhaps, all part of the effort to know ourselves by knowing our past and, if the past is painful beyond comprehension, to put it into a framework more bearable and apprehensible." Fair enough. But it also remains the playacting of an incredible, massed-weaponry, meat-grinder violence that the word "carnage" just doesn't comprehend: the stew-beef that any soldier knows—the hamburger, the brains, the liver and pancreas and intestines, the blood in buckets slopped all over the grass and other people; the bodies and parts of bodies lying around everywhere or still in flight killing and maiming other people. Real body mathematics are in order. One and a half gallons is a lot of blood. One hundred fifty or so pounds is a lot of meat. Then there is all that bone. And this doesn't even begin to take in the ear-shattering, brain-rending noise and concussion.

In a roughly parallel film, I would propose, there has been at least one creditable attempt at a solution of this problem concerning the realistic representation of Civil War combat and combat injury. This is the one arrived at in the opening of the 1990 Civil War film *Glory*, where fifty-five seconds of Matthew Broderick as the young Captain Robert Gould Shaw at Antietam somehow supply the thing that is missing in four hours of *Gettysburg*. Further, it is achieved precisely through the unique capacity of film to combine spectacle with horrific concentration of focus.

Here, as if on parade, a union regiment advances across open ground toward Confederates behind a fence line. The boy-officers walk out in front of the formation, Broderick as Shaw among them, pointing with drawn swords. Their swords are very big and very heavy. The Confederates open up with artillery first, gouging large holes in the advancing ranks. Then, at close range, the riflemen let go with volley fire. The young Union officers lean into the flying lead as if in a storm. Their legs continue to take them in the direction their swords are pointing while, with their heads and shoulders, they cannot help turning involuntarily away, cringing at the danger ahead. Just in front of Broderick, another officer's skull explodes. Broderick is hit by some of the bloody spatter. Then he too is knocked to the ground by an exploding shell. Reaching for a sharp cut on his neck, he draws back his hand and finds blood. He collapses in fatigue and horror. As he lies there, another wounded soldier tries to scuttle crablike off the field on the stumps of his legs, which have been taken off just above the ankles.

At the dressing station, the young officer has the shell fragments removed by a gossipy orderly while watching another man having his leg sawn off and listening to his bellowing and shrieking for mercy. But even now, we realize, the hospital suffering is anticlimactic. Broderick has been, as they say, to see the elephant. The rest of the movie will be a study of character indelibly shaped by a memory of those images of horror at Antietam.

It is the absence of horror in any such palpable dimension that remains the most striking and disturbing thing about *Gettysburg*; for it so immeasurably reduces those countless moments, conflating the big view with the human dimension, in which one does sense the grand, mysterious, awful presence of history. Who could not be moved by Colonel Chamberlain's speech to his mutineers? By Armistead's tears at having to face his old friend Hancock? By the mad grin, the moment's rictus of insane bravery that flashes across Pickett's face? It is epic. Texans, Virginians, Georgians, Alabamians, the doomed, gaudy Trojans, break themselves against the stolid, Greek-like resolve of New Yorkers, Pennsylvanians, Massachusetts and Maine men. The authentic and, in its way, sincere handsomeness of *Gettysburg* is that it does crank the American Civil War and its greatest battle down to the human scale. Amid all the din and spectacle and, yes, even glow, *these were people*, it tells us. But just then where it is most moving and lovely, as with so many of the productions of the Civil War history industry, it is also most pernicious. These were people, it needs to tell us, but they were also meat. And *it was slaughter*: mass slaughter; indiscriminate slaughter. Factory-style slaughter, the way pigs or chickens or cattle are slaughtered, except with far less delicacy as far as damage to the meat is concerned. To further the corporate mathematics, at Gettysburg alone around fifty-three thousand of the people involved wound up in the basic condition of meat, killed or injured by the time the three days were concluded. Those too badly hurt to leave with the departing armies suffered in field hospitals hastily erected by the Sanitary Commission, precursor of the Red Cross. Others rode out on wagons screaming things like "God, why can't I die?" and "My God, have mercy and kill me!" and "Stop, for God's sake take me out and let me die by the road."

But, as with wars and rumors of war, so with reenactments and rumors of reenactments. A handsomely packaged property and some good marketing can usually take care of the meat problem. Or certainly at least it seemed so, according to an item in an early 1998 issue of *Civil War Times Illustrated*, in which the business of doing battle at Gettysburg announced itself as continuing in full flourish. There, in a lavish, full-page ad, with artwork by popular illustrator Don Troiani, "Civil War Heritage, Inc." of "PO Box 1292, Fort Washington, PA," trumpeted its sponsorship of "the Civil War event of the decade." The occasion so heralded was the 135th anniversary of the battle. The title: "Gettysburg, From Start to Finish." Scheduled for July 3–5, 1998, it was described as "A stirring, living history experience featuring five battles." These included "First Contact; the Wheat field; Little Round Top; Culp's Hill"; and of course "Pickett's Charge." Prominently billed as being in charge were "Confederate Commander Chuck Hillsman and Union Commander Dana Heim." Advertised coordinating events included both Federal and Confederate cavalry competitions—with separate events listed for Pistols, Sabers, and Carbines. Somewhere in between the two was also promised a "Civil War wedding." As prominently featured, however, were the attractions of an interactive media tent featuring "your favorite artists, authors, music, and Talonsoft CD-ROM gaming." Talonsoft CD-ROM gaming. *Pace*, Bruce Catton. Gettysburg had truly become *The Final Fury*. Or, as a competing manufacturer put it in its advertisement in *Civil War Times Illustrated*, "War may be hell, but with the right software, it can be kind of fun."

Meanwhile, for anyone who had worked up an appetite after all the fun and make-believe slaughter, there now existed a nearby addition to the local culinary scene. Conveniently located where the Emmitsburg Road meets Steinwehr Avenue, just a half mile north of the Bloody Angle, was General Pickett's Buffet. His truth is marching on.

4
What Lady Butler Knew

Among the most widely reproduced cautionary images during the US invasion of Afghanistan a decade ago was a classic of nineteenth-century British military art titled *The Remnants of an Army*. Painted at the height of Victorian empire, it was singularly bleak and inglorious. Indeed, the titular "remnants" numbered two: a lone, exhausted rider—Dr. William Brydon, a military surgeon—and his nearly dead horse. The army in question was an 1842 British formation of sixteen thousand forced into a catastrophic sixty-mile retreat from Kabul to Jellalabad during the First Afghan War. For some time, Brydon was thought to be the sole survivor. Eventually he was joined by a handful of others.

Painted in 1879, *The Remnants of an Army* commemorated one of the great disasters in the history of the British Army. In radical contrast, an 1882 painting from the same hand memorialized that army's greatest victory; to this day it remains accordingly one of the most stirring battle portraits in the history of British art. Titled *Scotland for Ever!*, it depicts the famous mounted charge of the Second Royal North British Dragoons—the legendary Scots Greys—at Waterloo. The attack had been long enshrined in British military legend, and the painting—with its oncoming mass of wild-eyed galloping horseflesh and howling red-jacketed cavalrymen—quickly found its own place in popular artistic tradition and has continued ever since to be among the most widely reproduced in the genre.

Both canvases, along with hundreds of others, were painted by a woman, Elizabeth Sotherden Johnson, better known to the world as Lady Butler. Living from 1846 to 1933, she never experienced a war or witnessed a battle. Yet from nearly the beginning, war somehow became her great artistic subject and, in her painterly hands, a subject of more than occasional artistic greatness. Along the way, her colorful, upper-class personal history was itself worth a movie. The beautiful, intelligent, talented daughter of a British eccentric of independent means and a cultivated mother with significant gifts as a pianist,

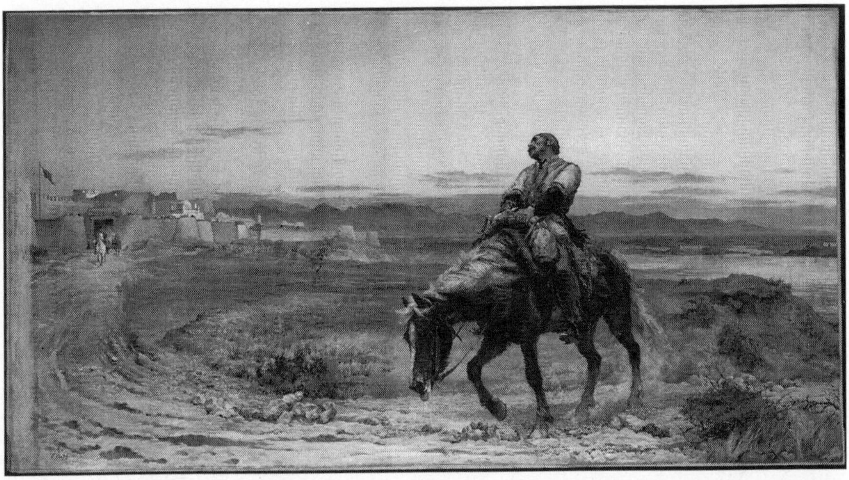

Figure 4.1 *The Remnants of an Army*, Lady Butler, 1879. Tate Britain, London, England.

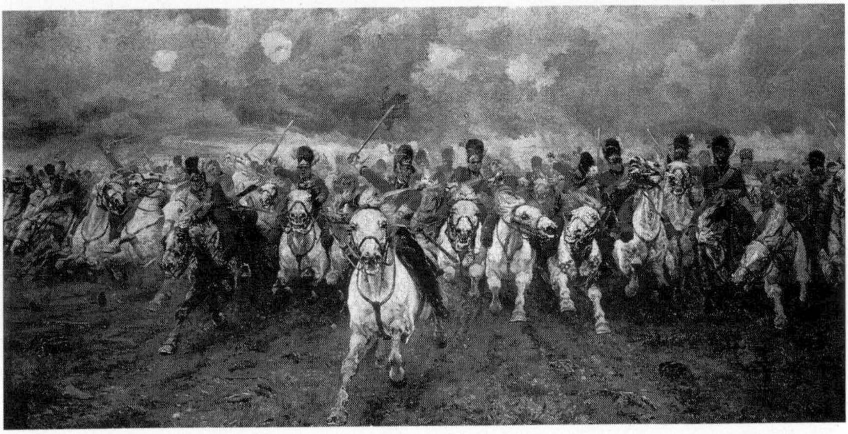

Figure 4.2 *Scotland Forever* depicting the cavalry charge of the Royal Scots Greys at the Battle of Waterloo, 1815, during the Napoleonic Wars, Lady Butler, 1881. Leeds Art Gallery, Leeds, West Yorkshire, England.

singer, and watercolorist, she led an independent life devoted to painting studies, enjoying an early professional career. In her early thirties, she married an older British military officer, William Francis Butler, who rose to become a lieutenant general and was briefly in command of British forces in South Africa on the eve of the Second Boer War before being cashiered for his public anti-imperialist pronouncements. Retiring to Ireland, General and Lady Butler took up residence in Bansha Castle, County Tipperary. Butler became a member of the Irish Privy Council and a strong sympathizer of the Catholic emancipation and Irish independence movements. Falling somewhat out of popular favor for her own apostate Irish sympathies and increasingly bleak depictions of the ongoing wars of empire, Lady Butler nonetheless pursued her career for several more decades. At the time of her death, this model of genteel Victorian and Edwardian womanhood had amassed a body of work making her possibly the greatest battle painter in British history—if not in European and American history as well.

What was the secret of Lady Butler's military art? What did she somehow know about war and soldiering and the lives and deaths of men-at-arms that granted her work a power of both physical and emotional evocation that outdid most of her male competitors? At the time, various attempts were made to "explain" her. On one hand, she was praised for a uniquely visible concern—at odds with other practitioners of the great, operatic battle painting of the era—not for great captains, fancy uniforms, or gold braid, but for common soldiers. (At the turn of the century, her sister, the poet and critic Alice Meynell, went so far as to claim, "Lady Butler has done for the soldier in Art what Mr. Rudyard Kipling has done for him in Literature—has taken the individual, separated him, seen him close, and let the world see him.") On the other, she was as enthusiastically proposed to be a singular, if not preternatural evolution of her sex, a warrior art-goddess in the mold of the ancients. (Another of her Waterloo classics, her portrayal of the famous clash at Quatre Bras, forced the estimable John Ruskin—famously on record as asserting that women could not paint—to confess, "It is amazon's work this; no doubt of it, and the first fine Pre-Raphaelite picture of battle we have had.")

A third characterization, commingling many aspects of the first two, is perhaps most directly to the point, having come down to us from the artist herself as she looked back over a long and celebrated career. "I never painted for the glory of war," she wrote in a 1922 autobiography, "but to portray its pathos and heroism." To put it simply, she somehow knew what the soldier knew. That is, she seems to have set out at once to show the savagery of battle and the pathos of its aftermath, that is, its direct effect upon the combatant; at the same time, she found inspiration to honor the age-old traditions of soldiering with their larger and enduring elements of individual and collective bravery and self-sacrifice—for want of a better word, heroism.

Here, the central piece of evidence must be the bleakly moving 1874 *Roll Call*, (or, more properly, *Calling the Roll after an Engagement, Crimea*), a depiction of the depleted ranks of the battle-weary Grenadier Guards attempting reassembly on a snowy morning in the aftermath of battle. The backdrop is gray, muted, elegiac. Against this landscape, the uniformed survivors attempt to present their re-assembled ranks, with gaping holes denoting the places of

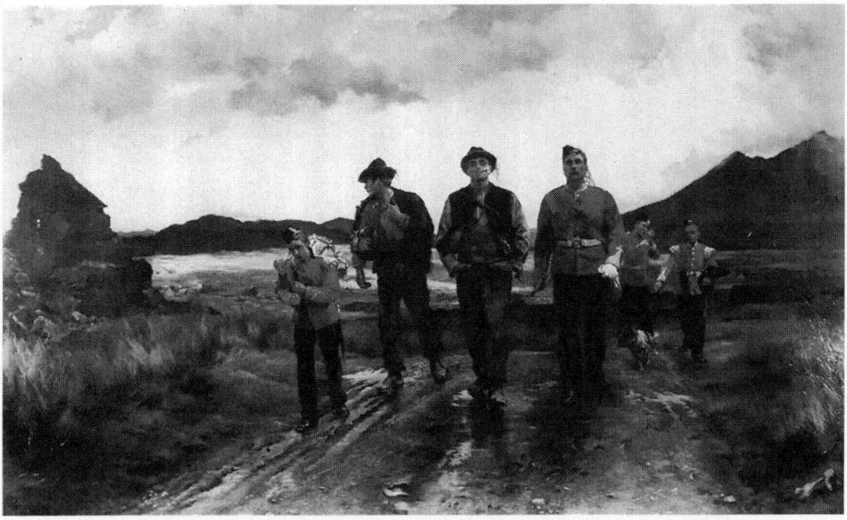

Figure 4.3 *Listed for the Connaught Rangers*, Lady Butler, 1879. Bury Art Gallery, Lancashire, England.

those who have gone. One understands that the "roll call" in question is an attendance roster of the dead. Still, the impression is that of a disciplined familiar military formation. Men in ranks help other men, attended silently by NCOs and officers. The depiction is, in a word, soldierly. Purchased by the Queen herself, it was the painting that made Butler's career.

The Roll Call also stands as central chronologically for the artist in her own unique career of military representations. She is surely one of the laureates of "the thin red line," as it was called in those days—a misquotation, as it turns out, from journalist William H. Russell's description of the Sutherland Highlanders in the Crimea as "a thin red streak tipped with a line of steel"—fighting the now all-but-forgotten engagements of the old wars of empire. But her best work also extends to the khaki-clad mass combatants of late nineteenth- and early twentieth- century battlefields ranging from the South African veldt to World War I Palestine and Flanders. In classic moments, we see a forced march with Wellington on the Peninsula; the retiring columns of wounded at Inkerman and Balaklava; the desperate band of holdouts against the Zulus at Rorke's Drift. In the pale light of a new century, we see Lancers in the retreat from Mons, and dusty, plodding infantry in France passing a roadside crucifix.

The paintings bear witness of the changes in the ways modern wars came to be fought. They also chart the evolutions of a sensibility that kept faith with the soldier even as the wars of the world changed. The pathos is there in perhaps the saddest picture Butler ever painted. With the title *Listed for the Connaught Rangers*, it depicts two hale conscripts from the Irish back country marching down the road toward enrollment in the regiment. Their civilian togs contrast with the military peacockery of the recruiting sergeant and his drummer boys. They have taken the Queen's shilling; shortly they will enter the world of war in which each roll call may be their last. A very late work, in contrast, in its eloquent austerity, still testifies to the possibility of the old soldierly virtues of loyalty, determination, and willingness to sacrifice. A watercolor painted in 1914 and titled *Patrick, Au Revoir!* depicts a single figure on horseback—an officer in modern uniform rendering a hand salute. The soldier in question has already been at war. His officer turnout is that of the regular, albeit in the muted tones of the army in France, a divisional headquarters of which he is about to join. Shortly, he will be badly wounded at First Ypres, invalided home, and then returned to duty to serve in Macedonia and Palestine. In many ways (that is, save for his survival), his will be the experience of the British regular soldier of the Great War. Already part of the remnants of yet another army, he is named Patrick Butler. He is the artist's own son.

5
Qingdao and the Archaeologies of War

The attractive coastal city of Qingdao in Shandong Province, China—now a high-end seaside resort and major naval headquarters, as well as a center of finance, technology, and education—retains a unique identity as a kind of palimpsest of its distinctive role in the wars between the great Asian and Western powers of the late nineteenth and early- to mid-twentieth centuries. On the ground this involves still highly visible traces of occupiers ranging from the Germans and the Japanese to the post World War II Americans. As to the historical record, the place becomes the text of its own ongoing re-inscription as an abstract or epitome of the twentieth-century conflicts eventuating in the rise of modern China.

The story begins with the peculiar circumstances leading to the role of the city, still of major interest to historians, as the site of the single battle of World War I fought in Asia. The year was 1914. On one side were the Germans—along with a small, somewhat accidental contingent of Austro-Hungarians. On the other, assisted by a small force of British and Empire troops, were the Japanese, with the latter greatly ambitious (after notable victories in both the Sino-Japanese and Russo-Japanese wars of 1891–94 and 1904–1905) to demonstrate their worthiness to take a place on the world stage among the great modern military powers. Known to history as the Siege of Tsingtao, the main action was a land battle whereby a combined Anglo-Japanese invasion force in late October and early November succeeded in defeating and expelling the German garrison of a heavily defended anchorage of the Imperial Navy, established in 1898 under the title of the Kiautschou Bay concession and developed into a colony centered on a modern European-style city.

Meanwhile, as regards the Kiautschou German fleet (under threat of being bottled up in their own harbor) the battle was already extending itself into a strategic naval dimension, with the Imperial East Asia Squadron—initially dispersed to various Pacific possessions—reconcentrating and attempting to sail for home while pursued by elements of the British Navy. Of considerable

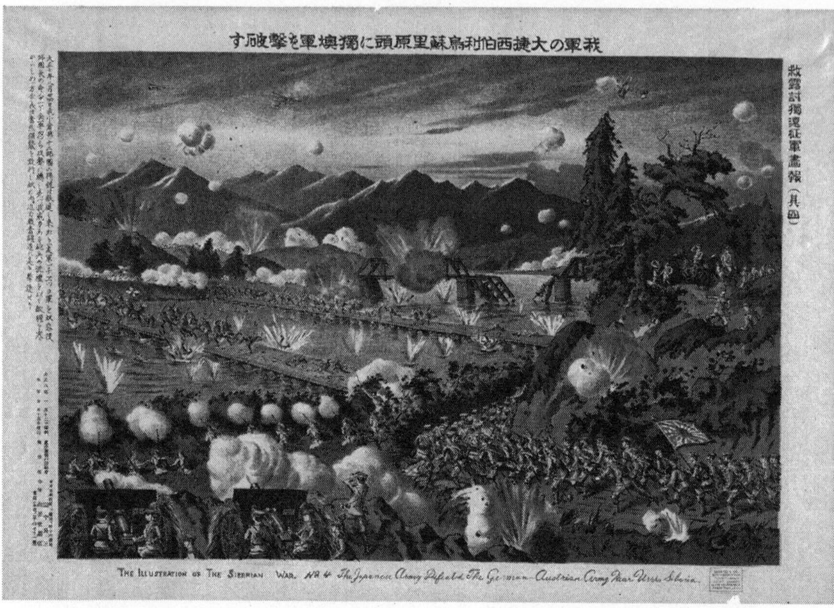

Figure 5.1 *The Siege of Tsingtao*, Japanese print illustration.

news interest at the time was the saga of one breakaway element, the cruise of the raider *Emden*. The main combined fleet action, however, eventually took the form of a long, southeastward chase toward the tip of South America and its opening into the Atlantic, resulting in two major sea battles. The first was a serious loss for the British at Coronel, off the coast of Chile, where the German Admiral Graf von Spee sank two enemy cruisers at the expense of three sailors killed. The second, however, proved a disastrous defeat for the Germans, in an engagement off Argentina now called the first Battle of the Falklands. This time von Spee—whose namesake World War II battleship, with no small irony, would go down thirty-five years later in the nearby River Platte estuary—lost his own life along with five of his seven ships.

By the end of 1914, when the land and sea engagements were over, Germany was finished in the Pacific and on the Asian mainland. The big winner in the region was Japan, having quickly absorbed various German outposts in strategic island groups that included the Marshalls, Marianas Carolines, and others. In China, Japan claimed both Qingdao and the entire surrounding Shandong concession, where by terms of the Versailles Treaty they would remain as occupiers until 1922. (They would return as conquerors in 1937.) And it is exactly in these terms—as it is my purpose to show here—that a relatively obscure World War I incident would have immense military and political consequences far beyond its own military dimensions. The newly occupied Pacific territories, with the benefit of decades-long fortification, would be shaped into a system of oceanic strongpoints, many of which would become the sites of World War II island battles whose names—Kwajalein, Eniwetok, Saipan, Tinian, and Peleliu—remain written in blood in both Allied and Japanese memory. Concurrently, the extended Japanese occupation of Qingdao and the surrounding Shandong concession would come quickly to be seen by the Chinese as the bitter fruit of betrayal at Versailles and foster a distrust of the victorious World War I Western Allies that lasted well past the World War II era; more importantly, within Chinese domestic politics, it would also generate the seminal May Fourth movement against the fledgling Nationalist (Guomindang) government, now regarded frequently by Chinese historians and others as the opening of the people's revolutionary struggle for liberation. The archaeologies of war at Qingdao, in short, remain a geopolitical text of their immense human and historical reverberations.

Both parts of the story may be said to originate in a general land grab by various Allied powers ensuing in the more or less immediate occupation of a defeated Germany's former Pacific and Asian possessions, with the wartime and immediate postwar division of spoils in turn ratified by the 1919 Versailles treaty. Here the Japanese were joined by ascendant regional powers, including Australia, New Zealand, Great Britain, and, of course, the United States. The distributions of individual properties were complex and frequently scrambled by various territorial ambitions, including strategic military concerns and the desire for important natural resources. Precisely in this manner, as evidence of Western strategic thinking, many of them would shortly serve as a template for Japanese conquest in the early stages of the new Pacific and Asian war.

As regards such developments in terms of English and Commonwealth allocations after World War I, typical would be the former German New Guinea, including the Bismarck Archipelago and Bougainville. These would go to Australia, only to become targets for almost immediate conquest in the great Japanese campaigns of 1941. Over the next four years, all would become major, long-term Allied battlefields: British, Australian, New Zealand, and American. Nauru, an important phosphate island, was jointly held by Australia, New Zealand, and Great Britain until likewise falling under Japanese occupation as another early World War II conquest and fortified reoccupation. It was left as such for the remainder of the war.

And then there would also be the German Solomons, which had gone to Britain in earlier colonial horse-trading dating back to 1899. Like the rest of the New Guinea region, they too were quickly overrun by the Japanese. Accordingly, here would come to prominence for World War II Americans, beginning to fight their way back against the early Japanese tide, a first dread collection of Pacific War island names earning permanent enshrinement in national memory as among the most desperate initial battles of the war. Guadalcanal, Tulagi, Gavutu, Savo, Santa Cruz, the eastern Solomons: on land and sea, US marines, army soldiers, sailors, and airmen successfully undertook the arduous, bloody process of fighting their way back across the great fortified network of Imperial Japanese military outposts in the Pacific. By the time these initial campaigns were declared complete in early 1943, the Americans had suffered 7100 dead, with the loss of nearly thirty naval vessels and more than six hundred aircraft; Japanese figures were thirty-one thousand dead, nearly forty ships, and seven hundred to eight hundred planes.

As to the subsequent grand sweep of the American war in the Pacific, particularly as the enterprise neared the home islands of Japan, the bloodless Japanese victories under the Versailles treaty would continue to comprise an ever-enlarging inventory of World War II strategic objectives, not to mention an expanding list of names where sacredness to American memory became measured by the ghastliness of facts and figures, as Japanese forces fought to the death. The retaking of the Marshall Islands required US Army landings and ensuing battles at Kwajalein (from January 31 to February 31, 1944, with 372 Americans killed and 1,592 wounded, against 7,870 Japanese fatalities) and Eniwetok (from February 23 to 28, with US 262 killed and 757 wounded, against Japanese 2,677 killed).

In the strategically crucial Mariana Islands chain, Guam had been held by the pre-World War I United States as a prize of their 1898 victory over the Spanish in Cuba and the Philippines. As with New Guinea, it suffered immediate World War II Japanese invasion and conquest in the great first wave of Imperial victories. Invaded on December 8, 1941—from staging bases in the Northern Marianas that had been owned by Japanese since 1919, such as Saipan and Tinian—it was quickly reoccupied and, like the rest, invested with major fortifications. One by one, they would have to be retaken. US recapture of Guam came first, on July 21 to August 10, 1944, with strategic concentration on a major military target defended by substantial Japanese forces. It also involved poignant human concern for citizens who had endured three years of Japanese occupation and brutalization. Casualties came to US 1,747 killed and 6,058 wounded, against Japanese 18,000 killed. (Guam civilian deaths under Japanese occupation were estimated at 10 percent of the total population.) Saipan and Tinian followed, with Saipan alone nearly doubling the Guam casualties, registering US 2,949 killed and 10,364 wounded, against Japanese 30,000 killed. Tinian, fought over between July 24 and August 10, 1944, would add on another US 508 killed and 1571 wounded, against Japanese 8,010 killed. The latter two proved of particular strategic importance and were quickly rebuilt as major US Air Force B-29 bases for the bombing of Japan, including the final atomic missions to Hiroshima and Nagasaki.

A different strategy attended the Caroline Islands, where Japanese fortification of a major harbor at Truk Lagoon produced what seemed an almost impregnable, Gibraltar-like fortress dominating the South Pacific. As such, it became a major determinant of Allied planning. Here, though, the decision was to forego land invasion in favor of alternative targets in the region, while still attacking and reducing by sea and air. The decision was a wise one. With minimum loss of American lives and weaponry, Truk and adjacent Japanese positions were essentially bypassed and left to rot. The extended outcome for the Japanese was notably severe. Ships sunk at anchorage included three cruisers, six destroyers, two submarines and more than thirty transports and merchant vessels. Air attacks claimed three hundred planes. But the worst was to ensue for a garrison force at its height numbering nearly forty-five thousand imperial army and navy troops. By the end of the war, vast numbers, insofar as can be reckoned, had died of starvation.

Not so fortunate for the American casualty roster was the military outcome of battles over the last, seemingly minor German island group claimed by the Japanese in 1919. These were the Palaus, unfortunately dominated, as US planners came to see it—in mistaken estimate of strategic necessity—by the strong point of Peleliu. The larger operative problem was the planned American reconquest of the Philippines, specifically Gen. Douglas MacArthur's fear, seconded by naval commanders, that Japanese airfields in Peleliu would endanger landings at Leyte. In this, strategic thinking was more than woefully incorrect on the part of everyone involved. The result was one of those dreadful convergences of history where catastrophic casualties became measured by military pointlessness. Peleliu itself turned out to be not only strongly fortified but fanatically defended. Among other things, after nearly five decades of mining, the core of the island had in fact become a labyrinth of underground tunnels and redoubts, with many containing suicidal last-ditch resistance forces that had to be reduced as combat ground on by sealing them up with bulldozers. In US Marine lore, with the highest casualty rate of killed and wounded for any island in the war, the campaign of September-November 1944 came to be mentioned in same breath with Iwo Jima and Okinawa. The final combat figures would include 1,794 US killed and 8,010 US wounded against 10,695 Japanese killed and 202 Japanese work troops taken prisoner.

Proving equally crucial to subsequent military history, meanwhile in consequence of the small 1914 Anglo-Japanese victory over German land forces initially described, were a series of parallel developments events on the Chinese mainland, beginning with the Japanese occupation of Qingdao and the surrounding Shandong concession as a major expansion of the Empire's role in great power politics in Asia. Here again events of the World War I and interwar eras would heavily influence the unfolding of the even more terrible world conflict to come. As early as 1915, with the Western Allies heavily committed to the war in various European theaters, Japan sought new concessions from the Chinese under protocols that came to be known at the time as the Twenty-One Demands. These proposed the expansion of its suzerainty over the former German holdings into Manchuria and Mongolia, to include combined Sino-Japanese ownership of major enterprises in mining and metallurgy and the prohibition of rival cessions or leases to any other outside power. At least initially these Japanese attempts at economic and political domination over large mainland areas were successfully resisted by the Chinese through a process of drawn-out discussions yoked to a campaign of internal demonstrations of popular protest and Western expressions of international disapproval. Yet various skillful international agreements by Japan with powers including Russia, France, Britain, and the United States gradually undermined the Chinese position, helping the Japanese to place northern China in particular in a tightening noose. With the fall of tsarist Russia and the subsequent disorders of revolution across its vast Asian expanses, Japan prepared to fill the void. By 1931 the Japanese had become masters of Manchuria, rechristened as the imperial province of Manchukuo. This was followed in 1937 by a series of Japanese provocations eventuating in the Second Sino-Japanese War, properly regarded as the beginning of World War II in Asia.

But perhaps the most important geopolitical legacy in mainland Asia of the World War I Japanese conquest and subsequent occupation of German Shandong lay in far-reaching developments in Chinese political culture itself—specifically in the origination of the 1919 Chinese people's uprising now celebrated as the May Fourth Movement and widely regarded as crucial to the very birth of the modern People's Republic of China. Again, for the Japanese, the matter began as an opportunity to benefit from wartime Allied inattention and extend the occupation. By the time it came to postwar treaty ratification, what quickly came to be called "the Shandong Problem" had elevated itself in Chinese eyes into prima facie evidence of profound Allied betrayal. In this, the Chinese were correct. In the five years between the brief battle and the Versailles conference, secret agreements had been executed. The Chinese now discovered that, according to article 156 of the formal treaty, Japan would be allowed to retain indefinite possession of the province. Bitterly they protested their own case before the world, with their representative in Paris going so far as to say that conceding Shandong, the birthplace of Confucius, was analagous to Christians conceding Jerusalem. Most importantly, demonstrations were mounted across China, reportedly covering more than twenty provinces and one hundred cities. Chief among these was the one in Beijing, in legendary lore the first full expression of solidarity by Chinese revolutionary youth and now celebrated as the foundational event of the May Fourth Movement. In turn, as now heralded in official Chinese Revolutionary accounts, the spirit of the May Fourth Movement crucially energized the larger 1915–21 New Culture Movement, in which political mobilization in China shifted finally to a populist, properly proletarian base. Thus, according to the canonical narrative, was prepared the true ideological basis for the 1921 founding of the Chinese Communist Party.

Meanwhile, efforts at international protest took official shape. In 1921 the Chinese government unilaterally declared the end of its war against Germany and eventually signed the separate Sino-German peace treaty of 1921. The matter was further addressed at length by the Allies, with the US acting as mediator, at the Washington Naval Conference of 1922. Finally, in February of that year, a full eight years after the initial military action, control of Shandong was returned to China. Even then, it was declared that Japanese residents in Shandong would continue to be accorded special rights.

The rest of the story is familiar. According to longstanding extrapolations of legend fostered by current PRC ideological mythographers, the Chinese revolution properly began with popular response to the matter of Qingdao. To be sure, the founding of the party would itself be followed by long years of struggle, eventuating in such celebrated events as the 1933–34 Long March, the vast agonies of the 1937–45 Sino-Japanese War, the 1945–49 victory over the American-supported Guomindang dictatorship of Chiang Kai-Shek, and the expulsion of Nationalists to Taiwan—ironically, itself a prize lost in the first Sino-Japanese War of 1894–95 and returned only four years earlier at the end of the second (1937–45).

In these years, Qingdao and Shandong at large remained a coastal hotbed of revolutionary activity, intimately connected to this day with the rise of the Chinese Communist Party. The 1937 Japanese reoccupation brought with it notable brutality and repression. The old restored German prison reveals Japanese basement water dungeons, stocked with instruments of torture and mutilation. Old persons still alive in the city carry memories and stories of activities as communist guerillas in the hills up the coast near Laoshan, a chokepoint for the wartime interdiction of Japanese supplies. In Qingdao proper wartime victory is remembered as one last chapter of Western delay, equivocation, and prevarication, this time with the Americans making the city the new anchorage of US Western Pacific Fleet and headquarters of the occupying Sixth Marine Division. These forces were removed finally in 1948. The final victory of the Chinese Revolution would come one year later.

Thus—as the geopolitical upshot of a small, solitary, largely forgotten World

War I battle on the Asian mainland—would the war and occupation history of Qingdao come to provide a crucial link between the nineteenth-century age of empire in Asia and the Pacific and the current era, rightly called the age of the twenty-first-century Chinese colossus. And so the matter now stands vividly evinced by contemporary Qingdao itself as a kind of living archaeology. It had begun—on the pretext of the murder of two German Catholic missionaries—with a German Kaiser looking for a Chinese concession to put his recently formed nation on a comparable imperial footing with other colonial powers in the Asian and Pacific regions. The land location of the presumptive German acquisition was surely dictated by its provocative nearness to British Wei Ha Wei and American Tientsin (now Tianjin). The place chosen was Tsingtao, a small Shandong coastal village and fishing port on the Yellow Sea. Seized, occupied, and developed with signature German industry, in slightly more than a decade it was transformed into a complete colonial model of a European style small city—administered militarily by the Imperial Navy but also supplied with a colonial governor and boasting a complete civic infrastructure, including governor's mansion, main government headquarters, German church, prison, beer factory, military barracks, and multilevel command bunker complex with heavy gun emplacements on Qingdao Hill. For the Kaiser himself, the place became an obsessively regarded symbol of personal and imperial pride. He is indeed alleged at time to have said, "It would shame me more to surrender Tsingtao to the Japanese than Berlin to the Russians." Yet that is just what happened in Asia before a mainly European war largely of his initiation was three months old. (The fall of Berlin to the Russians would wait another three decades.) Meanwhile, China waited and endured: a false treaty; a second war of global slaughter, now regarded as an extension of the first; a renewed struggle against a Western-supported puppet "democracy"; a final victory of people's revolution.

Today, one place where such history can continue to be read is twenty-first-century Qingdao itself—a kind of living archaeology. Visible in the earliest German photographs of the village and still standing is a 1497 temple. Nearby, within easy view, is the city's best-known symbol, a pagoda pavilion at the end of a recreational pier—with its roofline image known worldwide as the label trademark of the beer manufacturing company "Tsingtao," still the preeminent Chinese brand. The beer factory itself tells a good story, with a German late-nineteenth-century brewery building approached from the old city side, and a twenty-first-century silhouette of high industrial storage tanks—tall beer cans, with name blazoned lighted in giant green letters on top—most visible from the airport downtown freeway. In the old German section of town, still largely preserved as if in nineteenth-century amber, villas, offices, and busi-

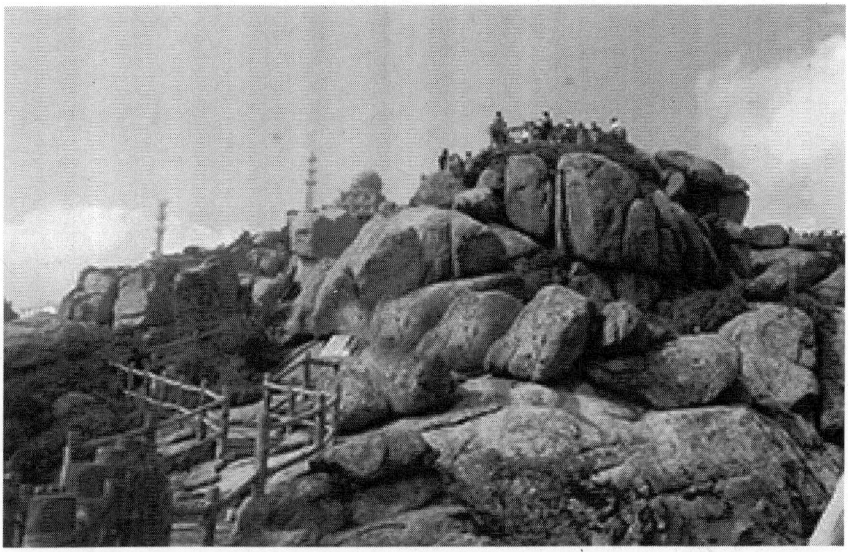

Figure 5.2 Qingdao Hill Park, Qingdao, China.

nesses blend in with distinctly Japanese structures, both of early and later occupation. An old downtown service club, now a warren of apartments, eerily recapitulates its own history of German, Japanese, and American occupiers. As nearly anywhere in the place—now described as a "small city" of eight million—one notes the constant juxtapositions of the Old and New China. In the heart of downtown is a teeming outdoor produce market. A block away stand shining glass and metal business towers. At the harbor, two ends of an enormous elevated freeway project come close to final connection to the new Jiaouzho Bay highway bridge—the world's longest, it is claimed, connecting Qingdao directly with the key industrial district of Huongdao. The entire city is now rimmed by a shimmering arc of beachfront development: a twenty-five mile coastal promenade forms a necklace of parks, beaches, and expensive resort and residential properties. In a new city center halfway down the promenade, high rises and skyscrapers house banking, investment, and banking headquarters almost without number. The Crown Plaza hotel showcases a Bentley-Lamborghini dealership. Nearby shopping venues include Prada, Gucci, Hermes, and Starbucks. The beach development extends past the sailing pavilion from the 2006 Olympics up the coast toward Laoshan. Here the analogue might be Silicon Valley. Everywhere one looks, clusters of construction cranes loom over new showplace university facilities, corporate headquarters, and technology campuses. Meanwhile, out in the shipping channels of the Yel-

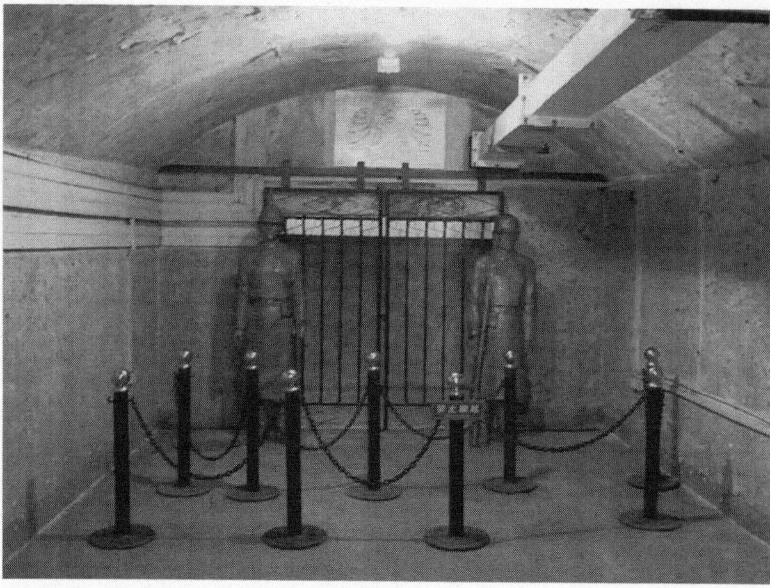

Figure 5.3 Bunker entrance, Qingdao Zhongshan Park, Qingdao, China.

low Sea, new container vessels, tankers, and naval ships, as far as the eye can see, head daily for the old harbor the Germans once coveted as Kiaouchou.

In China, history now means ubiquitous, nonstop upbuilding of the future on the excavations of the past. In business, industry, technology, and infrastructure, the country might be best described as a boundless continental big dig. Revealingly, in Qingdao one digs backward as well as forward. While the cityscape is cratered by station construction for a new underground railway, it has also carefully preserved the historical section centered on German concession. This includes, most eerily, the underground bunker fortress up on Qingdao Hill. Inside, in various chambers and simulations of activity, stand life-sized effigies of German World War I soldiers and sailors, at once somehow garishly entombed yet strangely alive. It reminds one of the others still down there in the battleships and cruiser trying to make it home under von Spee off the River Platte.

In the Pacific, the bunkers dotting the old American World War II island beachheads stand as numerous as a vast literature of countless volumes, multiple accounts of nearly every island campaign. Most of these Asian-Pacific geographies, like twenty-first century China, now stand as independent nations. Many of them have become world travel and business destinations in their own right. Of all the sites mentioned among the Asian and Pacific legacies of the 1914 Siege of Qingdao, there does remain one that can no longer be visited. That place is Eniwetok. As if in ritual reprise of monstrous birth, upheaval, and erasure of the utter destructiveness of twentieth-century war, the latter, it may be recalled, was obliterated a few years after World War II as part of the program of US nuclear weapons testing—vaporized, to be exact, in the explosion of the world's first hydrogen bomb, and thus erased from the very archaeology of creation.

6
Ralph Vaughan Williams's Long Journey Out of War

"Died some," intones the narrator of Ezra Pound's *Hugh Selwyn Mauberly*, "pro patria, / non 'dulce' non 'et décor' . . . / walked-eye deep in hell / believing in old men's lies, then unbelieving / came home, home to a lie, home to many deceits, / home to old lies and new infamy." Thus reads one of the most celebrated post–World War I anthems for doomed youth. (The latter phrasing, as will be recognized, is that of the young British soldier-poet Wilfred Owen, aged twenty-five, himself killed in Flanders a week before the German surrender.) Such poetic expressions of generational protest, written by contemporaries or by slightly older figures like Pound, comprise one of the great genres of the war and are reflected as well in a larger history of Anglo-European and American survivorship writing: Robert Graves's *Good Bye to All That*, Vera Brittain's *Testament of Youth*, Erich Maria Remarque's *All Quiet on the Western Front*, Ernest Hemingway's *A Farewell to Arms*. "You are all a lost generation:" Hemingway claimed to have gotten the famous line—used as an epigraph to his 1925 novel of war-ruined expatriates in Paris, *The Sun Also Rises*—from a conversation with Gertrude Stein, who in turn is said to have heard it originally it from a French garage-owner complaining about the curious anomie of a young mechanic assistant who had survived the war.

Thus in life and art alike, the experience of fighting and dying young became a signature motif of World War I on the western front and elsewhere, as did frequently also that of surviving the war but returning home too physically or psychologically damaged to resume anything resembling the patterns of peacetime existence. But they are not the only ones. As a battlefield survivor and artist, the English composer Ralph Vaughan Williams represents a noteworthy departure from the pattern in any number of respects, both experiential and aesthetic, having gone to war old and having survived far into a fabulously creative later life, in the process fashioning one of the great musical careers of the twentieth century. Vaughan Williams was forty-one when he enlisted, forty-three when deployed to western front, and forty-six

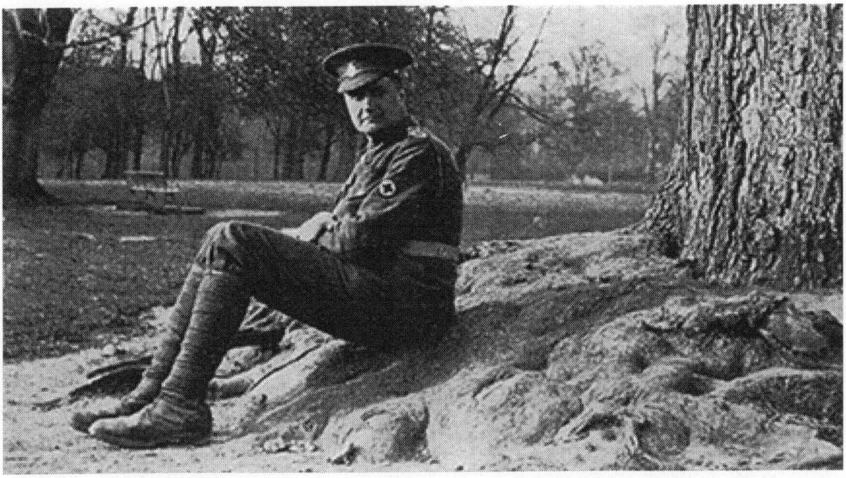

Figure 6.1 Vaughn Williams, as stretcher bearer in World War II. Ralph Vaughan Williams Society pamphlet.

when demobilized in 1919. (The only comparable English cultural figures that come to mind are the poet Edward Thomas, aged thirty-eight, and the politician Raymond Asquith, aged thirty-six, both killed in action; or the novelist Ford Maddox Ford, aged forty-three, who served briefly as a rear-area transport officer before being variously reported as having been "gassed" or "shell-shocked.") When Vaughan Williams died at age eighty-six in 1958, he had written a full nine symphonies, along with nearly countless other orchestral and choral classics—operas, ballets, film scores, concertos, fantasias, oratorios, masses, songs, carols, hymns, and ballad cycles—both secular and religious. By comparison, surviving British literary counterparts such as Robert Graves, Siegfried Sassoon, and Edmund Blunden—all active combatants—all lived long postwar lives with relatively productive careers but evinced a lifelong pain and anger over their experience of the war, their sentiments manifested in pronounced forms of estrangement, personal and cultural, from postwar life. Thus we see Graves in Majorca, with his reconstructions of the ancients and recondite poetic mythmaking; Sassoon with his endless autobiographical revisions and struggles with his culture and sexuality; Blunden with his extended Asian sojourns and polite academicism. "Never such innocence again," writes their successor Philip Larkin, capturing the mood of chilly alienation exactly. Ralph Vaughan Williams, in contrast, somehow came back from World War I determined to make England once more his home and to remake twentieth century English musical art—in the fullness of its richness and possibility—as the vehicle of an ever-evolving and culturally embracing creative modernism.

This strikes one as particularly remarkable given the unusually vivid and immediate character of Vaughan Williams's service, first as an enlisted stretcher bearer in France, where he survived the Somme; in Salonika, where his medical unit was deployed to support a malarial mini-Gallipoli; and then back in France near the end, where he served again at the front as an artillery officer. Nor was his time unattended by the loss of friends or artistic compatriots, most notably with particular poignancy, the composer Frank Butterworth. Pound again: "There died a myriad,/And of the best among them." Vaughan Williams indeed never got over Butterworth's death or the idea that had the latter lived he would have been the great composer of his generation. In all these respects, to borrow the title of Blunden's memoir of life in the trenches and its aftermath, the post-1918 world of Ralph Vaughan Williams would be one in which musical composition would never be free of undertones of war. The difference lies in what Vaughan Williams tried to do with them as an attempt to address the experience of the war through the reintegration of Anglo-European classical music tradition into the patterns of subsequent twentieth-century life and culture.

To cite a commonplace in Vaughan Williams studies, to listen to the composer's music at nearly any point is to be "never quite sure whether one is listening to something very old or very new." Moreover, it is also to experience the continuous achievement of a lifelong modernist historical and cultural project, with the composer confirmed in his artistic commitment by the defining experience of the war, during which he spent nearly five years away from formal composition. Indeed, this character of sustained commitment now seems evident in nearly everything the composer wrote: portended in the prewar "Linden Lea"—Vaughan Williams's first well-known musical production, a pastoral song derived from a poetry text in the Dorsetshire dialect by the cleric William Barnes (1800–1886), with a melody resembling that of a folk tune or a popular hymn but born of the composer's own musical imagination; and equally fulfilled in *Hodie*—a Christmas cantata written in the very last years of the composer's life, with a libretto taken from poetic and literary texts by John Milton, Miles Coverdale, Thomas Hardy, George Herbert, and others but with the traditional melodies of the English hymnal updated by the composer into the tonalities of a mid-twentieth-century modernist polyphony. Everywhere in Vaughan Williams we thus find the complex modernist project of cultural reconstitution and re-connection, the great provisional resynthesizing of the ancient and the experimental; the commonplace and the visionary; the vernacular and the epiphanic. The symphonies alone, a full nine of them, take us from a self-conscious Edwardian and Georgian parochialism into the cosmopolitan world of the late nineteenth- and early twentieth-century modernist pantheon, with echoes of hymnal and folk melodies and of fellow English composers of the era enlarging into invocations of the great Europeans—Ravel, Bruch, Mahler, Prokofiev, Rachmaninoff, and others. Likewise, the great choral works, in a venerable Anglo-European sacred lineage—*Toward the Unknown Region* (1905–07), *Five Mystical Songs* (1911), *Sancta Civitas* (1926), *Dona Nobis Pacem* (1936)—honor the traditions of Byrd, Tallis, Bach, Handel, and their inheritors even as they move into the secular, frequently experimentalist compositional metaphysics of a "cheerful agnostic." "There is no reason why any atheist shouldn't be able to write a good mass," Vaughan Williams once famously said. From the standpoint of embracing the modernist project of culture in its various forms, that is just the point.

This is to posit, then, that beyond everything else Vaughan Williams's modernist project of musical creation, for all the attempts of interpreters at various categorizations was much like Eliot's "tradition" or Pound's "kulchur"—though happily, without a trace of the fascist mystagogy of either. In Vaughan Williams's case, this might be best identified as the "Englishness," described by both Peter Ackroyd and Alain Frogley as a common characterization of the composer's work, in Ackroyd's phrasing, a general character of "lyric melancholy. To move again to literary ground, in this respect "England" for Vaughan Williams becomes much like Joyce's Ireland or Faulkner's Mississippi, a creative precinct wherein the twentieth-century artist pursues the modernist effort of restoring the vision of the human to the stern, impassive mechanics of History. And thus, equally, "pastoral," as interpreted by Frogley, may be seen to correspond rather exactly with that term as used by Paul Fussell in regard to the British literature of the Great War, whereby is invented a dominant twentieth-century mode of Irony, of complex cultural inscription and dissonant, often parodic, revision. To this may be added, as briefly outlined above, a larger, complex syncretism of cultural invocations and appropriations—in some cases taking the form of harmonious confluence and in others of jarring juxtaposition—that is no more or no less evocative of the modernist paradigm (again to choose the two most obvious analogues) than Eliot's syntheses of the Hindu scriptures alongside the British metaphysicals or Pound's of the French troubadours alongside the Chinese classics. "These fragments I have shored against my ruin," says the narrator of Eliot's *Waste-Land* at the end of his labors. It is the very paradigm we see here in Vaughan Williams the modernist composer, the post–World War I project of the artist as the artificer of culture, the provisional creator who somehow puts the world back together after the end of the world.

A proximate explanation for such largeness and continuity of creative purpose, of course, may partly have been a fortunate matter of age and experience. In comparison with the younger Butterworth, for instance, it now seems notable that when Vaughan Williams went to war, besides having spent more than four decades of being alive in the late nineteenth and early twentieth centuries, he also already had a substantial musical career behind him. In turn, he eventually outlived the war and its immediate aftermath by a full four more decades, in possession moreover of his large creative powers to the end. In both of these connections, he further "experienced" the war in his own, notably formative ways. Unlike Graves, Sassoon, Blunden, Owen, or, quite probably, Butterworth, he never had to kill anyone in France; but as his wife Ursula put it acutely, at the Somme in 1916 he certainly saw many people killed in all the myriad ways of modern industrialized warfare. "Working in the ambulance gave Ralph vivid awareness of how men died." Afterward, the vision of war was always there in his major compositions—though with elegiac purposes frequently overstated, especially in works of the immediate postwar decade such as the Second (*London*) Symphony and *Missa Solemnis*. He never wrote a War Requiem, though he lived through not just one but the two greatest armed conflicts in history. Still, it would be accurate to say that with few exceptions the vision of war generally is a presence in everything he wrote afterward. At the same time, it is never unmixed, existing in a given work as the function of a particular time, place, and creative enterprise. If the *Pastoral Symphony* speaks to the experience of the 1914–18 trenches, for instance, it is precisely in the complex ironic register ascribed by Fussell to the postwar poets working in the same deeply English vein, at once of the war and in its disturbed aftermath. So the composer himself famously wrote: "It's really wartime music—a great deal of it incubated when I used to go up night after night with the ambulance wagon at Ecoivres and we went up a steep hill and there was a wonderful Corot-like landscape in the sunset—it's not really lambkins frisking at all as most people take for granted." So the stern menace and challenge of symphonies Four and Six are said by musical historians to envision a new landscape of war—the dissonant, angry Fourth, charting the 1930s darkness of a new march into the abyss; the post–World War II Sixth with its bleak, atomic landscape, a world of silent destruction, as with Farley Mowat's Keatsian entitling of his memoir of that war—"and no birds sang." Yet these, too, as Heffer points out, both exist in their own distinct musicological relations—the first being associated with *Job, a Masque for Dancing*, an extremely complex and innovative mixed-media composition, a ballet based on the strange iconographies of the illustrated version of the scriptural text famously produced by William Blake; and the second, an allusive homage to the music of his beloved friend Gustav Holst, coupled with compositional strategies newly explored while writing program music for World War II documentaries. (In between, it might be mentioned, one also accounts contextually for the Fifth, frequently noted for its lyrical otherworldliness—a melodious recuperative 1943 contribution to wartime morale.) From the same era, as much might be said of the complex associations of the 1926 *Sancta Civitas*, the 1936 *Dona Nobis Pacem*, and the 1939 *Five Variants on Dives and Lazarus*. In the first two, expressions of postwar hope may be seen as complicated by an increasing sense of the imminence of new global catastrophe. In the last, surely the most hauntingly beautiful of all his compositions, precisely on the eve of new European war there arises a pure music of human supplication, a plea for brotherhood and mercy.

Such achievement of a rich, cosmopolitan modernism, to be continued in the decades after 1939, might now also seem to have been culturally prefigured in a remarkable early personal history, at once deeply parochial and liberated. The son of a churchman, on his mother's side Vaughan Williams was descended closely from both the Wedgwoods and the Darwins in a family world imbued with their history of involvement in emancipatory scientific inquiry. An educational passage including Charterhouse, Cambridge, and the Royal College of Music produced intellectual associations with the philosophers Bertrand Russell and G. E. Moore and musical studies with Hubert Parry. Further study abroad with Max Bruch in Berlin and Maurice Ravel in Paris was conjoined with new creative friendships with fellow English composers, including Gustav Holst and Frank Butterworth. All this took place by the turn of the century. In the larger musical world of the day, Vaughan Williams first made his mark in 1904 as a coeditor of the *English Hymnal*, locating and transcribing original traditional melodies and contributing several of his own composition. His first celebrity as a composer came with the greatly popular *Fantasia on a Theme by Thomas Tallis*, accompanied the same year by the *Sea Symphony* (no. 1), an experimental work for chorus and orchestra with lyrics by the American poet Walt Whitman. There followed the well-regarded *London Symphony* (no. 2) in 1913, and *The Lark Ascending* in 1914.

The fairly standard account of Vaughan Williams's post–World War I development as a composer is sketched above. The 1931 *Pastoral Symphony* (no. 3), based largely on a celebrated misplaying in the final movement of bugle notes from "The Last Post," the British equivalent of the American "Taps," is often reckoned an elegy for lost comrades and friends. (Indeed, one memoirist goes so far as to record a purported wartime glimpse of Vaughan Williams as a "doctor" resting between patients and attending to the solitary sounds of the melody in question.) Similar quasi-religious postwar purposes are frequently ascribed to the *Mass in G Minor* (1922), in spite of Williams's reputation as a lifelong unbeliever. And in both cases, such readings may be partially correct as far as they go. The decade of the 1920s, after all, encompassed the great years of the literary-cultural emergence of the Anglo-European and American generation of the war, including Graves, Sassoon, Owen, Remarque, Hemingway, Dos Passos, and others. Still, to accept such a spiritualistic interpretation wholly is also to play false to the larger contexts of an already major career—a career, to be sure, interrupted by the deeply personal experience of the war and now assimilating the composer's deeply personal creative responses to that experience—but also one unfolding anew into an extremely diverse and eclectic body of major contributions to postwar English musical culture for decades to come. Just to begin, for instance, with the roughly ten year period just after Vaughan Williams's military discharge in 1919, *along* with the *Pastoral Symphony* and the *Mass in G Minor* appeared a classical *Piano Concerto in C*, several attempts at folkloric ballad opera (including *Hugh the Drover*, *Old King Cole*, and *Sir John in Love*), and extensive experimentation with various meditative, mystical, and sometimes explicitly religious forms: *Flos Campi* (1925), a composition for viola, wordless chorus, small orchestra; *Te Deum* (1928) for the installation of Cosmo Lang as Archbishop of Canterbury; (1928) *Three Choral Hymns*, (1930); and the aforementioned *Job—a Masque for Dancing.*

Along with the works already described, the wide-ranging creative energies of the immediate postwar decade also may be said to have extended into the various productions of the 1930s. The 1934 popular masterpiece *Fantasia on Greensleeves* seemed self-consciously to partake of the folk origins of the composer's prewar music, perhaps for that reason still remaining an audience favorite. The direct influence of the war itself, on the other hand, shows itself self-consciously in the foreboding, painful *Dona Nobis Pacem*, with lyrics from Walt Whitman's *Drum Taps* poems about his service in the American Civil War, analogous to the composer's on the western front as a stretcher bearer, wound-dresser, and hospital attendant. At the same time, program music and dramatic compositions included *Five Tudor Portraits* (1935), a *Serenade to Music*, from famous passages devoted to the subject in Shakespeare's *The Merchant of Venice*, and *The Poisoned Kiss* (1936), an opera fashioned after Nathaniel Hawthorne's "Rappaccini's Daughter." Writing for numerous film documentaries related to the 1939–45 war effort (*The 49th Parallel, Coastal Command, The People's Land*, and others) in turn supplied further evidence of Vaughan Williams's complex understanding of the new, mass media potentialities of the project of modernism, the continuing connection of the virtuosic challenge and complexity of classical composition with a genuine popular tradition of British cultural expression through music. Meanwhile, besides the two symphonies—the melodious Fifth, debuting at the midwar 1943 Proms, and the 1946 Sixth, conversely noted for its grim postwar bleakness, various other compositions of the 1940s included the *Oboe Concerto* (1944), the *Concerto for Two Pianos* (1946), and the 1949 *Oxford Elegy*, a work personally honoring his lifelong friend and fellow English composer Gustav Holst, with texts from two favorite Matthew Arnold poems, "Thrysis" and "Scholar Gypsy."

Nor did the aging composer slacken creative pace with another decade about to begin, completing *The Pilgrim's Progress* (a long opera project he had been working at off and on since before World War I) and writing for the BBC the celebratory accompaniment to a documentary on the polar explorations of Robert Falcon Scott, eventually also to become the basis of Symphony no. 7, the *Antarctic*. That symphony appeared in 1953, along with two more, numbers 8 and 9, in the mid 1950s. They were joined just before the composer's death in 1958 by *Hodie*, a Christmas oratorio, with the conclusion sounding rather like that of Mahler's *Resurrection Symphony*—though with the ironic pastoralist's characteristic choice of subject, one might opine, in the pagan winter holiday so much beloved of the English as opposed the springtime Easter festival of the traditional church.

Here, with the final flowering of a signature Englishness in musical homages to figures as various as Holst, Bunyan, and Scott of the Antarctic, along with a valedictory religious work such as the *Hodie*, one may be tempted to see Vaughan Williams as having succumbed to the parochial nostalgia of English cultural history or the late life solace of the English church. Yet here once again this would be a complete misreading of the composer's lifelong attitude toward the relationship between the particular tenor of his individual productions and the larger intellectual and creative designs of musical modernism. Constructions of the secular imagination on one hand—folklore, history, literature, the visual arts—and those of the sacred on the other (Biblical texts, church liturgy, iconography, architecture) all continued to appear in Vaughan Williams's music to the end with equal respect as *complex forms of culture*, no more or less privileged than other imaginable counterpart forms. As Alain Frogley has importantly written on both points, there is a vast difference in Vaughan Williams in the first case between English nationalism and a sense of English nationality, and in the second between English religion and the cultural fact of a long tradition of English religiosity. To help one's fellows to attempt to live in the world of the modern, as seems the point in so much of Vaughan Williams's music, is to use such cultural legacies as may be available to help re-create a recognizable world of history and tradition in which the individual person, to use Frogley's image, may feel himself or herself to be a not incidental inhabitant of the landscape.

From a musicological standpoint, any such myth of Vaughan Williams's going quietly in his last decade is equally dispelled by evidence of the ongoing adventurousness of his new experiments in modernist technical inventiveness and eclecticism, his continuing attempts, if one may so phrase it, to help create the century's myriad new languages and possible architectures of composition. In this respect, the final symphonies may now serve as an abstract or epitome of the later career. The documentary origins of the *Sinfonia Antartica* (as he elected to call his seventh) have been mentioned in their connections with wartime experimentation in new multimedia constructions for film and television of the musical, the visual, and the verbal. At the same time, the score, perhaps best described as a symphonic and choral tone poem in five parts—complete with wind machine—also proves dense with literary and musicological allusion to other cultural texts. The program notes alone cite Shelley's "Prometheus Unbound," Psalm 104 of the English Bible, Coleridge's "Hymn before Sunrise in the Vale of Cluny," and Donne's "The Sun Rising." The Eighth, frequently described as a somewhat lighthearted work, is a novel rewriting of the traditional four-part invention—allegro, adagio, scherzo, and rondo—here substituting a fantasia, a scherzo, a cavatina, and a toccata. The first movement, described by the composer himself as "seven variations in search of a theme," was hailed by one reviewer as "the most sophisticated, civilized and universal music he has ever written, with an oddly melodious opening in a minor key leading from one strain into another into a final dizzying waltz-like swirl." The same reviewer called the Scherzo the wittiest music Vaughan Williams had composed. Offered another, it sounded perhaps as if "Shostakovich had become a Cockney with atavistic memories of the Cotswolds." The Cavatina, defined as a song for a single instrument, duly devotes itself to the string section alone with major solo passages for violin and cello; the Toccata in turn moves the composition to an energetic conclusion notable for a display of percussion—including gongs, bells, xylophone, celesta, glockenspiel, and vibraphone—happily described by the eighty-three-year-old symphonist as "all the 'phones and 'spiels known to the composer."

The Ninth, completed just before Vaughan Williams's death in 1958, seems even more boldly to forge from the self-consciously allusive and personal into the unknown. Program notes at the time suggested connections in early movements with Hardy's dark novel *Tess of the D'Urbervilles*, a particular favorite of the composer, and the dark Wessex landscape on which it is set. An early title, indeed, for the opening section was "Wessex Prelude." The second carried headings for particular sketches including "Tess," "Salisbury," and "Stonehenge." Such portions are also said to reprise important musical echoes from the composer's own career. A stark, atonal, brass-dominated opening fanfare yields to individual responses by solo violin, harp, oboe, and flute, each playing a precise, correct, brave melody, but with the series abruptly ended by a return to the menacing brasses of the opening. The usual reference made to the style of such passages connects them with a particular musical favorite of Vaughan Williams, his beloved *St. Matthew Passion*. Part two begins with what sounds like a low cornet or bugle; it is a baritone flugelhorn; drums begin a steady rhythm; the march continues until the conclusion. The flugelhorn opening recalls, according to some interpreters, a much earlier composition, *The Solent*. To others, it goes as far back as *The Sea Symphony*. The steady percussion, as noted by the composer himself, is meant to invoke "the ghostly drummer of Salisbury Plain," a familiar local story collected and pseudonymously published among *The Ingolsby Legends* by a local cleric, the Rev. R. H. Barham. As variously noted by Vaughan Williams biographers, such cultural and spiritual geography meant nearly as much to Vaughan Williams as his own native countryside—so much that he once walked the entire literary circuit of the region with his beloved friend Holst. Well known also was his abiding love for the town of Salisbury and its ancient cathedral. But in the realm of the deeply personal, there is more to the memory, one may suggest. In 1914, Salisbury Plain was also the place where the forty-one-year-old composer underwent his basic military training as a private in the British army. To use once more Blunden's apt title, such a landscape, even at the remove of more than forty years, surely must have carried last undertones of war. The opening and concluding brasses of the first section frame starkly the plaintive lyrical statements of the individual solo instruments. The unexpected menace of the flugelhorn becomes possibly one final, darkening reprise of "The Las Post." The drums are those to which Ralph Vaughan Williams may have marched in that very place in the first passages of his journey into war. The remaining story of the symphony is quickly concluded. Part three throughout sounds like a dance. At first it sounds like a danse macabre; then it sounds like a Morris dance; then, jocular, playful, abrupt, it vanishes. Part four begins with a lyrical three-four section much in the vein of the composer's early teacher Ravel; briefly there is a return to the earlier, contemplative passages of small, solo instruments; but again, the brasses encroach, contesting for the dominant strain with woodwinds and strings, becoming dominant in stern final chords but then in turn yielding in release to quiet strings. The strings disappear into silence.

We need not be too somber about the last symphonies or such other late works of elevated spirit as *Hodie* as part of some final Vaughan Williams passage to virtuosic sublimity. Throughout his life and career, even to the end, it is rather accurate to envision Ralph Vaughan Williams in the happy warrior persona that served as his public face. For a composer of works frequently notable for their fineness of execution and almost unearthly beauty, he was also hardworking and hard-nosed, with a pronounced vernacular directness. Someone is alleged to have told him once that Fauré wrote his *Requiem* on his knees. The impenitent English popularizer Vaughan Williams is said to have replied that he wrote the *Missa Solemnis* "sitting on his bum." He firmly believed—and said so in many places—that he thought the main point of the hard work of twentieth century English modernist musical creation was to help people find it in themselves. "His missionary beliefs in music-making," in Heffer's words, became pronounced in the years after the war through a new commitment "not just to resume composing, but to teach and to encourage others to make music." And so throughout the ensuing four decades he devoted unstinting support and personal presence to such musical gatherings as the Three Choirs, Glyndbourne, and the Proms. Closer to his birthplace, the provincial Leith Hill Musical Festival remained as important as any other single object of professional commitment in the course of his lifetime. So among his proudest productions remained the hymn, at once a product of invention and tradition. One favorite, "Come Down, O Love Divine," took on "Down Ampney," as its familiar title. Down Ampney was the name of the place of his birth.

Somehow in keeping with the age of the Internet, the global village of electronic communication, Ralph Vaughan Williams's twentieth-century modernist legacy of music keeps in touch with cultures both cosmopolitan and local. Among the first of the great twentieth-century composers with major modern recording projects devoted to the standard body of work, Vaughan Williams further remains the cynosure of assiduous electronic curators, collectors, and preservers. Perhaps most heartening is the current availability of virtually the whole canon, major and minor, on YouTube, with English, American, European, South American, Australian, and Asian performances—both professional and amateur—produced for formal programming or locally recorded. One finds available, for instance, the popular *English Folksong Suite* in stirring performances by the Eastman Wind Ensemble or Sir Adrian Boult and the London Symphony Orchestra. Meanwhile, on the computer display page, ready to be queued for viewing just below these are others every bit as enthusiastic by the Kanawah, West Virginia, County High School Band and by a youth orchestra playing in a park in Singapore.

In the large or small, were one to attempt a signature term for Vaughan Williams's compositions from start to finish, one could surely do worse than recall that ascribed by Warner Berthoff to Herman Melville, who spent his last years working on the manuscript of *Billy Budd*. In a world of war, writes Berthoff, the tragedy of the handsome young sailor, falsely accused of mutiny yet condemned to die by the inexorable military laws of the sea, becomes simply a fact of things—of which myriad accounts will be written, frequently in direct contradiction of each other. Yet the tale nonetheless becomes a testament neither of acceptance nor of resistance, says Berthoff, but rather a grand statement of Melvillian magnanimity. So Vaughan Williams seems to have been imaged by literary and artistic contemporaries, such as the exile Elias Canetti. "The most wonderful pure man, Ralph Vaughan Williams," Canneti called him, "the composer and pride of the nation, great-hearted, independent, with no notion of aristocracy, submissive, but without acute rebellion, a man one would like to cover pages and pages about."

In conclusion one might identify this as precisely the spirit emanating from the most memorable and most characteristic artistic productions of Ralph Vaughan Williams, the survivor of the Great War who went on to become the great twentieth-century modernist musical composer. Were one to choose a particular *Billy Budd* moment in Vaughan Williams, one might search in a number of places. For reasons outlined above, an apt choice, biographically and artistically, might be the valedictory Ninth Symphony, to which the musicologist Alain Frogley has devoted an extended compositional analysis highlighting its meticulous late-life inventiveness and technical complexity. Another might be the *Serenade to Music*, which in its sublime beauty and compositional virtuosity is said in its first performance to have moved the fellow composer Rachmaninoff to tears. Yet another could be the oratorio *Sancta Civitas*, the composer's favorite among his choral compositions, with textual inscriptions of the *Phaedo*, the *Book of Revelation*, and the Taverner Bible charting the progressions of the musical score toward a chastened postapocalyptic vision of grace.

The fact of the matter is one might choose almost as readily from many places in the prodigious body of composition. Personally, I would give the award to another of the short works, the briefer *Five Variants on Dives and Lazarus* (like *Billy Budd*, something of a musical novella in multiple renditions), written just at the chronological midpoint of Vaughan Williams's post–World War I career in 1939, at the heart of the dreadful century, as the dark memory of the slaughter of 1914–1918 spilled over for many survivors such as the composer himself into the prospect of another even more monstrous and horrific. For me it remains his most melodiously beautiful. I would also claim it as his most humanly poignant and most compositionally precise. It is also a work, for those of a modernist bent, with a characteristic Vaughan Williams history. Commissioned for the 1939 New York World's Fair as expression of the spirit of English culture in music, it arises in fact from what might be called a scriptural anecdote, a small human story, biblically obscure, though among the most frequently represented in medieval church iconography. Not to be confused with associations of Jesus and Lazarus, it is the parable of the rich man and the leper, a specific rendition of which appears only in Luke 16:18-31 and has no traces in the other Gospels. In the version referenced by Vaughan Williams, the text in turn invokes its own complex history as a cultural figuration. Dives and Lazarus: the former derives from the Latin tradition, a word meaning "rich man"; the latter comes from the Hebrew "God is our help," which from the Middle Ages onward became further synonymous with "leper." The parable, similar to that of the Good Samaritan passing by the stranger on the side of the road, is frequently cited as having a moralistic conclusion giving one of the most notable New Testament renderings of the vision of the afterlife. Frequently ignored is a notably cruel and punitive element. Dives, consigned to eternal torment without hope of mercy, sees Lazarus taken to dwell forever in the bosom of Abraham. The possibility of human connection, either of Dives in repentance or of Lazarus in forgiveness, we are told, is for all time abridged across the abyss of history. Again, the transforming beauty of musical rendition lies in Vaughan Willliams's rewriting his particular account out of a familiar magic and mystery—in this case, as in so much of his work, from a well-known English melody of the folk song tradition ("Come All Ye Faithful Christians," extant in a number of regional versions though best known through its rendition as a carol).

A first performance of the Vaughan Williams set of complex musical variations on such a theme met with great acclaim in 1939, becoming immediately embraced as a permanent part of the repertoire. Less known is how it came to be reprised on film in 1947 during the gray, mournful, austere period of post-1945 recovery for the documentary *The Dim Little Island*, in which the composer appears in person along with three other figures reckoned proper exemplary spokesmen for the encouragement of a sturdy, striving postwar morale spirit—an industrialist, a naturalist, and a popular cartoonist. In the composer's section, he speaks over the melody, commenting on the music, its history, his quiet pride in what it says about the English spirit, his belief in music itself as a basis of cultural cohesion. "Listen to that tune," he says. "It is one of our English folk tunes. I knew it first when I was quite a small boy, but I realized then that here was something not only very beautiful, but which had a special appeal to me as an Englishman." Such music, he says, unites the culture at all levels from that of the musical virtuoso in the concert hall through practitioners in the schools and choral festivals to "those who play and sing for their own spiritual recreation in their own houses." So the national life is founded on "those great tunes, which, like our language, our customs, or laws, are the groundwork upon which everything must stand."

Thus, as with so much of Ralph Vaughan Williams's work, again one directly connects the concept of magnanimity with another more specific and peculiar to the composer—the idea of music and community. And thus one is not surprised to know that *Dives and Lazarus* was the selection chosen to begin a Westminster Abbey memorial service for him in 1958. *Five Variants on Dives and Lazarus*: composed exactly at the darkest moment of mid-passage in the four decades of life the composer was vouchsafed after 1918 and played once more at the end, no better selection could have honored the musical memory of what he had fervently wished to be both his own and his century's long journey out of war.

7
History and Memory in the Great War Paintings of John Singer Sargent

On a recent visit to London, I made my way south of the Thames to the Imperial War Museum, with the particular goal of reencountering the significant sections devoted to the British experience of the Great War, specifically those concerning the experience of the western front: what my countryman Paul Fussell—author of *The Great War and Modern Memory* and himself a World War II infantry lieutenant in northern Europe—has called "the matter of Flanders and Picardy." Following Fussell, I was further pursuing the memory of my own combat experience in the Vietnam War, as a young officer of upper-middle-class origins and elite education leading soldiers from a conscript, largely blue-collar army, and of our shared identification with the British generation of the trenches—Graves, Owen, Sassoon, and others. "Someone had blundered." Across the decades of the misbegotten wars of the century, we all understood what that meant: when the politicians and generals get to moving lines on a map, it's the junior officers and enlisted men who pay the price, usually getting sent out to the end of nowhere to die for next to nothing.

All this was on my mind as I walked down Westminster Bridge Road, crossed over the museum grounds and joined a line of early arrivals moving up the stairs. There I found a stark white banner, colored with a single scarlet poppy. I was to see, it announced, a special exhibition on the British experience of the Great War, in commemoration of the ninetieth anniversary of the cessation of hostilities on November 11, 1918. At the entrance to the exhibition proper, I encountered a handsome, well-dressed woman perhaps in her eighties, looking at a violin in a display case. The instrument was described as having been lost in France by its British owner during the Battle of the Somme in 1916, only to be discovered some fifty years later in a French barn and restored to its owner. His name and unit were given, along with a photograph of him as a young enlisted soldier. "Astonishing," I think I must have whispered, or some such thing. She turned and looked at me. "It was my father's, you know." There she stood—the daughter of the man in the photo. She went on. "He told me that he was ordered to drive his truck up to Thiepval. When he got to the place where they'd told him to go, there was no one anywhere. Then he looked down and saw that he had been driving over a field of dead bodies."

Ninety years after a great silence had descended over the trench lines stretching from the North Sea to the Swiss border, this seemed to me a uniquely heartbreaking British western front moment, and it prefigured the tone of much of the exhibition, which was largely British Expeditionary Force (BEF) in emphasis. Decent attention was given to other theatres of operation and to the sacrifices of other nations, Allied and enemy; throughout, Fussell's phrase stayed in my head—the matter of Flanders and Picardy. A special section conjoined the fates in that region of war of Raymond Asquith, a major in the Grenadier Guards and the son of a prime minister, and the poet Isaac Isaac Rosenberg, an enlisted man and a Jew, both killed in 1916. On display was Wilfred Owen's poetry manuscript of "Anthem for Doomed Youth," with hand emendations—some of them rather peremptory and brutal—by Siegfried Sassoon. The editing had been done at Craiglockhart, a military hospital in Scotland for shell-shocked officers, who called it "Dottyville." Another Dottyville text was a letter by Sassoon, describing his own journey there—whence he had been committed after publishing a notorious declaration of refusal to serve further in what he described as an insane, immoral war. He was supposed to have been accompanied to Craiglockhart, Sassoon wrote, by fellow officer and poet Robert Graves. Graves, himself on the verge of breakdown, had stupidly missed the train, and Sassoon had made his own way to the loony bin with his unhinged escort officer arriving a good deal later.

Near the end of the exhibit, a small auditorium offered a continuous screening of *The Battle of the Somme*, a purported documentary shown to British audiences during the war. Suffice it to say that the action represented had not the horrific violence which has come down to us as a metonym of pointless western front slaughter—with sixty thousand British casualties in that single battle suffered in the first three hours. But even now this seemed a graphic and disturbing film; how truly awful it must have been then, I thought, if they were willing to show such things to civilians at the time.

I made what I took to be an exit into an art wing familiar to me as part of the permanent collection. And there I came face-to-face with the artifact that would launch me toward the meditations on history and memory that now become the subject proper of this essay. Had this enormous painting, filling an entire wall, always just been there, I wondered, escaping my particular notice on an earlier visit? Was the shock of it in its juxtaposition with the foregoing exhibit? Whatever the case, it nearly took me to my knees: an extremely large John Singer Sargent canvas from the western front, titled *Gassed*—a canvas, to

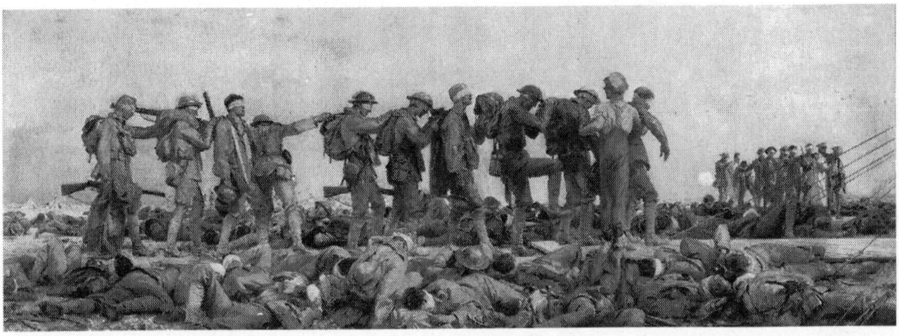

Figure 7.1 *Gassed*, John Singer Sargent, 1918–1919. Imperial War Museum, London, United Kingdom.

be exact, twenty feet wide and nine feet high. The figures in a central grouping are roughly life-sized, all of them blindfolded, shuffling and stumbling, some helmetless, many with bandaged wounds, their gear torn and makeshift, a few still with their Enfield rifles carried in various disorderly ways. They are moving left to right, nine of them in total, each attempting to keep his hands on the shoulders of the man in front of him. The file is further divided into groupings of three and six, interrupted by the figures of two medical corpsmen attempting to keep them organized. They are backgrounded by a vista of sky and bare-ground landscape, where one sees large numbers of other soldiers. One of the men in the main group is stepping notably high, trying to avoid some unseen obstacle. The obstacle, one realizes, is likely one of a vast accumulation of fellow casualties who carpet the ground as far as the eye can see. Off to the right, another such column of the blinded leading the blinded advances, this one attended by two vaguely angelic hospital orderlies in white gowns. Amid the vast spectacle of humanity, there appears not a single recognizable human face. The dominant colors of the bottom half of the painting are those of earth; the entire top half is devoted to an empty grey sky. A sickly yellow tone—the color of the gas itself—reflects from every surface, including the human figures.

The date and provenance of the painting are well known. They follow from Sargent's 1918 commissioning by a quasi-official War Artists Memorial Committee, followed by a personal letter of request from Prime Minister David Lloyd George to go to the front as a government war artist. As Sargent himself observed, it seemed initially an unlikely assignment for a figure of his age, background, and experience. He was, after all, in his sixties, an American expatriate-cosmopolitan of long standing, a renowned society portraitist enjoying a refined, elegant lifestyle of a kind of Henry James fastidiousness. His trepidation was marked: "Would I have the nerve to look," he asked himself, "not to speak of painting? I have never seen anything in the least horrible—outside of my studio." All this notwithstanding, he was given a proper quasi-military kit and shortly transported into the area of British military operations, landing at Boulogne where he was taken to main Army headquarters and a cordial meeting with Haig himself. Next, accompanied by an appropriately well-born and cultivated escort officer, his long-time friend Sir Philip Sassoon, he was sent to a portion of the front occupied by the elite Guards Division. There he enjoyed another orientation meeting with the divisional commander General Fielding and a briefing on the newest Allied breakthrough weapon, the tank, including a test ride. He met up with his acquaintance Churchill, who, exiled from government for his sponsorship of the Gallipoli nightmare, was serving a brief stint in the trenches and, it seemed to Sargent and others, fighting his own war. He got a visit to ruined Arras. Meanwhile, he found himself filling numerous pages of notebooks devoted to troops in various uniforms, poses, duties, attitudes; he sketched gun carriages, supply trains, trench fortifications. He had several dangerous brushes with enemy fire. On August 11 he was alerted to a large party of gassed British being assembled at a casualty clearing station on the Arras-Doullens road; this proved the genesis of the "big" or centerpiece painting that had been stipulated as a part of his commission. It was not, as things turned out, the "big" work most suitably proposed as one of the peculiar expectations of his assignment—the bright idea, no doubt, of some sponsor who saw possibilities in Sargent's American birth: a large-scale depiction of coordinated activity between British armies in the field with newly arrived combat troops of the American Expeditionary Force (AEF). To this end, he had spent some time with the American Twenty-Seventh Division commanded by General O'Ryan. But the whole assignment ended shortly when Sargent was struck with flu, part of the great pandemic, and evacuated to England at the end of October.

Altogether the experience made for a lot of art. In addition to *Gassed*, there were countless smaller paintings, sketches, studies, watercolors, and drawings. Although he could never seem to get the British and Americans together, as was suggested for his master commission, he did manage to paint the AEF. *Arrival of American Troops at the Front*, for instance, is a large canvas divided into two columns, left and right, one of Americans moving forward into action, the other of French troops being withdrawn. The Americans, generically tall, handsome and healthy, properly uniformed and equipped, all with helmets, gas masks, packs, and bedrolls, carry their rifles in ready position at right-shoulder arms. The marching unit moves in orderly rank and file, eight to ten abreast, as part of a column stretching infinitely backward. In middle distance are two officers, both on light-colored horses. Far more prominent,

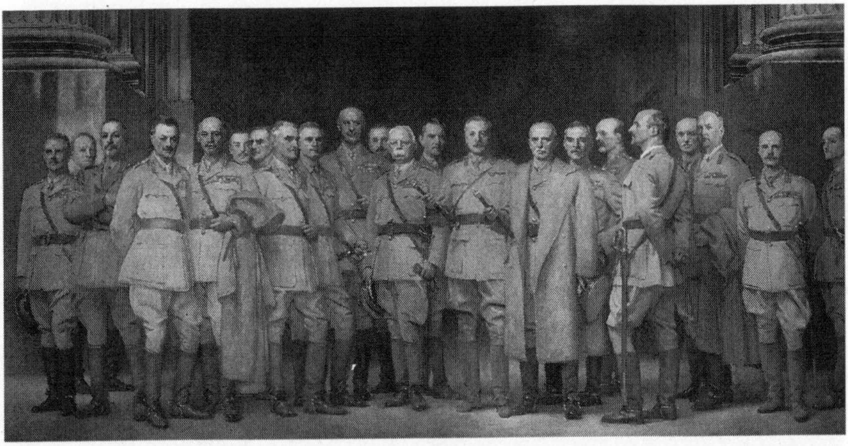

Figure 7.2 *General Officers of World War I,* John Singer Sargent, 1922. National Portrait Gallery 1954.

to the left of the marching column, is a double column of trucks advancing in parallel. On the right side of the canvas, balancing the advancing Americans, is a disordered crowd of French being withdrawn. There is the occasional Poilu helmet, but most are bareheaded, several with skull bandages. One carries a rifle carelessly in his right hand; another has his slung over the shoulder. No machine transportation is visible.

Rather more frequently reproduced are paintings with characteristic British and French subject matter, a number of major oils all painted during 1918. They include *Ruined Cathedral at Arras*; *The Road*; *Army Convoy*; *Shoeing Cavalry Horses at the Front*; and, above all, *Gassed.*

Gassed. In any circumstances, on the day I stood in the Imperial War Museum, ninety years after the armistice, the painting would have been a shock. In my case the shock was accentuated by a sense of standing at a further, quite personal intersection of history and memory created just the previous day by a visit to the National Portrait Gallery, where I had viewed another vast war-related painting by Sargent—commissioned a few years later—*Generals of the Great War*. The sense of horrific congruencies that overcame me could not have been more exact. I had been looking at a precise counterpart of the painting in the Imperial War Museum. The canvas is almost exactly the same size as that of *Gassed.* The standing figures are of similar proportion. They are not, of course, enlisted men, infantry, medical, or support troops. Their uniforms, immaculate headquarters khaki, are clean and red-tabbed. Most wear officers' belts and full decorations. There is the occasional sword. To a man they wear polished riding boots. All seem distinctly middle-aged or older. None are wounded. They are visibly clean, in good health, none of them seeming the worse for their experience of the Great War.

Assembled as if at the portico of some vast edifice—suggesting, perhaps, St. Paul's or Westminster Abbey—and posed so as to take the eye from left to right, as they never would have congregated naturally—are twenty-two figures, all individually recognizable from photographs or personal portraits. Virtually everybody is there. Haig is slightly to the right of center, surrounded by his major western front army commanders—Rawlinson, Horne, Plumer—and chiefs of General Staff, including Robertson and Wilson. French, relieved after the British Expeditionary Force debacles of the early war, has the consolation of standing as part of the Haig assemblage. But the dominion commands have not been ignored. Birdwood and Monash represent Australia and New Zealand; Smuts, Lukin, and Botha, South Africa; Byng and Currie, the Canadians. Nor have the far-flung fighting fronts been neglected. Gallipoli, East Africa, Salonika, and Mesopotamia are represented. There is Lambart from Italy and Allenby from Palestine.

We know a good deal about the provenance of this work as well. Commissioned by a South African magnate (Sir Abe Bailey) for the National Portrait Gallery, it was part of a massive triple project: major army, navy, and civilian political figures. (As revealed in another part of the Gallery, Sargent wound up doing the last, as well.) For the artist, there was no concealing his sense of oppression in having undertaken a tiresomely laborious assignment. "How am I going to paint twenty-two pairs of boots?" he wrote. He found his answer in the vintage Sargent way: producing—through conscientious sittings, for which the studies exist—twenty-one society portraits of exactly the sort he had made a career of painting. But it is the overall effect that somehow takes command and mocks the pretense. It is in their faces, hands, necks—the color of their skin—how pink and plump and babyish so many of them look. They all have the complexion of Winston Churchill in every adult portrait. Or perhaps it is more that they all look like babies the way a lot of babies seem to look like Winston Churchill. They certainly do not look remotely like the men who had been gassed. If one will excuse the cliché–because it is flatly true—they are in the pink. That is the dominant tint overlaying the painting, as obvious as the sickly yellow tone that permeates the surfaces of *Gassed*.

During this commission, Sargent's work was further complicated by concurrent obligations arising from other large, demanding projects and assignments, some of them transatlantic. He made several trips back and forth to Boston, attending to a late-life pull of home, a certain patriotic connection, in the broadest sense, at least to his own culture and class. The most famous of these later commissions was *The History of Religion*, the lavish mythological murals for the Boston Public Library. But he also agreed to do some work for the new Widener Library at Harvard, a kind of American coda, it turns out, to his British Great War commissions. Specifically, he was asked by the trustees to create murals for the great second-story landing of the vaulted marble entrance hall; the theme was to be the commemoration of the sacrifices of Harvard men who had served in the American forces of the Great War. Two panels were requested. The results are still there to behold on the way to the computer terminals. On the left, almost purely allegorical, is *Death and Victory*. At center, a helmeted, muscular, immaculately uniformed and equipped American doughboy stands astride the body of a fallen comrade, albeit neither with visible wounds. With his left arm he holds closely in a final embrace a hooded female death figure; with the right, in presumably a last heroic gesture, he lifts triumphantly heavenward a beautiful nude female figure of victory. The second painting, on the right, divides subject matter and theme in the middle, counterposing a certain heroic combat pictorialism with a rather more complicated design of allegory. To one who knows Sargent's other war-related work, the painting looks a good deal like *Americans Moving Toward the Front*, without the presence of the French. At a slight diagonal with the vast Atlantic to their left, a marching column of youthfully fine-featured doughboys in campaign hats moves relentlessly forward; to the right several of them, as if part of some joyous metaphysical victory parade, respond with a wave, a nod, an outstretched hand to the welcome of figures representing Helmeted Mars (Britain); Death, again shrouded, oddly androgynous, with downturned broken sword (the Hun); and Victory. The latter is female and impossibly beautiful; she is suckling an infant at her breast; she wears the red Liberty Cap. She can only be, of course, France.

One could go all the way back and summarily do a good bit with the grand cultural symbology of Sargent at war, starting with the bizarre schizophrenia of the big British paintings and winding up with the almost ludicrous American jobs. On the British account, *Gassed* must surely still compel us through a vision of twentieth-century, mass-casualty warfare, the victims of the weaponry of terror stumbling mutely about a landscape carpeted with the fallen. The individual soldiers comprise scattered parties of the lost, helpless and unmanned, the blind truly leading and led by the blind. The *Generals*, for all the historical interest and, in some cases, genuine distinction of the individual portraits, evokes the great historical cliché of the red-tabbed, champagne-swilling, chateau-dwelling butchers, safe and warm from the horrors of the battlefield, residing amid their staff retinues in immaculate isolation. Alan Clark refers to them as the "Donkeys." He records his source as the memoirs of Field Marshall Erich von Falkenhayn, which feature a purported conversation between the great German commanders Ludendorff and Hoffman. (Ludendorff: "The English soldiers fight like lions." Hoffman: "True. But don't we know they are lions led by donkeys.") The German "Löwe" translates directly into the English "lions." Donkeys more properly comes out as "asses." The asses. Let it be so written. For their part, the American paintings attempt to chronicle reinvigoration of Allied will through infusions of New World power, confidence, and historical idealism. *Americans Moving Toward the Front* shows, one is obliged to conclude, what Sargent genuinely saw to be a new sense of physical energy and hope filling the Allied ranks with the entry of the Americans into the war, their fresh, healthy, spirited formations moving relentlessly forward. (And he was not alone in this. See, for instance, the moment of watching a group of Americans moving forward recorded in Vera Brittain's *Testament of Youth*, a passage of parallel emphasis on their energy, optimism, health and even physical stature.)

The Widener murals comprise more of the above. As noted, they are also certainly a response by the old Bostonian Sargent to particular personal imperatives of culture and class. They represent the Harvard of Alan Seeger, who could not dally while America dithered and joined the French Foreign Legion as an enlisted soldier and died at Verdun, but not before leaving the world with possibly the most famous of war-poems in English to come out of the great conflict, "I Have a Rendezvous with Death." The murals also celebrate the gallant martyrdom of pilot officer Quentin Roosevelt, son of a US President, in his dying so revered by the French that his solitary grave at the site of the fatal crash remained for decades a shrine apart from the official military cemeteries. It is said that many Harvard alumni remain mortified by the images' overblown allegorizations. In spirit, there seems little to separate them from Pershing's alleged proclamation "Lafayette, we are here!" The knightly atmospherics seem no more oppressive than the decorativeness of the Pre-Raphaelites; the images of marching columns evoke the eye-catching modernist graphics of the better recruitment posters; the illustration of mythological figures appear no more outlandish than those found in fine editions of Milton, Homer, or Dante. The hooded personifications of death, if anything, invoke something of the great mystery of the Augustus St. Gaudens's *Kwannon* sculpture commissioned by Henry Adams for the grave of his wife.

An explanation for much of this strange jangle of styles across Sargent's paintings of the Great War must surely lie in the artist's own complex, late-life understandings of cultures at large. A great cosmopolitan, he could not have been stupid about demands of particular national narratives, elevated to the status of what we call cultural myth. And surely his paintings reflect an acute sense of the dynamics of war, history, and memory for the British along with the Americans, for the British as distinguished from the Americans, and as certainly for the Americans as distinguished from the British.

Yes, he did it all massively on commission. But abroad or at home, wherever that was, audience expectation itself was a problematic question of the highest order for Sargent—an absolute determinant of how he wished to look at a project, to set the terms of its composition and representation and for whom, when, and where. At the same time, it was never a question that couched itself in political or ideological abstraction. It was always an artistic problem. As T. S. Eliot once commented famously on Henry James, Sargent's art, in its complex cultural cosmopolitanism, was the product of a mind so fine it was never violated by an idea, let alone ideology. James did renounce his American citizenship in protest of his government's refusal to come in on the Allied side. Sargent stayed American—though he might have gone over if a knighthood had been in it for him. But he also lived long enough and was able to continue his work as an artist to make a substantial record in his paintings about complex Anglo-European and American attitudes toward the Great War in history and memory. To put it simply, he had been asked to witness and paint history. He also surely understood how, as the work of a major representational artist, his painting would become the basis of memory. How did he do it? Not to put too opportunistic or cynical a construction on it, he did it depending on the terms and requirements of a particular commission. He did the western front as he imagined the War Artists Memorial Commission would choose to have it remembered—hewing rather precisely to specific instructions, although he never produced the suggested big painting of combined Anglo-American arms. He painted the British and Commonwealth general officers as he imagined the National Portrait Gallery would choose to have them remembered. He did the American contribution to the Allied cause as he imagined the trustees of the Widener Library of Harvard University would choose to have it remembered. The enterprise was not completely under his control, of course, nor under that of his sponsors and patrons. He could not have known, in the case of *Gassed*, how people visiting the Imperial War Museum would find it remembered; in the case of *American Troops at the Front*, how people able to visit the Gilcrease Museum of Tulsa, Oklahoma (or to gain access to their website) would find it remembered; or how presumably the Cholmondeley family, still private owners of *American Troops Going Up into the Line*, a counterpart of *Arrival of American Troops at the Front*, must think of it now as having been remembered. Nor can anyone imagine how Sargent must have thought of all those Great War paintings, sketches, studies, among the tens of thousands of other paintings, sketches, studies that came out of a long, almost incredibly productive lifetime. In the end, one wishes certain proper ideological conclusions might be drawn concerning the larger cultural resonances of this account of certain paintings of the Great War in history and memory—even if nowhere ranking with Paul Fussell's explorations of the ironist Anglo-American sensibility of the postwar age or Modris Eksten's of the Franco-German birth of the modern. One might even settle just for Jake Barnes and Bill Gorton in *The Sun Also Rises* doing a little chorus of "Give me some irony and pity." Here the complex, enigmatic, art-haunted history of the paintings themselves becomes the point; and the point turns out to be one beyond irony, beyond pity, beyond even sadness. It is the realization that one culture's myth is another culture's absurdity; that one culture's glory is another's catastrophe. On exactly that point, in relation to the visual arts, one is drawn to the brilliant recent novel by Zadie Smith, *On Beauty*, and what may be its central pronouncement on the subject. Never mind that it is uttered by a distinctly confused, morally flaccid, and intermittently unpalatable character; a brilliant, unhappy, and confused English art historian; a Rembrandt specialist exiled to an American university in suburban Boston. His post, in one final do-or-die attempt at tenure, the next-best-thing-to-Harvard, that it is a pretentious, carefully honed poststructuralist zinger, the one he always uses in his opening lecture, hoping to drive off the great undergraduate unwashed who will never rise to the brilliance of his theoretical understandings. He is talking about the faces of art in relation to those of culture and ideology. Prettiness, he says, is the mask worn by power. He goes on: "Art is the Western myth with which we both console ourselves and make ourselves." The comment, that of a pretentious academic making his radical sallies against the privileged young, concerns Rembrandt, but it applies equally to the faces of history and memory in the works of a great establishment portraitist doing the Great War on commission. In either case, the context of its utterance makes it no less true for being so uttered.

8
The Great Party Crasher

"Mrs. Dalloway," "The Great Gatsby," and the Cultures of World War I Remembering

As might be expected in the wake of so immense a cataclysm, the decade after World War I proved an epoch rich in the literature of aftermath. This pertained equally to the cultures of both of the Western victor nations and of those defeated in the massive conflict. Literary war writing had begun to appear as early as 1917 with Henri Barbusse's *Through the Flames* and 1920 with an initial version of Ernst Junger's *Storm of Steel.* 1921 saw the publication of John Dos Passos's *Three Soldiers*, 1923 Thomas Boyd's *Through the Wheat*, and 1924 Jaroslav Hasek's antiwar absurdist satire *The Good Soldier Schwek.* There followed later in the decade an outpouring of combat narrative, with British literary memoirs including Edmund Blunden's *Undertones of War* (1928), Robert Graves's *Good-Bye to All That* (1929), and Siegfried Sassoon's *Memoirs of an Infantry Officer* (1930), as well as Vera Brittain's classic of remembrance and loss, *Testament of Youth* (1933). Novels of the same period included Eric Maria Remarque's *All Quiet on the Western Front* (1929), Ernest Hemingway's *A Farewell to Arms* (1929), Frederick Manning's *The Middle Parts of Fortune* (1929) (republished in 1930 as *Her Privates We*), and William March's *Company K* (1933). Drama included Maxwell Anderson's and Lawrence Stallings's *What Price Glory* (1924) and R. C. Sheriff's *Journey's End* (1928). The large body of British war poetry that brought to literary prominence such figures as Blunden, Graves, and Sassoon, as well as Edward Thomas, Ivor Gurney, Isaac Rosenberg, and others, found a culmination at the end of the decade in the publication of the previously uncollected works of Wilfred Owen. More general aftermath texts, involving recurrent modernist symbologies of death, disease, depersonalization, destruction, sterility, blindness, cynicism, and despair, likewise abounded. A short list of major works shaped in the image of the war might include Ezra Pound's *Hugh Selwyn Mauberley*, T. S. Eliot's *The Waste-Land*, E. E. Cummings's *The Enormous Room*, Thomas Mann's *The Magic Mountain*, Ernest Hemingway's *The Sun Also Rises*, and Louis-Ferdinand Celine's *Journey to the End the of the Night.*

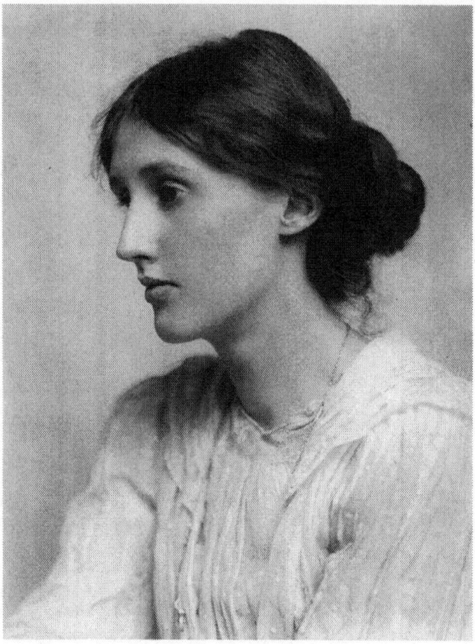

Figure 8.1 *Virginia Woolf*, George C. Beresford, 1902. National Portrait Gallery P221.

My purpose here is to draw into the orbit of such major canonical writings of the Great War—as it was still called at the time—two oddly paired but remarkably parallel texts, both well-known modernist classics of social realism/naturalism produced exactly at mid-decade. The first is Virginia Woolf's masterpiece of postwar English manners and class relations, *Mrs. Dalloway*; the second is its American counterpart, F. Scott Fitzgerald's *The Great Gatsby*. Both, by conventional taxonomy, are considered major twentieth-century extensions of the novel of society; at the same time, both represent departures in the tradition of the experimentalist art-novel, with their striking innovations in form and narration, their complex psychological explorations of inner consciousness, their modernist fragmentations, juxtapositions, and economies in structure and point of view. That is, if we remember them for their greatness as social texts in the long tradition of the novel of manners—the attempt to capture at a certain distinct point in history what Lionel Trilling once called "a culture's whole hum and buzz of implication"—we also respond to their extraordinary aesthetic achievement. As powerful social or political fictions, both are also possessed of an exalted, albeit haunting and ultimately tragic beauty. A major source of both their power and their beauty, I would propose here, lies in the subtexts of the British and American public cultures of World War I remembrance—through novelistic invocations not only of general popular culture iconographies of war memory but also of particular individual figures connected with the frequently conflicted visions of heroism and sacrifice arising out of the war.

In laying the ground for such a broad cultural and ideological argument connecting the two texts, it may prove useful initially to make a further note of a number of important and quite specific cross-cultural affiliations. To begin with, both are in large part novels of the city, centered on the twinned postwar cultural capitals of the Anglo-American world, London, and New York—albeit with pastoral elements involving, for Woolf's titular protagonist, memories of the English country house and, for Fitzgerald the great lawns and expanses of Long Island shoreline estates recalling an older vision of American nature. In the same sense of elegiac consciousness, both look back across the abyss of the war years to lives of youthful aspiration and possibility, *Mrs. Dalloway* to the late Victorian and Edwardian world of the young Clarissa Parry with her hopes of intellectual and spiritual self-realization, and *The Great Gatsby* to a boy named Jimmy Gatz with his Benjamin Franklin self-improvement schedules and golden dreams of success and romantic love. As emanations of postwar sensibility, both are fables of mechanization, abounding in imagery of cars, trains, autobuses, and airplanes; of crowded streets, bridges, and highways; of enforced rituals of urban deindividualization and anonymity. At the same time, both are society novels in the highly conventional sense of the rituals of traditional class arrangements, centering as they do on the idea of the party as a social gathering and post–World War I cultural microcosm.

In this, one should note, they share fictional ground with literary urban sites as diverse as the Paris of Hemingway's *The Sun Also Rises*, itself devised in wandering expatriate social panorama as a desperate, drunken, nonstop party of the war-damaged, a kind of moving "fiesta," as the original short version was titled; the Berlin of Christopher Isherwood's *Berlin Stories*, with the dark nightlife, the subterranean culture of the club and cabaret; the London of Evelyn Waugh's early novels about the dissolute bright young things of 1920s, such as *Vile Bodies* and a *Handful of Dust*; the New York of F. Scott Fitzgerald's other works of the era, including *This Side of Paradise*, *The Beautiful and Damned*, and assorted other tales of the Jazz Age. The cosmopolitan roster of doomed, merrymaking capitals of the world could be further expanded—Vienna, Prague, St. Petersburg, Madrid, Shanghai, Havana. Amid a spectacle of throbbing music and dance crazes, out of the cultural epicenters of a world afire with the excitements of modernism would come a steady production of books underpinning the desperate gaiety in one way or another with the spectral presence of the war, its continuing role in the memory culture of everyday life. Strangely ensconced amid the entertainments—whether the polite, carefully planned, albeit vestigial gatherings of survivor prewar elites, or (more often) the vast, vulgar, carnival displays of the newly mobile and meretricious—the Great War would continue to reach out and claim its latest victims.

Distinctively, in the two works directly at hand, major roles are enacted by characters suffering from the war-related mental disorder called at the time shell shock. Though various diagnostic explanations existed for the latter—it was first thought to be a kind of brain lesion, the result of concussion from artillery bombardment or other explosive ordnance. In the neuropsychiatric dimension, the concept would unfold over the decades of the century in an evolving set of terminologies that would include battle fatigue, combat exhaustion, and, most recently, Post-Traumatic Stress Disorder (PTSD). These, in both novels, are further surrounded by large casts of persons qualifying as war-damaged in one way or another, with the eventual cataloguing of the malady extending from specific injury in body and mind to broader imagings of physical disease and mental deracination. In *Mrs. Dalloway*, the chief representatives of war trauma include the mad, shell-shocked veteran Septimus Smith, but also the upper-class party giver and hostess Clarissa Dalloway, who has notably lost her health and her earlier vision of life through a near fatal infection with Spanish influenza. In Fitzgerald's novel, the two primary figures are the titular hero, Jay Gatsby—a highly decorated hero, as it turns out, of combat with the American Expeditionary Force in France—but also in considerable degree Nick Carraway, the first-person narrator who begins with substantial comment on his own war experience and its effects on his subsequent understandings of belief and value. And as with such characters, one shortly discovers, so with their worlds: we feel the death culture of the war continuing throughout the decade to spill over into somber public atmospherics and grim monumentalism.

For both nations, in fact, this was a matter of recent, postwar memory. In London's Whitehall, on November 11, 1920, the British dead of the war were honored with the dedication of the great Cenotaph, literally the "empty tomb"; at the same ceremony, the body of a single unidentified British soldier was interred in Westminster Abbey. A year later in the United States, parallel scenes of remembrance were enacted in ceremonies at Arlington National Cemetery, marking the return home and the burial of an unidentified American at the Tomb of the Unknown Soldier. So throughout these contemporary novels of postwar social relations in the two victorious nations of postwar culture and power, the landscape of popular memory continues to be haunted by the wandering ghosts of Flanders, Gallipoli, the Izonzo, the Argonne.

For Woolf's novel of postwar London society, set somewhere around 1923, the more appropriate phrasing might be "high society," certainly in the terms projected for the Dalloway gathering in Westminster. For here, as in so much

English literary fiction, the drama of manners and class relationships being played out will eventually come to center on the highly arranged and formalized social gathering, with invitation determined largely by status, power, family tradition, and socio-political standing. To be specific, the culminating event toward which the novel tends from its first sentence onward is to be a single, very English party, given on the evening of the day in which the novel is set by the titular character—a well-born Englishwoman in her fifties—and her husband, a well-connected government functionary. The house is in the fashionable West End, amid the enclosures of fine dwellings and private squares, great parks, and royal palaces abutting Whitehall, the traditional seat of government and public ceremony. In keeping with the postwar mood of a small, ancient, island culture that has lost to death nearly a million of its young men—one in ten of its eligible males—with another two million maimed, mutilated, disabled, or otherwise wounded, the gathering, even nearly five years after the armistice, is to be somber, select, sedate, and reflective of traditional upper-class social rituals and observances. For all that will be written eventually about the 1920s English generation of "bright young things" (the daring, privileged, frequently outrageous sons and daughters of the postwar upper classes) by Evelyn Waugh, Nancy Mitford, and others, here will be no desperate revelry, garish costumes, jazz dancing, drunken or drug-addled public misbehavior. Presiding over the world of the novel, within and without, is an England undergoing an extended period of mourning and chastened remembrance. The one working class character featured in a major role, the ghostly representative of the war on the landscape of remembrance, is the shell-shocked English veteran Septimus Smith with his Italian war bride, Lucrezia—or, as she is called by the narrator, "Rezia." At the same time, in a strange thematic and stylistic partnering, Clarissa Dalloway comes to share this larger novel of shell shock as the great social disease of the twentieth century. A member of the ruling class generation of the war, she now lives out a life of memory of prewar hopes and enjoyments, of country-house life with lost romantic dalliances, male and female, mixed with reflection on present disappointments: an old suitor returned; a caregiver husband, affectionate but remote; amid the absences of the sons of old friends lost to the war, a grown daughter given over to the company of a dour female religionist. She feels old, tired, and invalided at age fifty-three—in fact barely recovered from her own legacy of the war, the great influenza pandemic that in 1918–1919 alone killed twenty to forty million inhabitants of the globe.

In Fitzgerald's American correlative to Woolf's representation of the social gathering as civilized entertainment, the partygoing that seems to be the central social activity in Fitzgerald's novel is frantic and nonstop. Jay Gatsby's parties in particular, as rendered to us through the eyes of the narrator Nick

Carraway, are big, lavish, drunken, brassy, and loud as only American entertainments can be. As models of class arrangements, they are as vulgar and various as the Dalloway gathering is polite and select. And so they are further interspersed with other frequently discordant social mixings and minglings at various levels of status and refinement, with their participants running the gamut of the American class system of the era. The book begins with a small dinner party at the old-money Tom and Daisy Buchanan estate of East Egg, he the wealthy Yale football all-American and polo celebrity, and she the well-born Daisy Fay of golden memory whom Jay Gatsby has now come to reclaim, dwelling across the bay from Gatsby's arriviste West Egg pleasure palace. The middle is marked by a sordid and confused, vaguely remembered drinking bout at the New York apartment maintained by Tom Buchanan for his mistress Myrtle Wilson. The culmination of the partymaking occurs during an ad hoc summer afternoon's event in a rented suite at the Plaza Hotel on Central Park, where a climactic confrontation involving Tom, Daisy, and Gatsby over their rivalry for her love extends itself on the homeward journey into violent death. Meanwhile, the novel immerses us in recurrent depictions of lavish Gatsby house party entertainment spectaculars, a kind of bacchanalian pageant of the Jazz Age. Here the subject truly is the postwar American 1920s, with the brief participation of US forces in the war subsumed into a quick orgy of patriotic rah-rah at home, while the nation, in Fitzgerald's own memorable phrasings, primed itself for the inevitable celebrations of victory. America was going on the greatest, gaudiest spree in history, he wrote, "and there was going to be plenty to tell about it." *The Great Gatsby* becomes testimony to that acute socio-literary recognition.

Here, the main victim of shell shock is the central character and titular protagonist, a mysterious wanderer on the postwar landscape. Jay Gatsby, we eventually discover, is a hero of the Argonne Forest, a solitary, elusive man who looks as if he killed somebody because he has, albeit in so doing saving his own cut-off battalion from destruction by several German divisions. There is also, however, the narrator, Nick Carraway, who frequently reveals similar symptoms—a pronounced sense of emotional detachment, a chronic reserve of solitariness, a tendency to live in memory. They are both figures whose eyes have looked out on the World War I spectacle of mass death. Amid the Jazz Age entertainments of their America—from the lavish, opulent, vulgar, entertainments thrown by Jay Gatsby at his estate on West Egg to which nearly everyone comes yet nearly no one is actually invited to the smaller scenes of labored festivity or furtive assignation—the two veterans frequently seem to stand as markedly apart from the scenes of postwar culture to which they have returned as do the disembodied advertising billboard eyes of the long departed oculist Dr. T. J. Eckleburg that look out in the text over the urban industrial wasteland that has become the American middle landscape.

Precisely as novels of the postwar metropolis, then, both *Mrs. Dalloway* and *The Great Gatsby* set out to detail the forms and relations of mid-1920s society culture, old and new, select and vulgar, tradition bound and brawlingly disordered. Meanwhile, the war itself intrudes upon the scene like the most unwanted of unwanted guests. Both novels yield to disastrous eruptions of violence at the end, with climactic scenes of brutal and graphic death. In the era of postwar social recovery and rehabilitation, the war becomes the great party crasher. Further, in both instances, the manner of the ghostly appearance would suggest the invoking of a well-known figure from recent war memory—in the case of *Mrs. Dalloway*, the highly decorated and politically controversial antiwar soldier-poet Siegfried Sassoon, and in the case of *The Great Gatsby*, the much publicized US Army hero of the Argonne Forest and Medal of Honor winner Major Charles Whittlesey.

These may seem large claims to status as contemporary war novels on behalf of two novels of manners regarded at the time as thematically and formally slight. *Mrs. Dalloway* we know to have been fashioned from two short stories. H. L. Mencken went so far as to refer to *The Great Gatsby* as "no more than a glorified anecdote." A letter from T. S. Eliot, on the other hand, described it as "the first step that American fiction has taken since Henry James." Here, something like this might be profitably said of *Mrs. Dalloway*. In homage to Woolf's fellow modernist voyager, it has been called a London mini-*Ulysses*. More to the point, it is a perfect Henry James "situation." Clarissa Dalloway, we are told in the novel's first sentence, has decided to go out and select the flowers for her party herself. The ensuing text follows her various journeys of the day, public and private, physical and mental, all beginning with a bright, vivid walking excursion, albeit in a city filled with traffic, noise, horns, and exhaust. An extended section appears on a royal limousine bringing downtown traffic to a halt. Later, pedestrians stop to descry the advertising message being written in the sky by an airplane. It is a machine world. Amid it all, Clarissa Dalloway, in keeping with her name, maintains some small bright excitement of hope. "Heaven only knows why one loves it so, how one sees it so, making it up, building it around one, tumbling it, creating it every moment afresh," she thinks to herself. "In people's eyes, in the swing, tramp, and trudge; in the bellow and the uproar; the carriages, motor cars, omnibuses, vans, sandwich men shuffling and swinging; brass bands; barrel organs; in the triumph and the jingle and the strange high singing of some aeroplane overhead was what she loved; life; London; this moment of June."

For it was the bright middle of June, she goes on. "The War was over."

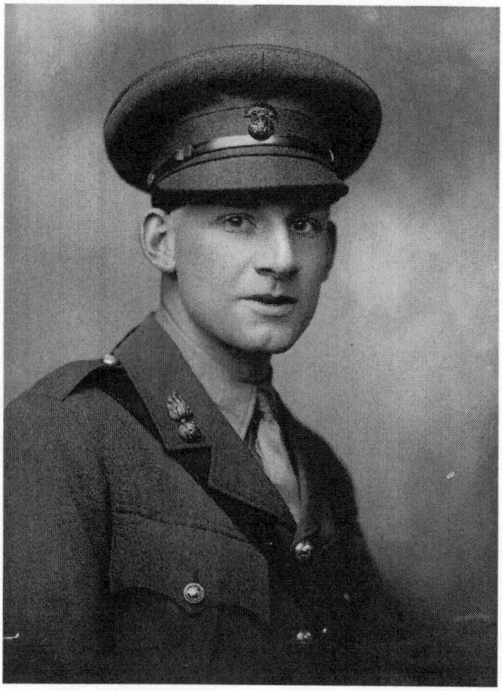

Figure 8.2 *Siegfried Sassoon*, George C. Beresford, 1915. Wikipedia Commons.

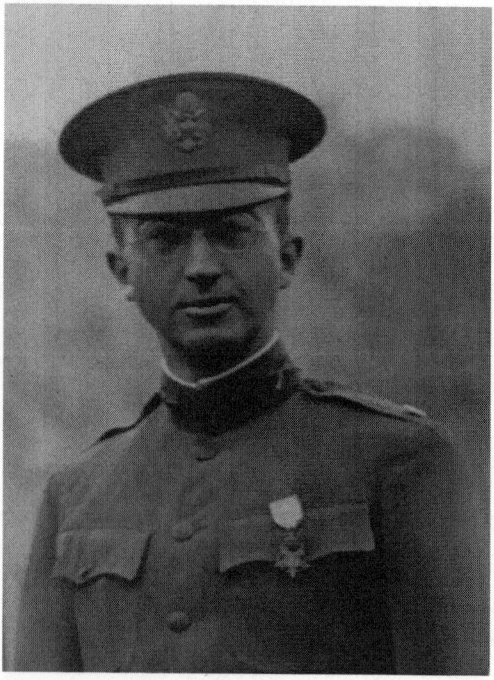

Figure 8.3 Major Charles Whittlesey, Commander of the Lost Battalion, 1918.

The capitalization is intentional. Indeed, the war broods over the novel and is mentioned recurrently in the opening pages. Mrs. Dalloway gazes shortly into the windows of a "glove shop where, before the War, you could buy almost perfect gloves." Her daughter's glum, religious friend Miss Kilman she recalls as having been dismissed from her school "during the war." In the rituals of postwar life, people carry on, their recent griefs notwithstanding. She remembers those for whom the war can never be over, "like Mrs. Foxcroft, at the Embassy last night eating her heart out because that nice boy was killed and now the old Manor House must go to a cousin; or Lady Bexborough who opened a bazaar, they said, with the telegram in her hand, John, her favourite, killed."

As for Clarissa Dalloway, this morning errand through Westminster launches her into her own landscape of remembrance. In various recapitulations of a life, we find out what might have been in its relation to new musings on what has come to be. She carries her own legacy of the great killing, the influenza that nearly took her away and left her permanently invalided. She thinks of the traditional ruling-class men in her life, all aging minor officials with small careers. There is the country-house recollection of an old might-have-been lover, Peter Walsh, clever, somehow failed and incomplete, out to India and back with his silly romantic infatuations. There is a meeting in the Park with Hugh Whitbread, an old childhood friend, impeccably dressed, a petty court functionary with the latest tales of a neurasthenic, hypochondriacal wife. Hovering in the background throughout the novel will be Clarissa's own caretaker husband, Richard, the partner chosen years back for a conventionally good but passionless marriage, a minor Westminster official, companionable, considerate, attentive, busy with the round of his nameless parliamentary committees. A contending, vivid countermemory introduces itself of a young woman companion of her premarriage years, the bold, heedless Sally Seton, and of a single, lingering kiss on the lips they once shared. It remains a vivid secret in a lifetime of civilized disappointments and banked passions.

Meanwhile, Clarissa Dalloway's physical progress takes her through St. James Park from the Westminster of sedate, elegant homes and court and embassy receptions, government parties and lunches. To the other side of the park, beyond the Serpentine and the Horse Guards Parade, is Whitehall, with the newly dedicated Cenotaph. At the far limit is the fashionable Bond Street hubbub and bustle of established shops and merchant houses—florists, tailors, jewelers, dressmakers. Now, it is also crammed with images of the machine present—automobiles, taxis, buses, the sleek, silent, armored limousine of some official personage.

A more immediate reminder of war-menace is also distinctly present in human form this morning in the immediate geography of Clarissa Dalloway's London. It is the shell-shocked, angry veteran Septimus Warren Smith, with his frustrated, increasingly helpless and resentful Italian war bride, Rezia. Amid a generation of the mutilated, paralyzed, grotesquely scarred and maimed, he seems visibly unmarked. But he is no less blighted and stricken, with his nightmares, hallucinations, and intrusive memory scenes. Indeed, such "hysterical men," as they were called, with their loss of nervous control, tics, tremors, outbursts, and frenzied motions, continued to appear in such numbers in the years after the war that an official inquiry was undertaken in 1920–22 under Lord Southborough, with various actions proposed in a well-publicized report that—according to recent scholarship—Virginia Woolf may have read. These included the establishment of a liberal support agency called the Ex-Services Welfare Society, treatment centers, and—as will be noted in the novel—isolation and confinement therapies involving rural group recovery homes. The official attitude of the government and military mandarins continued to pigeonhole shell shock as a somewhat embarrassing failure of masculinity: some men can take it, and some small percentage cannot. In contrast the antiwar liberal and literary intelligentsia increasingly imaged the idea of the military victim as the trusting, innocent, betrayed conscript, or, as often, as the keen, idealistic, quickly disillusioned young officer, both concepts emblematic of a generation of patriotic volunteers sacrificed for old men's lies. To this degree, in intellectual circles the figure often came further to represent postwar class conflict as well as changing ideas of gender roles.

Both of these are suggested by the presence of Septimus Smith in the world of Clarissa Dalloway, where, as a catastrophically failed man, he becomes singularly emblematic of a whole failed system of class, gender, privilege, and social administration. He is also a prediction in Woolf's prophetic genius of similar survivor victims of trauma across the long decades of horror to come, imaging uncannily the precise symptomologies of the various conditions we have now come to call PTSD. As importantly in the direct connection with World War I memory, Septimus, from his first appearance onward, becomes in the world of Clarissa Dalloway a kind of uncanny psychological double, sharing the novel with her in an arrangement of correlative and sometimes intertwined centers of consciousness. Though the two characters will never meet, he is the embodied presence of the war. Accordingly, by the novel's end, his world and Clarissa Dalloway's will intersect with shattering consequences.

For Septimus, it turns out, is in the last day of his life. A walking inventory of war-induced aberration—as rendered through the attendant recollections of his increasingly hopeless and resentful caretaker wife—his life has become a series of recurrent scenes of mental disturbance mingled with of endless consultations and suggested "cures." Now he has become simply worn down by the apparitions, the voices—the dead comrades appearing at midday, most particularly the officer friend Evans beckoning him back across the barbed wire and mud. He had been treated initially by the estimable Dr. Holmes, who was friendly, ingratiating, paternal, if somewhat ineffectual. Today he has come to see a Harley Street expert, the Olympian Sir William Bradshaw. The consultation is to take place at high noon; and so Sir William duly arrives at his chambers, full of degrees and honors, borne in his sleek monolith of a motor car. Dr. Holmes suggested there was nothing wrong with the patient that a little rest and personal discipline won't cure; in the alternative, he suggested confinement to a rehabilitation facility. One of his own, of course. Sir William pronounces with even greater confidence—his benign manner concealing even greater authoritarian menace—a diagnosis that is basically the opposite of his colleague's. A complete breakdown, he observes. Holmes has treated Septimus for six weeks, Sir William notes, and prescribed a little bromide. He is not impressed. Their own talk at the appointment runs no-nonsense to the war. The word recurs over and over. Septimus is in the possession of other words and other voices. "I will kill myself" he has already said. "I have committed a crime," he tells the doctor. The doctor privately interviews Rezia. They agree that he is very sick. He should go to a home. No, not one of Dr. Holmes's homes. One of Sir Willams's homes. For the moment, the doctor admonishes Septimus to avoid thoughts of suicide, and to think not of himself but his wife. "'Trust everything to me,' he said, and dismissed them."

Septimus has survived the military blunderers of the battlefield. Adrift among the civilian medical experts who would return the mad of the war to postwar sanity, he will die in the well-intentioned peace. Back at their lodgings, for a moment a kind of sanctuary, Rezia assures him that they will stand together against the experts, the judges, and their professional verdicts. Shortly he hears a conversation between his wife and Dr. Holmes, who has come, he says repeatedly, "as a friend." Muscling past Rezia, the doctor ascends the stairs. Neither Holmes nor Bradshaw will get him, Septimus decides. He throws himself from the upstairs window and impales himself on the spear tips of his landlady's iron fence. "The coward!" Holmes shouts.

The case of Septimus is not a solitary instance in fiction of the era. Rebecca West's *Return of a Soldier* (1918) and James Hilton's *Random Harvest* (1941), two of the most popular romantic novels of the war, center on domestic situations involving amnesiac shell shock victims. Woolf's depiction, however, was something else indeed. Some case can be made, and with reason, that the characterization of Septimus has much in common with Woolf's own lifelong experiences of surging, recurrent bouts of madness, the struggling toward momentary recovery only to be assaulted by new onsets. As wandering souls, they also share haunted but somehow vivid and affecting memories of same-sex intimacy with lost companions. (1925, the year of the novel's publication, would be marked by Virginia Woolf's sexual affair with Vita Sackville-

West.) There also seems to be her own pronounced resentment of the doctors, the male medical experts, alternately patronizing and bullying, kindly and authoritarian. Then as now deep trauma reaction mocked them as a malady beyond their power, the endless assaults of horrific, intrusive, unbidden memory. The beckoning voice of suicide: during a 1904 onset of madness Woolf herself had tried to take her own life by jumping out a window. Another in 1913 had resulted in a near-successful attempt with a drug overdose; more immediately, though sources differ on dates and degrees of severity, the early 1920s had also produced a wave of similar episodes. The dates notwithstanding, for Septimus as eventually for his literary creator, the apparitions and voices seem already to be there in 1925. The ones that would impel her—worn out with the struggles over the long years—to take her own life a decade and a half hence.

At the time of the novel's composition and publication, however, a source of peculiar insight into the passion of Septimus Smith may also have come from personal acquaintance with a corresponding war-connected figure with whom she was familiar on both social and literary terms. That figure was Siegfried Sassoon—probably the most notorious military celebrity head case to emerge from the war and to figure importantly in its literary aftermath. A notably brave and able officer in the Royal Welch Fusiliers, he is thought to have become gradually deranged by loss of his brother Hamo at Gallipoli and of an intimate prewar friend, second lieutenant David C. "Tommy" Thomas—the "Dick Tiltwood" of *Memoirs of a Fox-Hunting Man*. Increasingly bent on revenge, he turned to audacious stunts at the front lines, winning the Military Cross and earning from his men the epithet Mad Jack. Wounded and returned to duty, only to be sent back to hospital with trench fever, in England he next suddenly cast himself—at great peril under military law—at the center of a major political controversy by issuing a formal, public declaration of refusal to serve further in what he had come to believe was a prolonged, mishandled, and immoral war. Knowing that the ultimate penalty for such an action could be court-martial and military execution, he at least initially refused to back down. Instead, through the agency of well-placed friends (including his fellow officer in the Royal Welch Fusiliers, Robert Graves, and his first cousin, Philip Sassoon, aide-de-camp and personal secretary to the commander of British forces, Alexander Douglas Haig) he was transferred to the Craiglockhart Hospital for the Insane, which specialized in shell-shocked officers, and placed under the care of the noted expert Dr. G. H. Rivers. It was there, at the already-mentioned "Dottyville," that Sassoon read and made suggestions on the poetry of another inmate, Wilfred Owen. At the end of the war, a series of reassignments then led him back to the front lines, where his irrationally audacious if not downright suicidal behavior resulted in a severe head wound which placed him on indefinite sick leave until retirement from

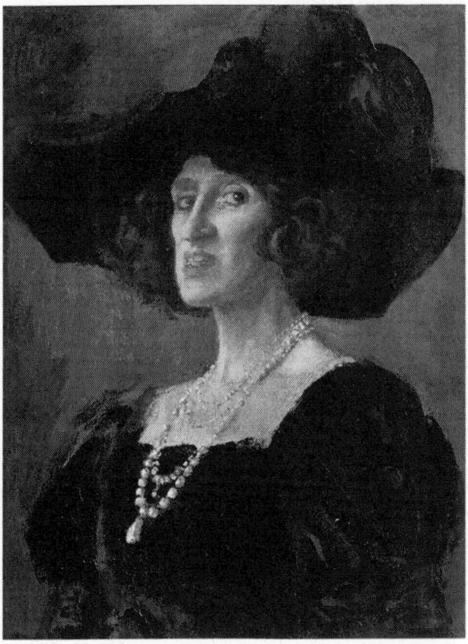

Figure 8.4 *Lady Ottoline Morrell*, August Edwin John, 1919. National Portrait Gallery 6095.

his commission in 1919. Over the same period, he had also become part of the fashionable Bloomsbury literary entourage, together with such notables as Philip and Ottoline Morrell, Lytton Strachey, John Maynard Keynes, and Leonard and Virginia Woolf. By his own account, he continued to suffer from various symptoms of mental disorder, including apathy, anger, recurrent nightmares, and in some especially severe instances, the hearing of voices and the sudden experiencing of visual hallucinations.

Meanwhile, he became a public literary figure of sorts as the book editor of the socialist *Daily Herald* and involved himself in the working class politics of the Labor Movement. This cemented his connections with the postwar literary intelligentsia. His relationships with Virginia Woolf included a favorable *Times Literary Supplement* review of his 1917 book of poems, *The Old Huntsman*, followed by at least one notable exchange of letters, before a dinner occasion during which he pleaded his lack of intellectualism. A closer female intimate, possibly the inspiration for Rezia, was the flamboyant and histrionic Ottoline Morrell, by whom Sassoon had been offered refuge at Garsington, the Morrells's country home and haven for conscientious objectors near Oxford, during the "Declaration" controversy. After this episode she continued to wish desperately to minister spiritually and sexually to his war tormented soul, a feeling unreciprocated by Sassoon, who rejected her continuing attempts at functioning as his would-be muse, mentor, protector, and social and literary promoter. "Rezia," or "Lucrezia," to give her full name, with its echoes in Renaissance literary and political scandal, may thus have served as a humorous reference to Morrell's exotic costuming and love of Italianate culture. Sassoon's own feelings, as a conflicted homosexual, may have been imaged by Woolf correspondingly in the Septimus Smith relationship with the young officer Evans. "I have committed a crime," Septimus cries out. Beyond his idolization of Dick Tiltwood, we do not know of Sassoon's relations with women or men before or during the war. It is certain that in the postwar period his need played out initially in a succession of love affairs with men, including the actor Ivor Novello, the actor Glen Byam Shaw, the German Prince Philipp of Hesse, the writer Beverley Nichols, and the young aesthete Stephen Tennant. The latter seems to have put an end to any further fantasizing on the part of Ottoline, who led a round of bitter merriment at Garsington. (To complicate matters further, eventually Sassoon would conclude an abrupt marriage in 1933 to a woman named Hester Gatty, followed by the birth of a son named George in 1936 and a divorce shortly after World War II.)

One finds certain small textual traces of Sassoon's shadow presence in *Mrs. Dalloway*. The young Septimus, it turns out, had been a boy of a certain literary bent—the kind with "fantastic Christian names like Septimus (or Siegfried) with which their parents have thought to distinguish them"—who came up to London with dreams of success and fame. He falls in love with his Shakespeare lecturer Miss Isabel Poole. When the war comes, he is one of the first to volunteer. In the war, "he developed manliness; he was promoted; he drew the attention, indeed the affection of his officer, Evans by name." He has committed a crime. The crime is the familiar one in the army. Evans was the affectionate young officer and Septimus the soldier boy. During a battle interlude on the Italian front, he goes on leave with Evans and meets Rezia. Evans is killed. Septimus marries Rezia and returns to England. He begins to go mad. Rezia is powerless, increasingly resentful. The war and its ghosts have claimed Septimus again.

The twinned psychological trajectories of Mrs. Dalloway and of Septimus Smith finally converge at the party. This is a day that has begun with Clarissa's pure delight in taking in the whole experience vast panoply of life, London, with her mission, a generous hostess's crowning touch of beauty, to buy personally the flowers that will complete the party. Her aesthetic appreciation of the world is fragile. She herself is but a step away from the clinical regime of the damaged and broken, the invalided. Just across the line, with the war the great abyss of demarcation is Septimus. The war has begun the final process of drawing him back into the realms of madness and death. Indeed, as the novel develops, she and Septimus have been shown to inhabit parallel universes, even down to the deepest springs of secret desire: Clarissa Parry and her wild, unconventional friend Sally Seton; Septimus and his officer friend Evans. Whatever the personal etiologies, the diagnoses are parallel. Nothing is really wrong with her, people think; some kind of nervous problem. Nothing is really wrong with him, people think; some kind of nervous problem. Queer people in the fullest sense, they are already, now or later, in the grasp of some remembered great doom.

The climax of a day that began with so great an appetite for the world comes at Clarissa Dalloway's evening party. Peter, having surprised her with his arrival back from India that very afternoon, returns. The old female love Sally Seton returns, now Lady Roseter, with her "five enormous boys." The daughter awakens a certain bemusement at her arrival with the dour Miss Kilman. In a high moment of the party, for the hostess as well as those in attendance, the prime minister makes his appearance. Sir Richard and Lady Bradshaw have arrived shockingly late. Clarissa overhears Sir William talking to her husband Richard about a Parliamentary Bill: "The deferred effects of shell shock." Then something about a suicide. A young man. Who had been in the army. "Oh, thought Clarissa, in the middle of my party, here's death, she thought." She is of course correct.

In the beginning, in the glorious June of a London day, Clarissa had found herself asking a dark question that has somehow been hanging in the air.

> Did it matter, then, she asked herself, walking towards Bond Street, did it matter that she must inevitably cease completely; all this must go on without her; did she resent it; or did it not become consoling to believe that death ended absolutely? but that somehow, in the streets of London, on the ebb and flow of things, here, there, she survived, Peter survived, lived in each other, she being part, she was positive, of the trees at home; of the house there, ugly, rambling all to bits and pieces as it was; part of people she had never met; being laid out like a mist between the people she knew best; who had lifted her on their branches as she had seen the trees lift the mist, but it spread ever so far, her life, herself?

She is drawn back to some old "image of white dawn in the country, as she read in the book spread open: '*Fear no more the heat o' the sun/Nor the furious winter's rages.*'" She goes on: "This late age of the world's experience had bred in them all, all men and women, a well of tears. Tears and sorrows, courage and endurance; a perfectly upright and stoical bearing." Across the abyss of the war, the same questions come back now at the end, their echo and embodiment in her thoughts now of the young man who, unbeknownst to her, had been there at the very heart of her world all those long, deadly hours ago, on Bond Street.

Had he "plunged holding his treasure?" she wonders. There are some over whom death holds this passion, this strange power of defiance. What, she imagines, if he had "gone to Sir William Bradshaw, a great doctor yet to her obscurely evil, without sex or lust, extremely polite to women, but capable of some indescribable outrage—forcing your soul, that was it." Thus "life is made intolerable." She goes on, "They make life intolerable, men like that? She felt very like him—" She thinks, "the young man who had killed himself. She felt glad he had done it, thrown it away. The clock was ticking." But for now, for herself, "she must go back. She must assemble. She must find Sally and Peter." The last of the conventional partygoers depart, even the tedious Whitbreads. Here is her daughter Elizabeth. Here is her husband and Elizabeth's father Richard. Tonight, she decides, she will stay on. She is not ready yet. Sally and Peter remain at the end. Sally opines that Richard has turned out rather well. "What does the brain matter," she says, "compared with the heart?" Peter lingers, as if to grasp one moment longer at Clarissa's avidity for the world. "What is this terror? What is this ecstasy?" he reflects. "What is it that fills me with extraordinary excitement?" It is Clarissa, he said, for there she was.

As with *Mrs. Dalloway*, so slim an introspective volume, required to carry such a weight of war memory, *The Great Gatsby* seizes upon a comparatively rather sordid minor incident on which to hang a great, war-haunted American tale. A bootlegger, "an elegant young roughneck" he is called by the narrator, once a young lieutenant, after coming back from the war, commits himself to trying to regain the prewar love of a woman of high social estate, now a wife and mother in a family of wealth and position, wooing her with his frenzied pursuit of status, money, possessions. For this, the young man so described, James Gatz, comes up with a preposterous, even mad concoction of a postwar identity: his wealth, his house, his "ancestral mansion," his legendary parties. He is Jay Gatsby. And it is all for the girl he remembers from before the war as Daisy Fay. The text is thus at bottom a social novel in the great tradition: the young man from the provinces, the American dream of success and romance rising to the status of post–World War I American myth. It is the great novel of the American 1920s, the Jazz Age, New York, Wall Street, the Big Money. Yet brooding over the text, as with the Waste-Land geography of the Valley of the Ashes presided over by the disembodied eyes of Dr. T.J. Eckleburg, is a vision of the haunted landscape of war memory. The two main characters, the titular protagonist Jay Gatsby, and the first person narrator Nick Carraway, are both combat veterans of the American Expeditionary Force, of the same infantry division. They have served in the same major battles. They return from the war visibly unwounded; still, both remain prisoners to their memory of having looked out on the landscape of death. As with Mrs. Dalloway and Septimus, Jay Gatsby and Nick Carraway are memory culture's walking wounded.

As is well known, American combat participation in the war was relatively brief. The physical costs, out of two million sent to France amounted to 116,156 deaths from combat and disease, with an additional 204,000 wounded during a set of brief but costly engagements in late 1918. Those determined to have suffered psychiatric disability numbered 159,000, with around half of these permanently discharged. As to postwar care for the latter, hospitalizations by 1921 numbered around 7500, with the figure rising by 1931 to 11,000. Public awareness concerning neuropsychiatric wounding seems to have been somewhat limited, perhaps understandably so in light of such relatively small figures for a populous nation as opposed to main combatants who had engaged in nearly five years of war with dead in the millions. Returned soldiers in need of support of various kinds also found help from major postwar voluntary organizations, including the American Legion and the Veterans of Foreign Wars, which enjoyed the support of the US Congress and major political figures. Further, through its own nineteenth-century mass Civil War, the US as a nation had some previous experience with the emergent military pathology. Indeed, in the aftermath of 1861–65 large numbers of veterans had been identified as suffering what was sometimes called "soldier's heart" or "nostalgia." Today we address such problems with elaborate diagnoses and therapies devoted to PTSD. Back then, as with World War I and eventually World War II, a familiar feature in towns and cities across America would remain the shell-shocked veteran with his vacant gaze and strange, shuffling walk, usually in the care of family or a local care facility, often called upon to lead the line of march in some Memorial or Armistice Day parade.

Certainly World War I combat trauma was a visible subject of postwar American literature. Hemingway, in the stories of *In Our Time*, created war-damaged characters such as Harold Krebs in "Soldier's Home," Nick Adams in "Big Two-Hearted River," and the blighted, benumbed, lost generation wraiths of *The Sun Also Rises*. Also noteworthy in this respect were many of the disturbed first-person narratives assembled in William March's *Company K*.

In Fitzgerald's novel, the titular protagonist is invested with myriad shadowings of the war. He is variously rumored to be a nephew of Kaiser Wilhelm, of von Hindenburg, and/or a German spy. Whatever his connection, he has that look in the eye. "You look at him sometimes when he thinks nobody's looking at him. I'll bet he killed a man." More directly, the legacy of combat is immediately there to see for anyone attuned to the symptoms in the victim of shell-shock. When we see Jay Gatsby, he is always alone. He touches nobody. Nick Carraway makes just such a crucial observation of Gatsby at the height of one of his lavish parties. During a signature musical performance by full orchestra of a work titled "Vladimir Tostoff's *Jazz History of the World*," says Nick, "my eyes fell on Gatsby, standing alone on the marble steps and looking from one group to another with approving eyes." He is not drinking; he actually grows more sober and stiff in behavior as the general hilarity increases. Nick concludes: "When the *Jazz History of the World* was over, girls were putting their heads on men's shoulders in a puppyish, convivial way, girls were swooning backward playfully into men's arms, even into groups, knowing someone would arrest their falls—but no one swooned backward on Gatsby, and no French bob touched Gatsby's shoulder, and no singing quartets were formed with Gatsby's head for one line." He is forbiddingly affectless. Such spiritual numbness is imaged both in his psychological dissociation and in his general social disconnection from the world around him. His lines sound scripted. He has quick angers. He is coldly violent. He frightens people. With his cars, his telephones, his speedboat, he is a man of the machine. With his mentors Dan Cody (the name vividly imaged in E. E. Cummings's Buffalo Bill poem of the era, the nation's "blue-eyed boy, Mr. Death") and Meyer Wolfsheim (who has fixed the 1919 World Series and wears cufflinks made of human molars), he too has become something of a machine—a ruthless gangster, a seeker by any means necessary of absolute power over his world. A war machine. When Nick, near the end of the novel, attempts to help him understand that Daisy, in spite of her love for him before the war, might also have loved her husband, his reply is chilling. "In any case," he says, "it was just personal."

As with Mrs. Dalloway, this postwar novel is full of machines: trains, taxis, trucks, cars. In the first of the three violent deaths with which the novel concludes, that of the sensuous and passionately bodied Myrtle Wilson, the murder weapon is an automobile. The victim is graphically mutilated. Her breast is described as hanging like a flap. In the second murder, that of Gatsby, the weapon is a revolver, of a sort a military officer would have carried in the war. The third murder is a suicide, that of the gunman, the deracinated George Wilson, a gas station owner, auto mechanic, and dealer in used cars.

A further determinant of the omnipresence of postwar memory culture in the novel is the fact that Nick Carraway, the first person narrator who becomes Gatsby's confidant, interlocutor, and eventual elegist, is himself a veteran. As the narrative develops, he and Gatsby appear to come quickly to a kind of unspoken identification on this basis, with Nick as surely drawn into Gatsby's psychological orbit as Gatsby is drawn into his. They have both been there, and they recognize each other for having been there. They belong to mysterious fraternity of those who have served in military close combat. Accordingly, Nick also carries his own psychological and social legacy of the war, an inventory of veteran mannerisms. He is detached, ironic, solitary. He rationalizes his way out of his own romance with Daisy's friend Jordan Baker by describing himself as "five years too old to lie to myself and call it honor." One has a good idea of where the old idea of honor got left behind.

He hits thirty in the book and envisions "the promise of a decade of loneliness, a thinning list of single men to know, a thinning briefcase of enthusiasm, thinning hair." Such reflections are frequently interpreted in a generalized social sense as Prufrockian. For Nick Carraway and Jay Gatsby, they also partake of the shared experience, both psychologically and socially transforming, of the western front. Nick knows what Gatsby knows. He knows something the others can only suspect, contrive, idly conjecture or spread rumors about. "You're worth the whole damn bunch of them put together," he shouts at the end of a last talk extending to the small hours of the morning. "I've always been glad I said that," Nick continues, "because I disapproved of him from beginning to end." It is Gatsby's response, however, that sticks in his mind. "First, he nodded politely, and then his face broke into that radiant and understanding smile, as if we'd been in ecstatic cahoots on that fact all the time." They have been; and it is the war that has brought them together at the beginning and at the end on Gatsby's dark lawn that last night.

It is indeed crucial to the narration, in this respect, that when Nick Carraway first meets Gatsby at one of his lavish parties, where he turns out to be, as Daisy's cousin and Gatsby's rental-cottage West Egg neighbor, one of the few people actually invited, their first connection hinges on their being momentarily nameless combat veterans of the American Expeditionary Force under Pershing. At this point, Nick does not even know that he is meeting his host. Their bond is already the war. Gatsby, in fact, recognizes Nick first.

> "Your face is familiar," he said politely. "Weren't you in the Third Division during the War?"
> "Why, yes," Nick replies, "I was in the Ninth Machine Gun Battalion."
> "I was in the Seventh Infantry until June nineteen-eighteen. I knew I'd see you somewhere before."
> We talked for a moment about some wet, gray little villages in France.

For the reader, it is a short soldiers' conversation, familiar, elliptical, comradely. As to the theme of war memory in the novel, it speaks a whole subtext. To borrow Edmund Blunden's phrasing, these are the undertones of war. Nick and Gatsby have both been members of the Third Division—which came to be known for its war record as the Rock of the Marne. Nick, in a nice techno-war touch, had served in the Ninth Machine Gun Battalion. Gatsby had been in the Seventh Infantry Regiment.

The latter is crucial. The full story emerges through Nick's eventual redacting of Gatsby's account of his experiences. It is the quite recognizable story of the legendary battle in the Argonne Forest, essentially that of the US Army formation that came to be known as the Lost Battalion. Gatsby's version tells it in succinct first-person: "In the Argonne Forest I took two machine-gun detachments so far forward that there was a half mile gap on either side of us where the infantry couldn't advance. We stayed there two days and two nights, one hundred thirty men with sixteen Lewis guns, and when the infantry came up at last they found the insignia of three German divisions among the piles of dead." We are never told what American decorations Gatsby may have received for his heroism. We learn that he was promoted to major—"and," he continues, "every Allied government gave me a decoration—even Montenegro, little Montenegro down on the Adriatic Sea!"

Appropriately, the narration occurs while Gatsby and Nick are driving in Gatsby's splendid, glittering juggernaut of an automobile. As it turns out, he has the medal in his pocket. He shows it to Nick. "To my astonishment," Nick recalls,

> the thing had an authentic look. "Orderi di Danilo," ran the circular legend, "Montenegro, Nicolas Rex."
> "Turn it."
> "Major Jay Gatsby," I read, "For Valour Extraordinary."

"Little Montenegro"; the "Order of Danilo." Ventured further are other, rather lovely details. In proof of the short, postwar sojourn claimed by Gatsby at Oxford, he shows a photo of himself as a quondam companion of the Earl of Doncaster. There was such a person. The contemporary of the fictional Gatsby, he too was a war hero, an artillery captain and winner of the Victoria cross. He was an Oxford man and a notable victim of shell shock. He was also a descendant of the Dukes of Bucceleugh. In the novel Nick Carraway mentions this as part of his own pedigree.

To be sure, in this vivid novel of historical realism/naturalism, noted for its many features of the *roman à clef*, inspiration for main arrangements of character and incident come from many places, not least the fictional imagination. (It is said that Fitzgerald got the idea for Dr. T. J. Eckleburg after being shown of a mock-up of the original dust jacket, an Art Deco rendering of Daisy's disembodied face over the lights of Manhattan.) It is often autobiographical. Scenes of Gatsby as a young officer in Louisville, with Daisy as the local belle with ardent suitors, recall Fitzgerald's courtship of Zelda in Montgomery while he was stationed at Fort Sheridan, Alabama. In other parts of the text, various elements register literary and popular culture sources. As noted, the naming of Dan Cody recalls both the Wild West killer-hero-showman Buffalo Bill and the title of the famous Cummings poem, itself published in 1920. Gatsby's New York underworld mentor/confidant, Meyer Wolfsheim, recalls the gangster Arnold Rothstein. Gatsby himself is also partially modeled on Rothstein, although he has also been noted as resembling other 1920s crime figures, including Max Gerlach, George Remus, Dapper Dan Collins, and Larry Fay.

However, it is as an embodiment of the culture of war remembrance, I would propose, that Jay Gatsby inscribes one of his most direct popular-culture models in the figure of the actual hero of the Argonne Forest Battle. This was the commander of the Lost Battalion himself, Major Charles Whittlesey.

At first any social connection between the New England Whittlesey and Jimmy Gatz from North Dakota may seem remote. In fact, however, Whittlesey was born in the Midwest, coming east as a Williams undergraduate and Harvard law student. Here, in the Gatsby connection, is where the story gets interesting. Even in school, he was nicknamed "the Count," remembered by friends and acquaintances as affecting a notably aristocratic demeanor. He then found work in New York after graduation, partnering with a fellow Williams graduate in a Wall Street law firm, though keeping an antiestablishment edge through his friendship with the socialist Max Eastman and brief membership in the American socialist party until he deemed the direction of its politics too extreme. Meanwhile, as an exemplar of the American citizen soldier and reserve officer in the Plattsburg mold, at the 1917 entry of the US into the war he took his active commission in the Seventy-Seventh New York ("Metropolitan") Division. Promoted to captain, he was assigned to the Meuse Argonne Offensive. Then, on October 2, 1918, over a brief span of days he was thrust into heroic celebrity with his command in the Argonne Forest of the unit of the Third division that came to be called The Lost Battalion. He was decorated with the Congressional Medal of Honor for his performance, along with the French Legion of Honor. There was even a special award for bravery from Danilo, King of Montenegro. At the same time, for all the mythification, there arose serious questions on how the battalion got to be "lost" in the first place and about the degree to which its agony was in fact a function of poor amateur officer leadership. Stories circulated about how the battalion had managed to get cut off by advancing too far ahead of units on flanks. Other rumors had to do with the sending out of faulty location coordinates with the result of drawing US artillery fire on the position. At the same time, as the commander of the pinned-down unit, Whittlesey had reportedly replied to a German surrender offer with four succinct words: "You go to hell." The casualty figures were certain. Of around 554 battalion members, 107 were dead, 63 missing, and 190 wounded. Only 194 were deemed operational. The killed and wounded rate reached 65 percent.

After his return to practicing law, Whittlesey was unable to shed his war celebrity and/or notoriety, being subjected to incessant personal demands on him by fellow veterans. "Not a day goes by but I hear from some of my old outfit, usually about some sorrow or misfortune," he said. "I cannot bear it much more." In public, he was repeatedly required to appear at major events of war remembrance, speeches, awards ceremonies, and honorary degree presentations. Most notable was a command performance in 1921 at the dedication of the Tomb of the Unknown Soldier, where he stood on the podium with two other Medal of Honor Winners, both up-from-the-ranks, Sergeant Alvin York and Sergeant Samuel Woodfill. Days afterward, he sought solace in a Caribbean cruise on the SS *Toloa*, a United Fruit Company floating party ship bound for Havana. Late after dinner on November 26, 1921, the first night out of New York, presumably in his dinner attire and after a good deal of drinking, he cast himself overboard—in some accounts first leaning over the rail and shooting himself in the head with a revolver. Almost nothing is known of his postwar family connections or other possible close relationships. In a last note to his close friend Bayard Pruyn, he wrote, "I'm a misfit by nature and by training." Among further letters to family members and friends were also found the Argonne Forest German surrender note and instructions for the captain of the SS *Toloa* on disposition of his luggage. There is a grave marker in the family plot in Pittsfield, Massachusetts. It is a cenotaph marked "in memory only."

As with Septimus Smith, in the mad Jay Gatsby we come to know the isolation, the mute inability to feel, the strange, off-tune, maladaptive phrases, the restless movement of unease. The assumption of an unreal identity underwrites a desperate attempt to have back the vision of the world the way it was before the war. But it is all an insane dream, the whole crazy scenario, the mansion, the landscaping, the furnishings, the car, the shirts, the famous scene in which their lavish waste and abundance move Daisy to tears. He is a hero; he is a gangster; he is a dreamer; he is mad.

Likewise, as in *Mrs. Dalloway*, in *The Great Gatsby* depictions of glittering social worlds culminate in acts/moments of extreme violence and graphic bloodshed. Septimus, the hopeless *isolato*, chooses suicide by defenestration and impalement. Gatsby, the deranged gangster-hero, floating on a raft in his ill-gotten swimming pool, is murdered by a jealous husband with a gun—a "gat," in gangster parlance, the instrument of his own trade—sent by another jealous husband with the money and reasons to want him dead. As a social outcome, it is as if he has contracted for his own murder and is waiting for death to come find him at last. The touch of war death dooms and corrupts everyone, everything. The disease of the twentieth century turns out to be shell shock. In both novels, the party is a wake. It celebrates the death of civilization as a sustaining force in people's lives. The instruments of death amount to whatever hard metal is at hand—an iron fence, a car, a gun. The scene of the crime is postwar London or New York. Whether by suicide, murder, or some combination of both, the operative diagnosis is death by reason of insanity.

This is the obvious thematic conclusion in these great novels of war memory. Beneath the surfaces of postwar social intercourse and class relations, shell shock becomes the diagnosis for a whole botched civilization. We can say of Septimus Smith that death had come to the party. Jay Gatsby, Trimalchio in West Egg, with the last guest departed, floats in the swimming pool on the last day of summer, waiting for the delayed rendezvous. So inscribed are the fates of significant cultural figures of war remembrance on which the two are modeled: Siegfried Sassoon and Charles Whittlesey. Sassoon would spend his remaining years on earth writing the war over and over, eventually calling a last bitter version *Siegfried's Journey*. Whittlesey would elect for cutting it short, tired to death of the endless retellings of the heroism and death in the Argonne. We can further say this of Virginia Woolf and F. Scott Fitzgerald themselves, veterans in a sense of their rare insight into their lives and times between the wars. Woolf's 1940 suicide we now know in large degree was attributable to her inability to go through it all again, the vast impending cataclysm, enduring the carnage of World War I only to wake up to the somber, wrenching, tragic aftermath of another great war. Fitzgerald, though famous for his remarks on his own lack of combat status, his rueful declarations about "the overseas cap not worn overseas," nonetheless possessed a profound understanding of the American and Anglo-European generations of the war. Anyone who doubts this need only read Dick Diver's soliloquy for the war dead in *Tender Is the Night* while on a visit to the old battlefield at Verdun. Fitzgerald's death, ironically, also came in 1940. His was of a heart attack, coming just as the US was about to enter the conflict in both the European war and the Pacific—induced by years of drinking and self-destructive behavior, a slow suicide. Both Woolf and Fitzgerald thus made their final arrangements with the great death they had somehow seen for so many years as inhabitants of the twentieth century. If not killed in action, they might be remembered at the very least, along with their war-damaged characters, as having died of wounds.

9
What Kurt Vonnegut Saw in World War II That Made Him Insane

(Along with Billy Pilgrim, Rabo Karabekian, Eliot Rosewater, and Others)

Toward the end of Kurt Vonnegut's literary and historical time travel narrative of World War II, *Slaughterhouse Five*, a boxcar load of American prisoners of war arrives in Dresden, Germany. It is quite late in the war, the spring of 1945, yet somehow a whole priceless metropolitan treasure-house of art and culture has been preserved from both Nazi militarization and Allied demolition. At the door of the boxcar stands Vonnegut's fictional protagonist, Billy Pilgrim, the once and future optometrist of Ilium, New York, for the moment dressed in a prison camp vaudeville costume of blue robe, fur ruff, and silver boots that makes him look rather like Cinderella. Here is what he sees: "It looked like a Sunday School picture of Heaven to Billy Pilgrim." A fellow POW standing behind him has his own, characteristically American take on the fantasy scene. "Oz," he says. The fellow POW in question is Kurt Vonnegut. Or so he tells us. "That was I," he avers. "That was me." And he has spoken so for his own good reason: "The only other city I'd ever seen was Indianapolis, Indiana."

What anybody sees, actually, if they are part of the POW cohort in question or the citizens who come out to greet them, will not be Dresden for long. Billy knows that. As he walks amidst the festive architecture—presumably in the company of young Kurt Vonnegut, the architect's son from Indianapolis—of the place called the Florence of the Elbe, "Billy, with his memories of the future, knew that the city would be smashed to smithereens and then burned—in about thirty more days. He knew, too, that most of the people watching him would soon be dead. So it goes." Again, the voice in the last sentence is really—if such a word may be used—that of the character named Kurt Vonnegut. It the death card he plants throughout the book—somewhere between the French "ça va" and the German "und so weiter"—a phrase he has warned us to expect anytime someone or something is about to die. (He tells us also that he got the idea from Celine.)

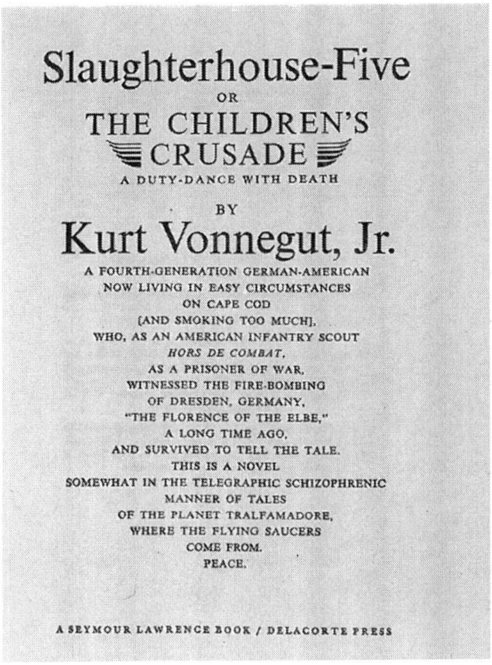

Slaughterhouse-Five
OR
THE CHILDREN'S
CRUSADE
A DUTY-DANCE WITH DEATH
BY
Kurt Vonnegut, Jr.
A FOURTH-GENERATION GERMAN-AMERICAN
NOW LIVING IN EASY CIRCUMSTANCES
ON CAPE COD
[AND SMOKING TOO MUCH],
WHO, AS AN AMERICAN INFANTRY SCOUT
HORS DE COMBAT,
AS A PRISONER OF WAR,
WITNESSED THE FIRE-BOMBING
OF DRESDEN, GERMANY,
"THE FLORENCE OF THE ELBE,"
A LONG TIME AGO,
AND SURVIVED TO TELL THE TALE.
THIS IS A NOVEL
SOMEWHAT IN THE TELEGRAPHIC SCHIZOPHRENIC
MANNER OF TALES
OF THE PLANET TRALFAMADORE,
WHERE THE FLYING SAUCERS
COME FROM.
PEACE.

A SEYMOUR LAWRENCE BOOK / DELACORTE PRESS

Figure 9.1 *Slaughterhouse-Five, or The Children's Crusade: A Duty-Dance with Death*, Delacorte, 1969. Delacorte Press, 1969.

During the thirty days in between, the Americans do not see much of Dresden proper. Their part of Dresden is called Schlachthof Funf—Slaughterhouse Five—part of the city's great centralized abattoir where animals are killed and processed for human consumption. Theirs is building number five in the compound. Number five, it turns out, is for pigs, although the fact no longer seems of any particular consequence. Germans like pig meat, to be sure; Jews abhor it; Americans think it makes great hot dogs. No one in Dresden in the early spring of 1945 is eating happily or well—except, in the case of the POWs, furtively and intermittently, of a strange, exotic substance they are forced to manufacture: a malt syrup specially produced by the Reich (in the beneficent spirit of *Kirche, Kinder, Kuche*) for expectant mothers. Always hungry on their prisoner rations, the GIs sneak sweet, golden ladlefuls into their mouths when no one is looking. Like angels in heaven, they become secret spooners, partaking of the ambrosial.

To compound all such ironies further, of course, is what happens to the POW denizens of Slaughterhouse Five during the great Allied firebombing raid that shortly smashes and incinerates the city, along with an estimated one hundred thousand of its non-combatant German citizens. What happens to the enemy aliens is precisely nothing. They spend the night safely entombed

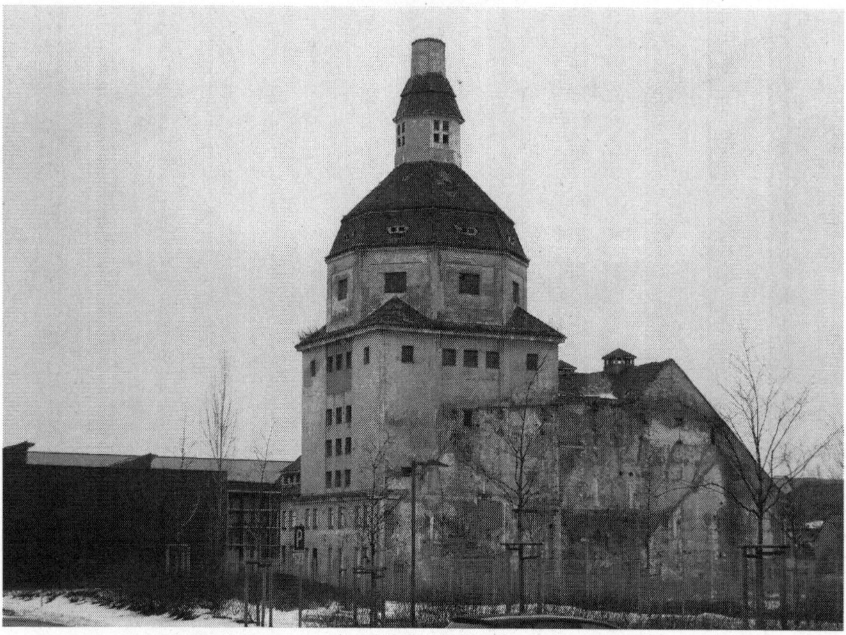

Figure 9.2 The slaughterhouse, Dresden, Germany.

inside the whited sepulcher that is their place of imprisonment while Armageddon rages on the outside. In the morning, after the great visitation of fire and sword has passed, they emerge to find the world gone.

It is to having been present for all of this that Vonnegut lays claim, amid the long authorial identification subtitle that fills most of the title page of his greatest and most famous book, *Slaughterhouse Five, or The Children's Crusade: A Duty-Dance with Death*.

> A FOURTH-GENERATION GERMAN-AMERICAN NOW LIVING IN EASY CIRCUMSTANCES ON CAPE COD [AND SMOKING TOO MUCH], WHO, AS AN AMERICAN INFANTRY SCOUT, HORS DE COMBAT, AS A PRISONER OF WAR, WITNESSED THE FIRE-BOMBING OF DRESDEN, GERMANY, "THE FLORENCE OF THE ELBE," A LONG TIME AGO, AND SURVIVED TO TELL THE TALE.

The basic claim is that of witness in the sense of bearing witness—to say what he has seen. In the more literal sense, the phrasing he uses in the memoir *Man Without a Country* probably gets it more accurately. "I saw the Dresden," he writes. "I saw the city before and then came out of an air-raid shelter and saw it afterward. . . ." In *Palm Sunday*, he is rather more specific. "When we came up, the city was gone." As Billy puts it to Montana Wildhack, his Tralfamadorian lover-muse, "It was like the moon."

What he did not see, from the inside of Slaughterhouse Five, was a full day and night of high explosive demolition of streets, buildings, monuments, houses, and living human organisms, followed by the towering cyclone of flame, the all-dominating, all-consuming pillar of oxidation; nor did he feel the giant vacuum that tore people's breath out of their lungs, that sucked their very bodies into the vortex. (He says in another place that the German guards ran up the stairs every so often while the bombing was going onto take a look outside. Is any of this what *they* saw?) Such death and destruction proper, presumably, the troglodytes of Slaughterhouse Five had to imagine. Or learn about from other sources: within the text, for instance, from a pompous Harvard professor named Bertram Copeland Rumfoord, the officially designated author of a one-volume history of the Unites States Army Air Corps in World War II—the big picture, so to speak—with whom Billy is briefly forced to share a room after a 1968 plane crash. Or from outside the novel, almost incredibly—even in a text where cosmic ironies compound cosmic ironies—from a work by the notorious Hitler apologist and Holocaust denier David Irving who, as a young English scholar-archivist, was one of the first historians to publish a book bringing the little-known story of the monstrous, and from a military standpoint, utterly gratuitous, raid to the attention of English and American readers.

What Vonnegut did see when it was safe to come out was surely quite enough to make him wish he had stayed inside—perhaps forever. Most famously fictionalized in *Slaughterhouse Five* and then corroborated in other texts—essay, lecture, memoir—this was the part he lived through in the days of aftermath, the part he would wind up carrying with him for the rest of his life. This was the part about corpses on the ground, with sublimated skeletons reduced to little, brown, charred bundles; or about entire families in basements and groups in shelters killed with bodies completely intact, victims of instant concussion and/or suffocation. The point is bodies—bodies everywhere. And, if my own experience of war is to serve as a measuring stick, bodies in very bad shape, disrepair, nasty disassembly. Human bodies by the hundreds and thousands, bodies that had to be dragged out of shelters, basements, collapsed public spaces, from the rubble of destroyed buildings. We see something of that at the very end of *Slaughterhouse Five*, where, in an evocation of Melville's Ishmael and Queequeg, Billy is paired with another POW—a tattooed Maori from New Zealand, captured at Tobruk—and sent off to begin excavating the post-bombing moonscape. The purpose of the excavation is to search for human remains. Soon they hit paydirt, of a sort. They have unearthed an entire chamber full of entombed, unmarked, dead human bodies.

"Thus began the first corpse mine in Dresden," says the narrator. There turn out to be hundreds of them. But soon the real horror begins. "They didn't smell bad at first, were wax museums. But then the bodies rotted and liquefied, and the stink was like roses and mustard gas"—in the latter case, not unlike that of the narrator's breath, he tells us, when he gets drunk as an older man and compulsively phones people at night. The stink and work prove too much for the Maori, who dies of the dry heaves, a kind of self-dismemberment. "He tore himself to pieces," says the narrator, "throwing up and throwing up." The Germans being Germans, they find a new and improved technique. "Bodies weren't brought up any more. They were cremated by soldiers with flamethrowers where they were. The soldiers stood outside the shelters, simply sent the fire in." This way to the ovens, ladies and gentlemen, one might say. Vonnegut settles for "so it goes."

The *Slaughterhouse Five* account tallies in many respects with a parallel description Vonnegut himself gave some years after the publication of the novel in the *Palm Sunday* fragment previously cited. For both its detail and the angry precision of its cold, grim, matter-of-fact impassioned first-person memory, it is worth quoting at length:

> Every day we walked into the city and dug into basements and shelters to get the corpses out, as a sanitary measure. When we went into them, a typical shelter, an ordinary basement usually, looked like a streetcar full of people who'd simultaneously had heart failure. Just people sitting there in their chairs, all dead. A fire storm is an amazing thing. It doesn't occur in nature. It's fed by the tornadoes that occur in the midst of it and there isn't a damned thing to breathe. We brought the dead out. They were loaded on wagons and taken to parks, large open areas in the city which weren't filled with rubble. The Germans got funeral pyres going, burning the bodies to keep them from stinking and from spreading disease. 130,000 corpses were hidden underground. It was a terribly elaborate Easter egg hunt. We went to work through cordons of German soldiers. Civilians didn't get to see what we were up to. After a few days the city began to smell, and a new technique was invented. Necessity is the mother of invention. We would bust into the shelter, gather up valuables from people's laps without attempting identification, and turn the valuables over to guards. Then soldiers would come with a flame thrower and stand in the door and cremate the people inside. Get the gold and jewelry out and then burn everybody inside.

Thus the details of the death-duty; or, perhaps more properly, the "duty-dance with death." Later Vonnegut would disclaim actually seeing the flamethrower incinerations. Perhaps they offer too conveniently parallel a literary

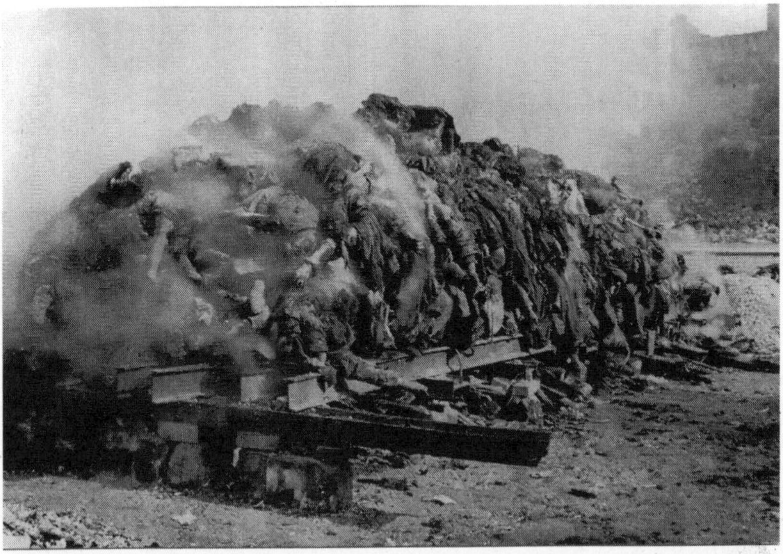

Figure 9.3 A pile of bodies awaits cremation after the bombing of Dresden, 1945.

figure to the industrial-style efficiency of methods being elsewhere employed at the same moment for the plunder, asphyxiation, and incineration of Jews. In contrast, if the author seems rather finicky on that point of truth-telling, the emphasis in the passage cited on intact bodies strikes one as eerily obsessive. On the other hand, maybe there wasn't much body substance left lying around of those who had taken the brunt of the high explosive followed by the incendiaries. Those little brown bundles may have been all that was left. As to the bodies Vonnegut and his fellow POWs did have to handle, what still comes to mind are analogous photographic images from the liberated death camps, with SS guards being forced to untangle and stack the twisted, mucky, disintegrating corpses of their victims. In Dresden, there just must have been bodies everywhere; and even those dead either of suffocation or of the rupture of cranial tissues and blood vessels due to shock and concussion would have started looking and smelling dead—as any soldier will testify—almost immediately. Within bare hours the first elements of decomposition, the particles and liquids of dissolving mucous membranes would have begun to mix with the residuals of emptied bladders and voided bowels. Within a day or so, the phrase "vast charnel house" would surely have come to mind. Vonnegut speculates on what German survivors must have thought as they watched him doing "such gruesome work" at gunpoint—and whether they felt justified. "But who knows what they thought?" he goes on. "Their minds may have been blank. I know mine was."

We know some further things from Vonnegut himself about the extended aftermath of Dresden. We know, for instance, that by May of 1945 his captors had marched his group of POW survivors out of Dresden in advance of the onrushing Soviet armies, only to abandon them in a strange wilderness, "a wholly ungoverned area," Vonnegut calls it, "somewhere in rural Southeastern Germany, near the border with Czechoslovakia." The account, in *Fates Worse Than Death*, is accompanied by a number of photographs in which a motley-uniformed group of ex-Dresden POWs, having availed themselves of "an abandoned Wehrmacht horse and wagon," resembles what might be charitably described as some kind of traveling circus. On the back of a big, long, coffin-shaped wagon someone has painted the letters "USA." (In a heartbreaking moment in *Slaughterhouse Five*, an old German couple scolds a fictionalized version of the gypsy band for their neglectful mistreatment of borrowed horses, their mouths torn, their hooves cracked and bleeding. The reproach sets Billy to soundless weeping. We suddenly understand the point of the epigraph to the book, a stanza from the Christmas Carol "Away in a Manger." "The cattle are lowing, the baby awakes," the lines read; "The little Lord Jesus no crying he makes.") The Vonnegut gang look as if they are escaping from something. Actually, they are wanderers, true strangers in a strange land, having just journeyed out of an unearthly valley, Vonnegut tells us, teeming with other "liberated prisoners of war like ourselves," "convicts, lunatics, concentration camp victims, and slave laborers," in turn mixed with "armed German soldiers," all waiting for the war to end. In a group photograph, we see the actual Bernard V. O'Hare. The actual Kurt Vonnegut, Jr., is there, too, lying in the wagon with his head resting against the back, stretched out full length, too tired and hungry to move. We see his face in relief, in silhouette, like a death mask.

The strange valley itself becomes a central subject of Vonnegut's *Bluebeard*, as the place where that novel's narrator and title character, an artist named Rabo Karabekian who was captured—as an American officer—during the Battle of the Bulge, has found himself after being marched into the countryside and abandoned by prison camp guards. The commander of a combat camouflage unit—assembled, with the kind of cartoon illogic of which only the army is capable, of painters—he is another damaged veteran, in this case with one eye, the other having been shot out during his capture. He has never forgotten what he saw there. "There may have been as many as ten thousand people below us," he recalls:

> concentration camp survivors, slave laborers, lunatics released from jails and prisons, captured officers and enlisted men from every Army which had fought the Germans. What a *sight*! And, if that weren't enough for a person to see and then marvel about for a lifetime, listen to this: the

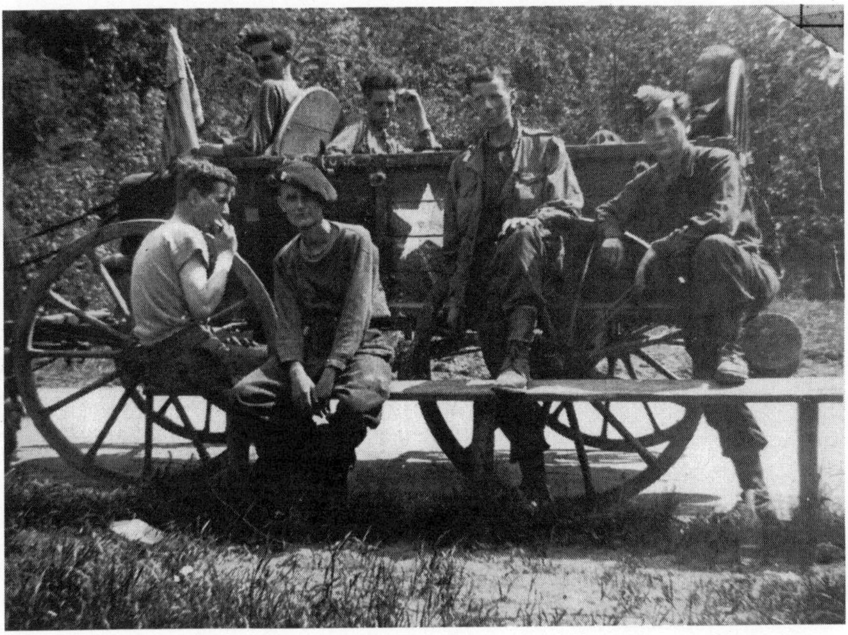

Figure 9.4 Kurt Vonnegut reclining in wagon with fellow Slaughterhouse-Five prisoners just after release at end of war, 1945, Dresden, Germany. Cincinnati Museum Center.

very last remains of Hitler's armies, their uniforms in tatters but their killing machines still in working order, were also there. Unforgettable!"

Karabekian has since gone on to become a pioneer champion and collector of American abstract expressionists of his cohort. Though not a distinguished painter in his own right, he turns out to be an obsessive one, and the subject of his great painterly obsession has very much to do with what he has seen. His *pièce de résistance*, in fact, will be a great mural of the valley he has passed through as a POW in the last days of World War II. He has described the place earlier to an old lover who has suggested he call it *The Peaceable Kingdom*. On canvas, as a realized visual phantasmagoria, it is more Hieronymous Bosch than Edward Hicks, with "an average," he observes, of "ten clearly drawn World War Two survivors to each square foot of the painting." (At first, he says, he has tried to make up a story and then paint the person belonged to. At some point, exhausted, he has given over the project, telling interested viewers "Make up your own war stories as you look at the whatchamacallit.") He has painted himself in, with a man clinging to his leg and looking up at him as if he were God. The man is dying of pneumonia and has two hours to live. He is a Canadian bombardier who was shot down over an oil field in Hungary.

There is an SS concentration camp guard who has thrown away his uniform, fearful of being recognized by a nearby crowd of his dying victims. His identity will be detected by anyone who notices the serial number tattooed on his upper left arm. There are Yugoslav partisans, a sergeant major in the Moroccan Spahis, a Scottish glider pilot, a Gurkha, a turncoat Ukrainian machine-gun squad in German uniform. Another old lover (platonic, he claims), observes that the painting is short on women. Not so, says Karabekian. At least half the concentration camp inmates and half the escapees from the lunatic asylums are women, albeit not looking their most thriving. But there are not any *healthy* women, she protests. "Wrong again," says Karabekian. "You'll find healthy ones at either end—in the corners at the bottom." They are German women, hiding down in the vegetable cellars. They know that the Russians are coming, and that with the Russians will come the rapes. Does the overall painting have a title, she asks? Yes, says Karabekian. As a panorama of the last days of World War II, it is titled *Now It's the Women's Turn.*

For my own part, as a veteran of the Vietnam War, I'd like to know what Kurt Vonnegut saw, particularly in combat, before Dresden, beyond the stories narrated by Billy Pilgrim and Rabo Karabekian. In *Slaughterhouse Five*, we have fictionalized scenes from the Battle of the Bulge, culminating in Billy's capture along with the narrator and the stupid, vicious Roland Weary. Two skilled infantry scouts initially part of the group have ditched the incompetents. These elite soldiers both die, shot from behind at roughly the time the incompetents are being taken prisoner. Amid the killing and capturing one recurrently hears a Cerberus-like barking dog. It is the kind of thing one remembers.

These details are more or less corroborated in an interview where Vonnegut describes the particular circumstances of his own, real capture. The two accounts both seem realistic depictions of, as Vonnegut puts it in the interview, people running around getting lost while trying to imitate things they'd seen people do in war movies. The feckless 106th Division had been thrown sacrificially into the line. Among its drifting personnel somewhere in Luxembourg (as far as anyone could tell) was a hungry, disorganized, castoff mob of Americans cowering in a big trench—six members, including Vonnegut, of a battalion scouting unit "and about fifty people we'd never met before." The denouement of the group's participation in the Battle of the Bulge proved swift and inglorious. "The Germans could see us," says Vonnegut, "because they were talking to us through a loudspeaker. They told us our situation was hopeless, and so on. That was when we fixed bayonets. It was nice there for a few minutes." Then the Germans started firing eighty-eight millimeter shells," Vonnegut continues. "The shells burst in the treetops right over us. Those were very loud bangs right over our heads. We were showered with splintered steel. Some people got hit. Then the Germans told us again to come out." It was nothing like the legendary heroism of the one hundred and first airborne in brave, encircled Bastogne. "We didn't yell 'nuts' or anything like that. We said, 'Okay,' and 'Take it easy,' and so on."

In other recollections, we learn a good bit about the actual Bernard V. O'Hare. He was Vonnegut's "buddy" under what was actually called the "buddy" system, from training at Camp Atterbury outside Indianapolis all the way through combat, capture, prison camp, Dresden, and home again until O'Hare's own death. We hear of other 106th enlisted men, including Tom Jones and his "buddy," Joe Crone, the model for Billy Pilgrim, again a story stretching all the way back to Camp Atterbury. Even in training, Crone turns out to have been a hopeless soldier. Jones recalls, "When we went on a forced march I had to walk behind him and pick up all the utensils falling out of his backpack. He never could do it right." Crone's death actually occurs in Dresden. "I bunked with him when he died," writes Jones. "One morning he woke up and his head was swollen like a watermelon and I talked him into going on sick call. By midday word came back that he had died." We do not know of what. Everyone had raging dysentery at the time. Vonnegut ventures a small suspicion that Crone may have just "let himself starve to death before the firestorm."

I must say I also wonder about another story, one that appears nowhere else in any of Vonnegut's World War texts save in *God Bless You, Mr. Rosewater* and describes the clinical etiology of the title character's lifelong madness while also explaining his childlike fascination with fire departments. In that story, set amid a kind of mini-Dresden firestorm of close combat, Rosewater, a brave, skillful, experienced, highly decorated US Army infantry captain, has gone catatonic after he has rushed a furiously burning building somewhere in Germany, allegedly defended by the worst of hardcore SS. In the smoke and confusion, he has shot down three Germans and bayoneted another. They turn out to be four volunteer firemen in gas masks, the last a fourteen-year-old boy.

The etiology of the particular thing that came over him, Vonnegut says—the fit of personal aftershock, so to speak, that suddenly made it imperative that he write in these odd, myriad, manifestly unhinged (and thereby true) ways about his own experiences and those of others like him in World War II—was his fury at the war in Vietnam, at the flagrant moral callousness of our leaders, and the insensate moral stupidity of our policies. "We could finally talk about something bad that we did to the worst people imaginable, the Nazis. And what I saw, what I had to report, made war look so ugly. You know the truth can be really powerful stuff. You're not expecting it." For this, many people at the time called him a literary cuckoo, an old vet gone soft in the head and, as one critic phrased it, sucking up to kiddie grievances. A pioneering critical study of Vonnegut's work during the era was actually titled *Insanity Plea.*

A lot of us who had been to Vietnam, meanwhile, somehow understood that he was writing about his war *and* our war. And he gave us the courage, however crazy it may have seemed at the time, to put into language what we saw and what we had to report. They diagnosed a lot of us as well, called us head cases. "Good luck," they always said before sending people out, recalls Michael Herr in *Dispatches*. "It was like telling someone going out in a storm not to get any on him, it was the same as saying 'Gee, I hope you don't get killed or wounded or see anything that drives you insane.'" What did they expect when they got us back? When you got home, writes the soldier-narrator Philip Dosier in Larry Heinemann's *Close Quarters*, people would say, "You know, you've got the oddest, strangest look in your eyes. Why is that, hey? What have you seen?" He goes on:

> "It is the look of the eyes, for a long time called the thousand-yard stare, that blatant sparkle of light which does not shine. The glassy milky eyes not of the trenches, but of the ambush. It is the thousand-meter stare cranked down to fifty, to five. It is seemingly perfect concentration, blind rage; simple pleading; incomprehension. A surrender to cool perfect murder that defies sleep and warm soapy water. It is a reach to see everything at once; the limit of wakefulness; an urge to live; to stay awake. Because to let the eye wander, to drop that gaze, to fall asleep and slip into dreams, is to die.

That is true, of course of all wars—the combat symptomology, one might call it, of all those who have dwelt on death's grey landscape. People still have quaint ocular expressions for this. "He saw combat with the 106th Division"; or, "he saw action in the South Pacific"; or, "he saw duty with the Special Forces." One supposes that is because memory and history always take place in the mind's eye. As to war as the worst thing that can happen to people in the world, on the other hand, there seem to be those who have a preternatural ability to see it; and, not surprisingly, they turn out to be the broken ones who return from wherever they have been with some strange power of witness. Not that it takes a particular battle or a particular war. Here, one is reminded of a singular moment of family conversation in J. D. Salinger's *The Catcher in the Rye* among the brothers Caulfield—Holden, the departed genius Allie, shortly gone to early death from juvenile leukemia ("So it goes," one is tempted to say) and the older D. B., (eventually to become the famous "prostitute" Hollywood screenwriter), on one of his short periods of home leave during four years of service in the US Army in World War II. "I remember when he used to come home on furlough and all," Holden recalls acutely, "all he did was lie on his bed, practically. He hardly ever even came in the living room." As it turns out, D. B. actually sees no real combat. Still, Allie suggests that being in the war for somebody like D. B., a writer, is surely not all bad, in that it gives him something to write about. D. B. counters by asking Allie who is the best war poet, Rupert Brooke or Emily Dickinson. It is a typical Salinger loaded question, with a side of Zen, but it makes the point; and it is a point, of course, that could only have been made in this 1950s novel about wise American children by a shell-shocked ex-World War II GI in his mid-twenties named J. D. Salinger. Nearly anyone *normal*, it is implied, would pick Rupert Brooke, the golden youth, royal naval brigade veteran of the doomed Antwerp expedition, famously dead of sunstroke followed by blood poisoning in the Aegean on his way to doomed Gallipoli (the strategic plans for both of those great fatal adventures, it should be put on record, issuing from the juvenile, hopelessly erratic warrior genius of Winston Churchill). Rupert Brooke, author of "The Soldier": "If I should die, think only this of me:/That there's some corner of a foreign field/That is forever England." D. B. knows the better answer to the question, although he never says why. But then anyone who knows Emily Dickinson also knows why. Emily Dickinson, riding out the endless months and years of Civil War deaths being reported back and mourned in New England—truly, as Drew Gilpin Faust has recorded it in her eloquent title, *This Republic of Suffering*. Emily Dickinson, like Emerson before her, with her attacks of psychosomatic vision disorder—hysterical blindness, one is tempted to call it—one can almost pick poems at random. For example, "There's a certain Slant of light":

> When it comes, the Landscape listens –
> Shadows – hold their breath –
> When it goes, 'tis like the Distance
> On the look of Death –

Mad, goofy, mostly inarticulate Billy Pilgrim is surely no Rupert Brooke, let alone an Emily Dickinson. For quality of simple human passion in vision *and* witness, though, the optometrist of Ilium, New York, is right up there with the best. And nowhere is he better than in a 1968 family scene issuing from a bizarre convergence of plot lines whereby Billy finds himself the hospital roommate of one Bertam Copeland Rumfoord, Harvard professor and designated official historian of United States Army Air Corps strategic bombing campaigns in Europe during World War II. Aboard a doomed chartered airplane carrying him, along with his father-in-law, to a convention of fellow eye-care professionals, Billy has been dropped out of the sky at Sugarbush, Vermont. He has fractured his skull. His rescuers are two Austrian ski instructors, speaking German behind their snow masks. Billy, accustomed to his time-travels among the Tralfamadorians, "supposed that they were part of an amazing new phase of World War II." As usual, he supposes right. In the same vein, he has just learned of the truly freakish accidental death of his wife, Valencia Merble Pilgrim, who has been killed while driving around in her closed car with a damaged exhaust system, by carbon monoxide poisoning (the early, experimental method the Germans used for killing transports of their victims until they discovered Zyklon B and got really good at it). The car was a Cadillac El Dorado Coupe de Ville, with a "Reagan for President" sticker on the back. It has been tail ended by a Mercedes, which has suffered a broken headlight. "But the rear end of the Cadillac," the narrator tells us, "was a body-and-fender man's wet dream." His daughter Barbara has arrived, stupefied with tranquilizers. His son Robert has been flown in on emergency "compassionate leave" from Green Beret duty in Vietnam. For most of his life after Dresden, Billy has just tried to be a good optometrist, somewhat lower than the physicians, a little above the lens grinders, helping people see. Now his work seems mostly to involve lying there in the hospital room, listening to Rumfoord pontificating. That, and the occasional attempt at witness. "I was in Dresden when it was bombed," he interrupts at one point. "I was a prisoner of war. . . . We don't even have to talk about it," he adds quietly. "I just want you to know."

Not surprisingly, if the preface to the twenty-fifth anniversary edition of *Slaughterhouse Five* is to be believed, Vonnegut himself seems to have been content to leave the message pretty much at that—although not without characteristic irritation at one more aspirant to the title of master pontificator. The person who made him feel impelled, one last time, to defend the quality of his own vision and witness was the conservative intellectual George Will. The "owlish nitwit" so named, Vonnegut says, had accused him of trivializing the Holocaust. Vonnegut's retort was simple. *Slaughterhouse Five*, he wrote, remained a book about which he has "no regrets."

> It is a non judgmental expression of astonishment at what I saw and did in Dresden after it was firebombed so long ago, when, in the company of other prisoners of war and slave laborers who had survived the raid, I dug corpses from cellars and carried them, unidentified, their names recorded nowhere, to monumental funeral pyres. Their corpses could have been anybody, including me, and there were surely representative among them, whether collaborators or slaves or refugees, of every nation involved in the European half of World War II.

He goes on: "The drama at Auschwitz," to be sure, "was about man's inhumanity to man. The drama of any air raid on a civilian population, a gesture in diplomacy to a man like Henry Kissinger, is about the inhumanity of many of men's inventions to man. That is the dominant theme of what I have written during the last forty-five years or so." Or, as the humble Billy Pilgrim might have said—in fact, did say—to the pompous Bertram Copeland Rumfoord: "I was there. I just want you to know. I was there."

Parts of the passage out of Dresden and into the valley are fictionalized movingly in *Slaughterhouse Five*. After being strafed and nearly killed by American fighter planes, Billy and the other POWs find themselves at an inn still being run by a blind innkeeper along with his wife and daughters. They know that Dresden is gone, but they do not hold it against the prisoners. They feed them with "soup and ersatz coffee and a little beer" and then bed them down. "Good night, Americans," the innkeeper tells them. "Sleep well."

10

Script by Stephen Crane, Novel by John Huston, Movie by MGM

In Hollywood's long tradition of rendering American wars on screen, the big-movie titles of the post World War II era roll in a grand, awful procession: *The Longest Day*, *Patton*, *Glory*, *Gettysburg*, *Saving Private Ryan*, *Apocalypse Now*, *Platoon*, *We Were Soldiers*, *Blackhawk Down*, *The Hurt Locker*. My proposition in this regard will be odd but simple: in the last great age of spectacular combat filmmaking, the weirdly cast, low-budget, low-technology, black-and-white 1951 Hollywood version of Stephen Crane's *The Red Badge of Courage*—directed by John Huston and released by MGM—remains among the most direct and moving popular representations of the experience of battle ever produced, whether literary or cinematic. Further, not least among its appeals is the degree to which it stands as the expression of a characteristic, albeit frequently accidental and composite genius to which the national imagination seems so frequently given—the result, one might say, of a kind of popular-culture convergence of the planets. (One thinks, for instance, of Hawthorne's publisher James T. Fields's marketing recommendation that *The Scarlet Letter*, initially conceived of as part of a tale collection, might be profitably re-engineered as a free-standing narrative for the novel market; of F. Scott Fitzgerald's being given an advance copy of the book jacket for the *The Great Gatsby* and writing the visual design into the novel; of Joseph Heller changing the title of his absurdly comic war novel from *Catch-18* to *Catch-22* because of a Leon Uris best-seller titled *Mila-18* about the 1956 Hungarian Revolution that used the number as a street address in Budapest.)

As to the critical status of the Crane-Huston-MGM *Red Badge*, this is a large claim to be making. As to the canons of critical history, it also becomes the basis of a good story to tell. Only thus does one begin to see how, among other things, the young literary journalist and popular-culture savant, Stephen Crane, himself not even born until 1870 but responding to late-nineteenth-century media reglorifications of the war such as the massive *Battles and Leaders of the Civil War* series published by *Century Magazine*, could produce a novel at once arguably the most realistic ever written about Civil War combat and, in anticipation of a host of now-familiar movie technologies—zoom lens, stop-action, jump-cut, montage, voice-over, and the like—do it in the form of a text reading uncannily like a filmscript. Only thus, in turn, does one begin to address the ensuing process, a half century later, whereby director John Huston—attempting to channel the ghosts of Stephen Crane, Matthew Brady, and D. W. Griffith in a black-and-white project largely filmed on his ranch in Calabasas, California, with a cast including Audie Murphy, (the most decorated US Army veteran of World War II), Bill Mauldin (the most celebrated GI cartoonist of the war), and a handful of character actors and directorial drinking companions—expanded Crane's compact naturalistic study into a complex, nearly three-hour, novelistic psycho-documentary of men at war. And only thus, finally, does one come to a proper appreciation of how, after Huston's wholesale abandonment of the project quite literally on the cutting room floor, a group of journeymen Hollywood moviemakers somehow managed to carve out the best of moving performances by Murphy and Mauldin, along with supporting actors such as Andy Devine and Arthur Hunnicut, and Huston "authentics" such as Royal Dano and John Dierkes, all while cutting the drama back into the to manageable shape of facing plots of cowardice and heroism and reinvesting the film with a voice-over narrative by James Whitmore, and thereby wound up with one of the best movies ever made about small-unit combat, right up there with *All Quiet on the Western Front*, *Saving Private Ryan*, or *Platoon*.

As may be already seen, what transpired here is an intensely American story, resulting in a characteristically American artifact. The 1951 Hollywood *Red Badge of Courage* emerges as a novel by Stephen Crane that was already a film; a film by John Huston that got turned back into a novel; and a hybrid final Hollywood synthesis that came out as a classic modernist reshaping of the post-1945 American war movie.

For all this—at any one of its major points a study in what might be called the strange alchemy of accidental genius—one needs no better starting place than the starburst life and career of Stephen Crane himself. We know well the story of his journalistic apprenticeship, his early personal and literary self-education, and his eventual celebrity adventuring as a military correspondent—though notably including no experience of war until well after *The Red Badge of Courage*. As to literary notoriety, his first novel, *Maggie: A Girl of the Streets*, the seduced-and-abandoned story of a girl of the New York tenements who descends inexorably into a life of sordid self-debasement and death, brought him public attention as a display of textbook naturalism. In characteristic contrarian fashion, it was accompanied by a polemical sneer by the young author at conventional devotees of literary moralism. "This book," he wrote, "tries to show that environment is a tremendous thing in the world and frequently shapes lives regardless." He went on: "If one proves that theory, one makes room in Heaven for all sorts of souls, notably an occasional street girl, who are not confidently expected to be there by many excellent people." Thus emboldened, he shortly turned his guns on the aforementioned highly prestigious Civil War series being published by *Century Magazine*. An initial version of *The Red Badge of Courage* was written quickly and published serially with the telling subtitle, "Private Fleming, His Various Battles." Only in book form did the novel acquire the classic designation by which it came to be known, "An Episode of the American Civil War." In either case, what emerged was a starkly naturalistic study of the experience of combat, centered on a handful of common soldiers in the Union Army. (Should proof of such consciously naturalistic intent again be needed, we have the final manuscript version in which the author, in some last-minute revisions, meticulously substitutes early references to his main characters by name with generic descriptions—the tall soldier, the loud soldier, a youthful private, etc.) His success was instant and more than literary, measured by the fact that many reviewers and soldier-participants acclaimed the book for its immediacy, accuracy, and veracity. All this the work of a young writer who had been born seven years after the fact.

Much of that achievement, as we now know, lay in Crane's assimilation of source materials, among them memoirs and personal narratives that served as almost forensic sources for realistic combat detail. In a precise connection with the Battle of Chancellorsville, noted by critics at the time, the Union coward in flight who renders the wound to his youthful counterpart is given a German syntax, and is thus identified as one of Howard's right-flank Dutchmen who were overrun by the audacious charge of Stonewall Jackson. As important was an ingenious use of techniques taken from both popular literature and the popular arts, an overall strategy made particularly successful through the author's adventurous use of narrative point of view. A sustained focus was thereby made possible through which the chief character's direct physical and psychological experience of combat was mediated by use of the impassive, albeit frequently sardonic voice-over narrator. One of the most perplexing features of the text at the time, it has remained to this day a subject of critical debate. Consensus now holds that the narrator's detached perspective exists initially at some remove from Henry's own consciousness; later, as he experiences some modest growth of perspective, the two lines of psychological vision become more consonant. Influential readings have sometimes ascribed the technique to Crane's interest in the contemporary visual arts, particularly painting. The narrator, who displays a vivid but meticulous sensory description of the observed particular, is described as being impressionistic and objective. The protagonist, in contrast, with his internalized observations of experience frequently rendered under intense psychological pressure, inclines for most of the novel toward the expressionistic and subjective. The two lines are frequently cited as explaining much-debated passages toward the end, during the march away from the battlefield, in which Henry's new perceptions of moral manhood come into consonance, if not complete unison. As plausible, on the other hand, is the explanation that Crane made use of a literary effect frequently visible in frontier storytelling—the antebellum genre frequently called Southwestern Humor—that found resonance after the Civil War in the work of such popular realists as Bret Harte, Ambrose Bierce, Hamlin Garland, and, of course, the master, Mark Twain. Here one again recognizes the familiar pairing of the self-controlled gentleman narrator with the interior dramatized language of the vernacular characters. Indeed, if one looks for something like influence here, it might very well be Mark Twain, with his own sardonic response to the *Century Magazine* series, titled "The Private History of a Campaign that Failed." Here also are the parallel literary signatures of narrative irony, the depiction of youthful romantic illusion fading into grim and unsympathetic deflation of military ardor, where death ultimately obtrudes with a conclusion in which we are left looking at a corpse.

The far heavier literary-cultural symbologies in Crane's frequently imagistic novel that become the signature of his aspirations as a modernist—Henry's sulking in his tent, his post-desertion wanderings behind the line, his encounter with a decaying corpse in a chapel of death, his witness to the passion and dying of Jim Conklin—are the poignant relics of incomplete education. We see vestigial prep school Homer, Virgil, Dante, Malory, Shakespeare, Bunyan, the Bible. Jim Conklin, in his rendezvous with death, enacts a ghastly parodic American Golgotha. The night scene with the cheery voice, the firelight brotherhood of the camp, provides a *Henry V* touch of Harry in the Night. Henry Fleming's return to action, his red battle anger, becomes the wrath of Achilles.

Such common literary references are further paralleled with attempts to recreate the visual atmospherics of familiar popular culture representations of the war itself in painting, illustration, and photography. The Civil War scenes of Winslow Homer come particularly to mind, along with the lithographs of Currier and Ives and the photographs of Matthew Brady and Alexander Gardner.

Beyond such literary and visual references, what now strikes the reader familiar with the Huston film—particularly in its MGM final iteration, in which many direct and concrete textual relations were restored—is how a pronounced movie style seems to be so frequently evident in Crane's text. The wide-angle opening scenes, with their portentous voice-over narrative, depict the figures of two monstrous armies arrayed against each other on the hills. Within two paragraphs, a kind of zoom lens strategy brings us into close, almost domestic focus on scenes of camp life, replete with decidedly unheroic scenes of clothes washing, hut furnishing, gossiping, and adolescent quarrelling. Then, following the dramatic establishment of the three main characters (Henry Fleming, Wilson, and Jim Conklin) and a flashback interlude of Henry's memories on leaving home to join the army, comes the quick cut to early action passages. In all this we find an almost an uncanny prophecy of the way the final version of the film works. As to the specific popular media provenance of the cinematic dimension of Crane's style, we must remain speculative. One thinks—given Crane's journalistic years in New York—that he may have known something of the protocinematic peep show style "kinetoscope" developed by Eadweard Muybridge and Thomas Edison, with the first such devices appearing in arcades in April 1894. By 1895 Edison had further developed an accompanying sound source called the Kinetograph. We will never know if Crane knew of these devices as he composed his own presciently cinematic text. We can say that, on matters of popular fascination, he was surely of that breed of observer exalted by Henry James as one on whom nothing is lost. In all this, we are surely on firm ground in acknowledging Crane—through his conflations of new literary and popular culture styles—as a precursor of the various technologies of artistic representation we have come to group under the heading of modernism. As a practitioner of advanced realism-naturalism, he seems to have assimilated the "veritism" of Hamlin Garland (his most influential literary predecessor) with the colorful popular newspaper style of Richard Harding Davis, his journalistic chief competitor. On the subject of war in particular, he also obviously anticipates not only the distinctly modernist literary ironies of such twentieth-century successors as Robert Graves, Siegfried Sassoon, Henri Barbusse, and Eric Maria Remarque but also the film techniques of such post–World War I modernist classics as *All Quiet on the Western Front*, *Grand Illusion*, and *What Price Glory?*

John Huston, in nearly every respect imaginable, had established himself during the interwar years as a film modernist in this sense. As a writer, he was largely responsible for the scripts of a host of classics, including *Jezebel*, *Juarez*, *Sergeant York*, and *High Sierra*. By 1941, in a new role as screenwriter-director, he gained three Academy Award nominations for *The Maltese Falcon*. During the war, he found his services required by Army Signal Corps as a maker of documentaries. Two turned out to be of particular note. The first, titled *The Battle of San Pietro*, dealt with the grim, hard facts of a no-name small unit combat in the Italian theater, regarded by many soldiers and civilians alike as a grimy, inglorious sideshow to the main action in the Pacific and in Northern Europe. The second, *Let There Be Light*, dealt with the post-combat experiences of soldiers both physically and mentally damaged by the experience of

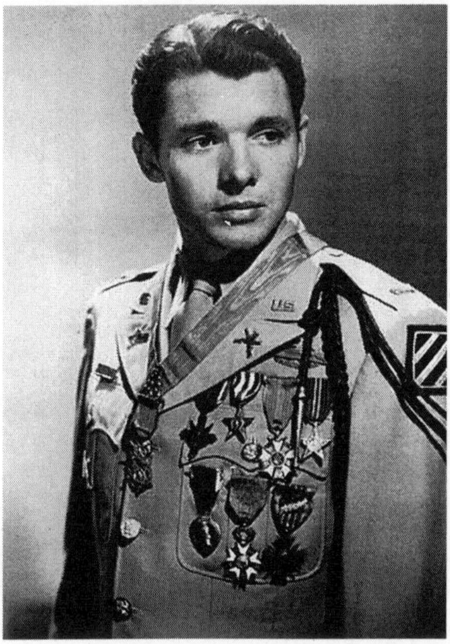

Figure 10.1 Audie Murphy in US Army uniform, World War II. US Army.

battle. Then, upon Huston's return to Hollywood, there followed a string of classics, including *The Treasure of the Sierra Madre*, *Key Largo*, and *The Concrete Jungle*. Meanwhile, he is said to have become increasingly impassioned about making a film version of Crane's *The Red Badge of Courage*, an idea he had allegedly been contemplating since World War II and his involvement in the two wartime documentaries, the first on the psychology of combat and of courage under fire, and the second on emotionally and psychologically disabled veterans—a subject and a treatment so controversial that the film was not released until 1981. This vision of overarching synthesis might also explain how the resultant initial Huston version, though accounts of final length differ, amounted to turning the book into a complex, cluttered, sprawling novelistic psycho-documentary about modern combat. As to casting, with Henry Fleming played by Audie Murphy, the most decorated US Army veteran of World War II, and Wilson by Bill Mauldin, the most celebrated military cartoonist of World War II, one wonders if Huston considered the three of them, counting himself, to be veterans of the Italian front in World War II, the slow, grinding, inglorious industrial war much resembling the Virginia campaigns of the Civil War.

The task would not be easy. Here would be a war film, albeit of historical and literary import, trying to attract the attention of people worn out on war

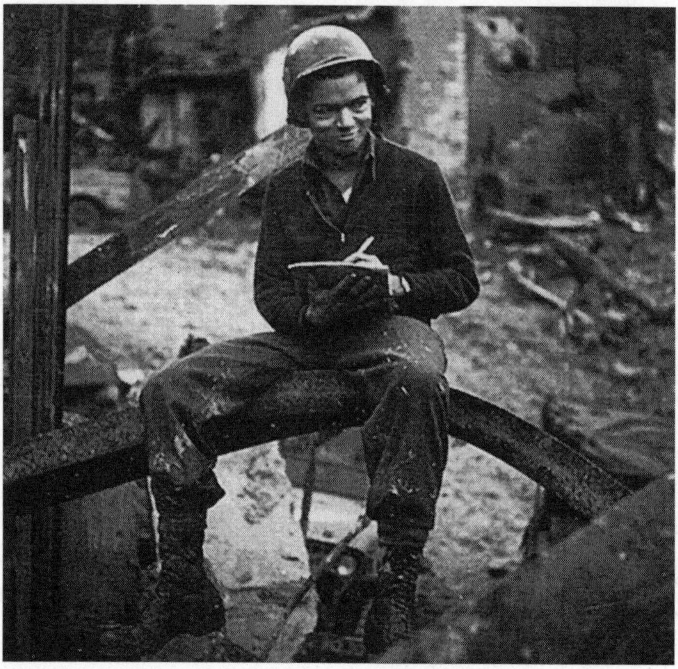

Figure 10.2 World War II cartoonist Bill Mauldin at work. US Army.

films. And not just guts and glory. By this time, World War II films themselves had entered a dark phase, with gritty offerings including *The Story of GI Joe*, *A Walk in the Sun*, and *Battleground*. The grimness was shortly compounded by the new presence of large-scale US military combat in Korea. It would be an ugly war, productive of some particularly ugly movies, several of which, more or less contemporary with *The Red Badge of Courage*, would share much of its grim, deterministic spirit. Nor was the path to any kind of antiwar (read anti-American) film smoothed by House UnAmerican Activities Committee proceedings against the Hollywood Ten, their culmination in court sentences of a year in prison for contempt.

Allegedly, it was Huston's producer and poker partner Gottfried Reinhardt who actually proposed the idea of a *Red Badge* project to MGM management —at the time, a set of contending egos locked into executive power wars. L. B. Mayer himself was dead against it. Executive Producer Dore Schary, on the other hand, was in favor. Schary allegedly enlisted the support of the New York management of the MGM parent company Loew's and its executive vice president Nicholas Schenck. There is now a certain supposition that Mayer basically let this happen, hoping that with a failed project Schary would seal his own fate. As it turned out the release of the picture coincided with Mayer's own departure from MGM. According to Lillian Ross, the latter was part of a process in fact engineered from New York by Schenck, euphemistically described as a "learning experience" for Schary.

Then there was the matter of turning Crane's novel into a film treatment. Huston wanted Norman Mailer; when he proved unavailable, Huston was told by Schary to do it himself. He duly prepared a treatment, as did his production assistant Albert Band. According to Band, Huston immediately threw his own in the waste can and went with that of his assistant. There is likely at least some truth to this, given the fact that Band is credited at the film's opening. Reinhardt's recollection was, "We finally shot, more or less, the book."

The chief legacy of the connection between Huston's experience in World War II and his commitment to the project was that he wanted a movie without actors. Or, more properly, he wanted a film with figures working as actors who had served their own apprenticeship in the crucible of war—and, for promotional reasons, one might surmise, were widely and favorably known for having done so. Murphy and Mauldin fit the bill perfectly. John Dierkes, a nonactor friend Huston met in wartime London, would play the third main figure, Jim Conklin.

On the face of it, none of these choices seemed like bad ideas. As things turned out, all of them would give Huston a lot of trouble. Frequently, moreover, the problems proved the result of insecurities and thin skins that only nonprofessionals would have. Murphy, the hero, found particularly objectionable a major change in characterization from the novel, registered in a scene where Henry actually admits to Wilson late in the film that he has fled the battlefield. The story goes that Murphy, the bona fide World War II hero, found the words of even a film confession of cowardice impossible to utter. In another version of the story, Murphy was offended by the indignity of making the speech to a rear-echelon military celebrity like Mauldin. The resolution came in yet another wholesale changing of the novel's Fleming-Wilson character dialectic, following to Mauldin's welcome suggestion that when Henry confesses to running Wilson does too.

As to Mauldin, the rancor of the GI cartoon satirist became fully aroused by all the prima donna business and command infighting. Indeed, not least among the dramatic participants, he may be said now to have actually brought unique acting abilities to the film, managing to combine the early adolescent braggadocio of Wilson with the later chastened sense of quiet manhood and also updating the buddy story through the Joe and Willie dogface humor so characteristic of the *Up Front* cartoon saga that had made him famous in his own right as a World War II soldier. He thus felt justifiable anger at being called "a raving dilettante" by Reinhardt. He also found considerable irritation in the hanging-about on the set by *New Yorker* correspondent Lillian Ross, whom he described to a *Time* reporter as "a pain in the ass." Finally, Dierkes, at a certain point, also seems to have begun take himself very seriously as an acting talent, asking why he was not given a private dressing room like Murphy and Mauldin. Huston obliged by attaching a nameplate to one of the portable toilets.

Other cast members contributed their own versions of imbroglio. A new addition to the Huston entourage, Royal Dano, playing the Tattered Soldier encountered by Henry among the procession of wounded where he shortly finds the mortally wounded Jim Conklin, suffered the consequences of some terrific acting—so terrific that it became, even for Huston, a distraction from the Henry Fleming-Jim Conklin encounter so crucial to the book. In the extended interlude, Dano had actually been accorded his own virtuoso death scene. Unfortunately, it added no dramatic relief, as in the book, where Henry runs from the shame simply of being asked where he had been hit. That proved just the point in the final film cut. Dano anguished over the exclusion. "Taking the baby and leaving the afterbirth," he called it. The overall cuts he similarly characterized as "going in and taking the wrong kidney." Among the no-name players, a happier moment was that of a surprise Huston sprung on the ensemble well into the film, when he cast the well-known character actor Andy Devine as the Soldier of the Cheery Voice.

Huston hoped, for reasons of historical authenticity, that the movie set would be created somewhere in Virginia. For reasons of economy, it wound up being all shot on Huston's own Calabasas ranch in California. Local problems arose. Pablo, Huston's adopted son, doubled on horseback for Tim Durant—himself a riding friend of Huston's—as the General. In Mauldin's opinion, he was "a smartass teenager. A not very bright Mexican boy. I didn't like him." More comic was the cameo appearance of a family heirloom, the Civil War sword of Huston's great-grandfather, Colonel William P. Richardson, which Douglas Dick, playing the lieutenant—"a classic jerk, a kind of knucklehead" Mauldin recalled fondly—promptly managed to stick through his own foot. Accordingly, the lieutenant's incredible, exaggerated limp in the last scenes of the movie proved to be anything but acting."

Chief among all the problematic movie features was Huston's choice to film in black and white. This went against the spirit of Crane's impressionistic/expressionistic style, which makes much of its painterly technique with its radical images and vivid splashes of color. A few additions capture such atmospherics, particularly the slow motion ballet of the flag carriers in the concluding final scene of combat. But overall one has the sense of the book being consciously rendered into something of a film noir starkness of black and white. Huston believed that his choice of film achieved something of the Matthew

Brady effect: "I tried to reproduce the feel of the photographs with a kind of bleached effect," he said. "I wanted the blond fields, the bright skies and foreground, contrasted with the explosive quality of the black-and-white." At the same time, it turned out to be a movie feature with much in common among combat films of the period. If anything, it actually seems to enforce its artistic seriousness by resisting the strained spirit of Technicolor guts and glory offerings in the ascendancy during the era—including Murphy's own garish big-budget reenactment of his own heroics in *To Hell and Back*. If anything, it now seems more of an age with contemporary Korean War films such as *The Steel Helmet* or *One Minute to Zero*, with their grainy black and white enforcement of a close, even claustrophobic sense of menace and hopelessness.

As to the third and concluding chapter in what might be called the making of an accidental classic, one must say that no single aspect of Huston's participation in the project seems to have proved so characteristic of his strange, mercurial genius as his leaving it. To be specific, in the wake of a series of disastrous preview showings of preliminary versions of the film, where audience members, alternately puzzled, bored, and amused, were witnessed leaving in droves, he simply departed for London to work on *The African Queen*, leaving others to salvage the picture. Conversely, one might also now propose that no provision of art turned out to be more purposeful than the largely arbitrary and expedient set of cuts and changes—themselves frequently the source of bitter disagreement between the remaining principals such as Producer Gottfried Reinhardt and MGM Vice-President for Production Dore Schary—in the process of arriving finally at a new version for popular release. According to one account, among the most basic of their guidelines for eliminating questionable dramatic material was to slash anything that preview audience members had laughed at. But there was also far more to the rescue effort than this. To capitalize on the cultural prestige of Crane's novel, the film now began with a traditional masterpiece theater-style shot of an opening book, with title and authorship prominently noted; and to further accentuate the "literary" connection, the full performance script was also given a voice-over narration, in most cases taken verbatim from Crane's text. Also integrated was a nighttime camp scene after Henry has returned to his unit, in which he is shown among his fellows, one reading his Bible, another tormented with dreams, another sleeping peacefully. On the eve of new battle, his previous cowardice undetected, the youth lies awake and open-eyed in his bedroll contemplating the morrow. On the other hand, cuts to the dramatic body were draconian to say the least, with the heavily edited final product now running barely over an hour. Major battle scenes had been reduced to two: one, early in the film, in which Henry Fleming, having successfully met a first test of battle, flees from a second charge by the advancing enemy; and a second, near the conclusion, in which he and his comrade Wilson are seen bravely leading a charge. As noted above, a long death scene by the young actor Royal Dano as the Tattered Soldier—considered by virtually everyone involved in the project the film's best dramatic moment, but also now seen in terms of its larger dramatic structure as a distraction—was summarily eliminated. So was Henry's cathedral-like encounter in the forest, amid his battlefield wanderings, with an open-eyed, decaying corpse—a scene from the novel recognized by Huston as so crucial to Crane's literary and psychological design that he had gone to the trouble of giving it two separate filmings. A scene of Henry's standing picket duty and entering into conversation with a rebel counterpart across the river, used to open the film, was moved to after the opening scenes of drilling and camp life. A scene in which Henry and his untested fellows, on the way into battle, are jeered by veterans was removed.

Yet in the process, I should like to propose, a great thing had come of an alchemy of accident: To wit, a collocation of professional filmmakers, skilled craftsmen from a major studio managed to bring forth an after-the-fact edited version of a film not only capturing much of the genius of Crane's masterpiece, but in certain serendipitous ways not only improving on it with virtues of focus and clarification but, in moments, adding to it a kind of avant-garde strangeness, an eerie experimentalist hyperreality.

This begins with the addition back into the film of the most distinctive literary element: narration. (In Francis Ford Coppola's classic of the Vietnam War, *Apocalypse Now*, Michael Herr's voice-over text of Conradian narration, relying heavily on the latter's celebrated book *Dispatches*, was similarly added after a fully dramatized film had undergone final editing.) Indeed, James Whitmore's voice-over—once it gets past an opening, flowery assertion of Crane's experience of authorship as a means by which he, like Henry Fleming, "became a man,"—succeeds throughout the film in underlining a number of the most complex and interesting ironies of the novel. Some comment, albeit taken directly from Crane, is borrowed from its original contexts for movie rearrangements of plot and character development. Some is altered to suit new dramatic purpose. Henry's inward wish that he, too, could have a "red badge of courage," for instance, is persuasively re-implanted into a Confederate sentinel's admonition that Henry, on picket across the river, step out of the light lest he wind up "getting one of those little red things." At the same time, we also hear the voice, unmistakably Crane's narrator, convincingly reshaped through gritty World War II black and white realism. (Interestingly, Whitmore served a similar function as actor-narrator in the World War II classic *Battleground* and would do so again in *Battle Cry*.)

As to dramatic reshapings, most of the film edits proved effective in providing new aspects of salutary focus and simplicity. The sentry scene that originally opened the film, for instance, was moved to a place following the early camp activities of Union Army housekeeping and rumormongering, with the latter in turn closed out in a brief close focus interlude of quiet emphasis on the "malaise" of the untested youthful private so carefully described in the Crane novel. At the same time, with reference to Crane's own fairly complex plotting and reversals, particularly in the second half of the text, scenes of Henry's return and subsequent heroism are brought into a sharp and manageable relief that the novel sometimes lacks. In the film, many of the complicated military ironies of war experience are simplified. In both the book and the film, during the first half of the action Henry runs but is not seen to run and is therefore not regarded as a coward. In the second part, he fights and is seen to fight and is thus accounted a hero. The movie basically leaves it at that, albeit with the small addition of the scene described earlier of Henry's and Wilson's mutual soul baring. But the supervening military ironies, particularly of Crane's last part, are helpfully cut away. It is necessary that Henry's and Wilson's heroisms, in a series of tentative advances and collisions that have all been part of a diversionary attack, become yet another version, as Crane calls it, of a "blue demonstration" in a battle (clearly modeled on Chancellorsville) that the Union army has lost. Here the matter is simplified into an immediate recognition that the regiment has not been fighting the main part of the battle and that another is going to get credit for victory.

Movie editors also addressed matters of performance that had troubled the film from the outset. Huston's choice of Audie Murphy to play Henry Fleming proved notoriously a "problem" all along. Neither he nor the dramatic scenario seemed satisfactorily to address the question of motive contained in the matter of "courage." How does one prove an abject coward in one encounter and then turn around in an ensuing one and become a hero? Where was the consistency? A Hollywood psychologist was consulted. Reinhardt and Schary exchanged lengthy views on the "story" of Henry Fleming. The final edits seem to have addressed the problem head-on, again with emphasis on focus and simplicity, thereby showing how closely the technical skills applied to the MGM film had come to Crane's own naturalistic mark. The resultant achievement, however unwittingly, was addressed in Martin Rubin's "filmic" critique. According to the latter, the film seemed marred by the "alienating effect" of Fleming's "too-abrupt reversal" of character from antihero to legitimate hero. "The character does not cohere at the level of a heroic reading, calling instead to two conflicting and contradictory responses. In effect, he asks to be identified with both as an antihero and as a more conventional hero in the John Wayne-Errol Flynn tradition. These two disparate approaches to the heroic do not support each other and instead tend more to cancel each other out." All one can say now is, "Just so." In the edits, as in the Crane original, the John Wayne-Errol Flynn analogy becomes just the point. In war, a cowardly man who stands and fights when surrounded by others doing so can also in the same company cross over the line of group behavior at times and perform solo acts on the battlefield as a military automaton, his earlier acts of fear and flight as strangely unconscious as those of the fire-eater he has become. This reflexivity was Crane's point. And the movie in its final form seems to suggest that he had been right all along. The distance between cowardice and bravery proves incredibly small. That was the meaning of combat. For a private soldier, at least, whether one runs like a rabbit or charges like a wildcat is largely a function of circumstance. This, in Lillian Ross's acute understanding, seems to have been "Huston's idea of the theme of the movie" as well, "which was simply that courage is as unreasoning as cowardice." But it took the filmmaker's final work to remove the essentially irrelevant point of motivation. Again, Rubin now seems to have gotten it right by getting it almost completely wrong: "Rather than presenting the hero as a remarkable or extraordinary figure," he wrote, "the film works more to demonstrate how he is a duplicable and interchangeable cog in an inevitable, unending cycle." Again, that seems to have been nearly everyone's intention. It took the MGM final edits to achieve it.

Oddly, virtually all contemporary reviewers seemed to sense the movie's permanence. *Time* called in "one of the best war films ever made"; *Saturday Review* "a classic of American filmmaking"; and the *New York Times* "a major achievement that should command admiration for years and years." *Newsweek* likewise concluded that it "bids fair to become one of the classic American motion pictures." The *Time* reviewer said it was "scrupulously faithful to the novel." This now may appear rather a naïve overstatement, except to the degree that art, in its various transmissions, has various ways of telling a truer truth. Here, the Crane story, on taking the materials of history and memory and transforming them into a classic of prescient genius, is something we can piece together from various biographical accounts. The story of the Huston project is similarly made available among other things by a Lillian Ross text sometimes called the best book ever written about moviemaking in classic era Hollywood. That of the MGM process of reshaping the creation into its only existing form must remain speculative and fragmentary at best. To be sure, it began in a Hollywood creative melodrama well founded in truth. Huston, simply washing his hands of the project, departed for London, on his way to Africa to direct Bogart and Hepburn in *The African Queen*. Whatever might remain of a director's cut vanished somewhere between the Dark Continent and the cutting room floor. Equally, apart from certain anecdotal reminiscences—somehow appropriate to Crane's own journalistic and frequently ad hoc methods of composition and revision—we will never know

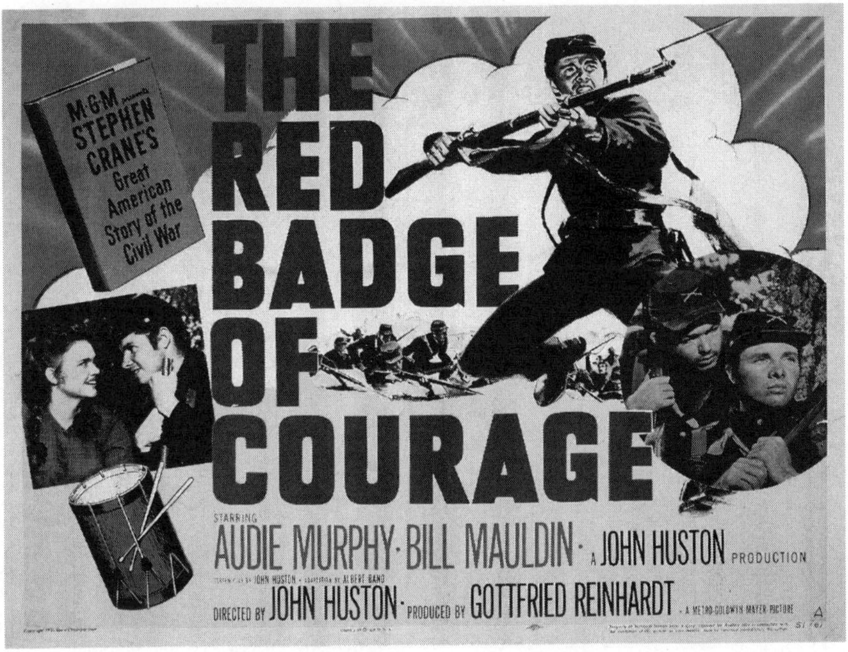

Figure 10.3 *The Red Badge of Courage* movie poster, MGM, 1951. Directed by John Huston. Metro-Goldwyn-Mayer, 1951.

all the participants, major and minor, in the complex editing work. Some important initial reshapings may be ascribed to the direct agency of technical experts. Bands said he made the first cut with the editor, Ben Lewis—Huston, according to Reinhardt, not having "not having the 'zitsflasche' to sit in the editing room to work on it himself." Others, such as the one really jarring editorial addition to the opening—the somewhat phony voice-over preface to the main narration—seem to have originated at the executive producer level with Dore Schary. Of the last installment in this transmission of a mystery of complex, novelistic heroism into an inspired film creation that continues at once to mystify and inspire, we must leave it there as well, somewhere between Africa and the cutting room. In the wake of watching a filmscript by Henry Fleming turn into a novel by John Huston, the MGM technicians and producers had been left with a mess on their hands. That mess ultimately became a masterpiece revealing its own strange pedigree of genius: *The Red Badge of Courage*—the movie.

II
In the Museo de la Revolucíon; or, The Ghost of José Martí

In Cuba, more than fifty years after Fidel Castro's triumphal entrance into Havana with his army of filthy, bearded, jungle fighters in their combat fatigues, the Revolution continues to write itself endlessly into history and memory. In today's Habana Centro, the old neoclassical Presidential Palace functions as the Museo de la Revolucíon, with its long, interconnected sequence of galleries comprising a densely documented chronicle of the Cuban struggle for independence from the earliest days of colonization to the present. The grassy, wooded square facing it is known as the Parque de la Revolucíon, containing at its shrine-like center the *Granma*, the leaky vessel used by Fidel Castro and his guerilla band to return to Cuba in 1956, as well as other relics from the history of the revolutionary struggle, ranging from vehicles and small aircraft to the mangled engine turbine of an American U-2 spy plane brought down during the 1962 missile crisis.

The museum itself proves an equally queer amalgam of period art, architecture, and historical display. The palatial office of the prerevolutionary dictator Fulgencio Batista is faithfully preserved, along with a memorial to the heroes of *13 de Marzo de 1957*, a group of youthful insurgents who proved nearly successful in storming the place and assassinating Batista there. For their heedless bravery, most of the fifty or so involved paid with their lives in the ensuing gunfight. (Unmentioned is the fact that the would-be assassins represented an anti-communist faction of the Cuban insurgency called the Revolutionary Directorate, and that their leader José Antonio Echeverría, who died in another gun battle nearby at the national radio station that was seized in the hope of broadcasting news of Batista's death, had been a longtime rival of Fidel Castro.) In a series of upper-level galleries, the outer rings of several floors are devoted to rooms crowded with displays on the history of militant Cuban anti-imperialist heroics, beginning with early independence movements and the nineteenth-century wars of liberation, followed by the interlude known in the US as the Spanish-American war and in Cuba as *La Intervención*, and then

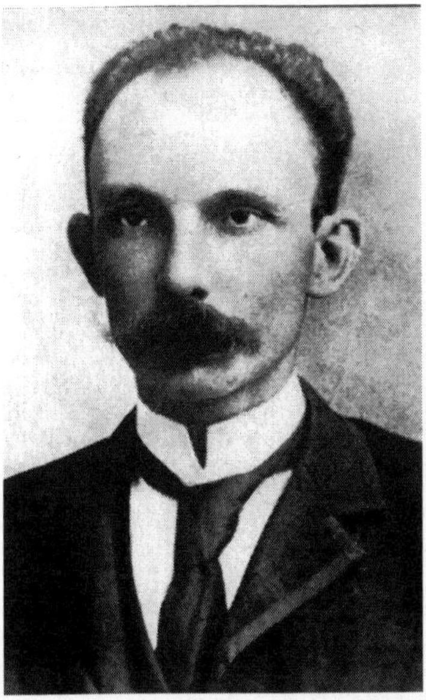

Figure 11.1 Photograph of José Martí. Artist unknown.

moving to the violent political struggles of the twentieth century (in the first two decades against the American occupation, in the 1920s and 1930s against the dictator Gerardo Machado, and in the 1940s and 1950s against Batista), culminating in the heroics of a band of *guerrilleros* in Oriente and the battles against puppet Batista armies that led to the heroic triumph of the revolution.

The effect of the exhibition overall is that which is surely intended: a vividly documented and illustrated "people's" version of the national narrative provides occasion for the ideological rewriting of collective history and memory. In the endlessly unfolding displays of early anti-colonialist independence movements, beginning with the struggles of native Taínos and coming up through such early revolutionary heroes as Manuel de Céspedes, Antonio Maceo, Máximo Goméz, Calixto García, and the peerless José Martí, the regime inscribes the long national legend of resistance and the battle for independence as its own Old Testament prehistory. In turn, the ensuing account of the twentieth century, with its equally dense documentation of early struggle against US imperialism, the dictators, the mobsters, the millionaires, the rise of the revolution, its great political triumph, and the ongoing heroic endurance of the new travails of military threat and isolation becomes a fulfillment of that earlier history as a kind of New Testament of world-historical struggle.

Accordingly, the larger effect seems a species of strange, mirror image, Latino-Marxist play on New England Puritan typology. The Taínos were peasant socialists. Manuel de Céspedes was a prophet of a postcolonial multiracial proletariat. The American gangsters were outlaw economic imperialists fronting for a larger capitalist corruption. The bloodstained clothing of twentieth-century revolutionary martyrs become the latest relics in a tradition of anti-imperialist self-sacrifice extending backward to figures as diverse as the native chieftain Hatuey, the *mulato* military giant Maceo, and the fallen liberator Martí. Above all there is Martí, and the attempt—as elsewhere in the capital, and, for that matter, throughout the island—to center the revolutionary narrative on the peculiar iconography of the great nineteenth-century inspirational figure, the spiritual father of the independence movement in Cuba now also become the sainted apostle of the *Revolucíon*. This requires something of a stretch. An extremely complex thinker and writer, as a revolutionary patriarch he was surely no Marx, no Lenin, no prophet of History as the inexorable unfolding of material relations and class struggle. Nor do his writings, although proposing a universal egalitarian concept of revolutionary liberation, promote anything more than a carefully hedged view of insurrectionary violence. As a working revolutionary, he spent major years of expatriation in the US, largely in New York, only to be killed in combat nearly instantly upon arrival back in Cuba to assume leadership of the eventually victorious 1895–98 revolution. Still, if anything, even on the part of an officially atheist regime, the atmospherics seem nearly everywhere to verge on the religious, with Martí the exiled Moses apotheosized as the revolutionary crucified Christ. In history, the revolution thus appropriates the colonial past and the role of major figures of resistance as its own myth of origin. In memory, it reconstitutes that narrative of history as revolutionary teleology. To borrow a literary analogy, within the overarching myth of the Revolution, elements of traditional Cuban history are here and elsewhere repeatedly made to serve a semiotic function not unlike that of Poe's "Purloined Letter," their meanings determined not by their own textual significations so much as by their ideological contexts.

Further, as if to ensure there will be no mistaking of the project, while the Museo version of the national narrative is being rewritten from within, so it is given a complementary ideological bookending from without. Here too is the attempt—analogous to the display of insurrectionary detritus in the park—at a framing iconography of armed revolutionary struggle, but one that has the effect of surreal, almost cartoonish improvisation. Foregrounding the entry into the display proper, a darkly dramatic passage centers on a guerrilla fighter tableau of two larger-than-life action figures in a jungle setting, striking appropriately larger-than-life heroic poses. Upon close inspection, they proved to be wax effigies of the traditionally twinned revolutionary martyrs, the sainted Che Guevara and Camilo Cienfuegos. It is as if one was entering the Revolution via some strange version of Madame Tussaud in the Sierra Maestra.

Then, at the end, appears a parallel imaging of the great US Satan. At the very departure doors, after many rooms of exhaustive immersion in documentary and photographic history, comes a wall displaying a set of humorous but somewhat childish murals. *El Rincón de los Cretinos*, it is labeled—roughly, the corral or roundup of the idiots. Cartoon caricatures duly appear of Fulgencio Batista, Ronald Reagan, and the two George Bushes. Batista is instantly recognizable in the neofascist military getup he used to affect—à la Hitler, Mussolini, Franco. Reagan is dressed as a Hollywood movie cowboy. Bush I is portrayed as Caesar. Bush II is a bat-eared helmeted Nazi trying to read a book he is holding upside down.

Such, one discovers, are the operations of revolutionary consciousness as a mode of ad hoc, composite, popular-culture remembering throughout the city and across the island, a vast, ubiquitous project of cultural and ideological syncretism, with continual mixings of story and image, of documentary and myth. The concept of the Perpetual Revolution, it might be called, or perhaps the Eternal Presence, the ceaseless engrafting of ideological legend upon a body of history and memory arising out of more than six centuries of struggle for Cuban independence, with no connection too strained or obscure, no juxtaposition of narratives or symbologies too far-fetched or even absurd.

A virtual equivalent, for instance, lies in nearby Vedado, in the visual and material symbology of the Plaza de la Revolucíon, the Cuban equivalent of Red Square in Moscow or Tiannamen Square in Beijing. Once the site of stem-winding three- or four-hour orations by the *Comandante*, it is on most occasions almost completely deserted. As if in futile competition with the others for totalitarian vastness, it now seems mainly a huge featureless asphalt space, a kind of gigantic parking lot. On the perimeter stand the national library and various government ministries—nondescript late 1960s- and early 1970s-style buildings strangely resembling those of a big US agricultural or engineering college somewhere out in the Midwest. One, as in the odd government high rise elsewhere in the capital, still bears a stylized outline image of Che Guevara. Nothing, on the other hand, as image or icon, can seen of Fidel Castro—testament, it is said, to his properly Marxist-Leninist attitude toward Communist Man, an architectural and monumentalist resistance to the cult of personality. What one cannot fail to note, on the other hand, is the central construction feature already presiding over the whole expanse—a bizarre museum-tower complex standing alone against the far perimeter, part space needle and part Washington monument, with the figure celebrated above and below again the sainted Martí. Further, here too one finds that the script of symbolic conjunction between larger national remembering and proximate ideological myth is one the Revolution has creatively appropriated for its own ends. In this case, the design competition for such a freestanding memorial turns out to have begun as early as 1938—with construction undertaken at the height of the Batista dictatorship in 1953 and completed just before the victory of the revolution in 1958. (It is alleged that the young Castro himself at the time attempted to defend the property rights of home dwellers in the area displaced by the huge construction project.) Now the Martí tower, too, site of the highest observation point in all of Havana, as with everything else on the landscape of history and memory, is part and fabric of the great Revolution.

Thus, across the island, the Revolution undertakes myriad other such deep-history piggybackings of revolutionary myth upon earlier traditions of Cuban historical resistance to oppression. Far to the east, in the traditional cradle of Cuban insurrection Santiago, lie the Moncada Barracks, site of the 1953 attack on the headquarters garrison of Batista forces during which the revolution was born. Named after Gulliermón Moncada, a figure of slave legend and general of the 1895 War of Independence in the model of Antonio Maceo known in his own right as "the ebony titan," they now stand as the 26th of July Movement Museum. Slightly southwest of the city, on a point of rocky coast near the town of Bayamo, is the 1956 landing site of the aforementioned *Granma*, now enshrined an island's length to the west. In a kind of creative updating of ideological legend, that piece of hallowed wilderness now has an environmental emphasis, as noted in its designation as Landing of the *Granma* National Park (Parque Nacional Desembarco del *Granma*). In the western war zone of guerrilla struggle, one may still visit a reconstruction of Castro's jungle headquarters, La Comandancia de la Plata. But one may find equally memorialized in those same regions earlier heroes of the struggle for independence in the eastern provinces, as far back as Hatuey, a Taíno chief who fought a guerrilla war against the Spanish in 1512 and was eventually captured and burned at the stake at Yara—itself to become again a nineteenth-century revolutionary station of the cross where a wealthy white plantation owner, Manuel de Céspedes, issued the "*Grito de Yara*," (the "shout" or "cry" of Yara) promising freedom to his slaves and calling them to join him in the first war of Cuban Independence. Similarly at various locations in the east, then and now celebrated as the fount of independence, are sites associated with military heroes such as Maceo, Gómez, and García, tracing out the histories of the agonizing Ten Years War of 1868–78, the Second Revolution (known as the Little War) of 1879–81, and the successful Third War of Cuban Independence, (1895–1898). But the big symbolic appropriation of heroic legend again centers on José Martí, whose mausoleum, built in 1951 as another Batista-era memorial project and featuring People's Army changing of the guard ceremonies, remains a well-established site of patriotic pilgrimage reminiscent of the tombs of Lenin in Moscow, Mao in Beijing, Ho Chi Minh in Hanoi, and the Tomb of the Unknowns in Washington, DC.

Particularly in this region of the major US-Cuban battlefields in the vic-

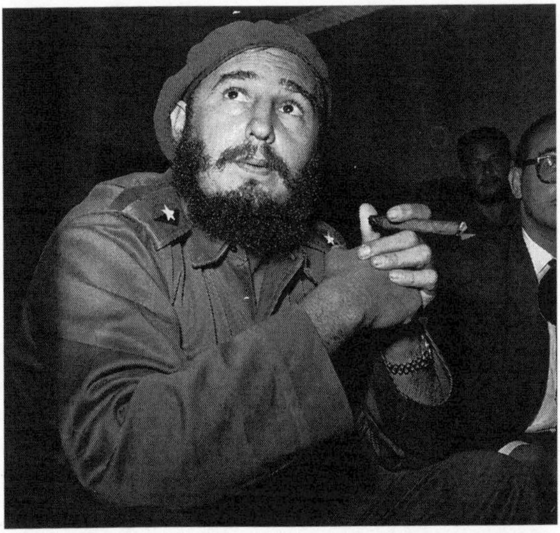

Figure 11.2 Fidel Castro news conference, 1961, old Havana Hilton, Havana, Cuba. *The Associated Press.*

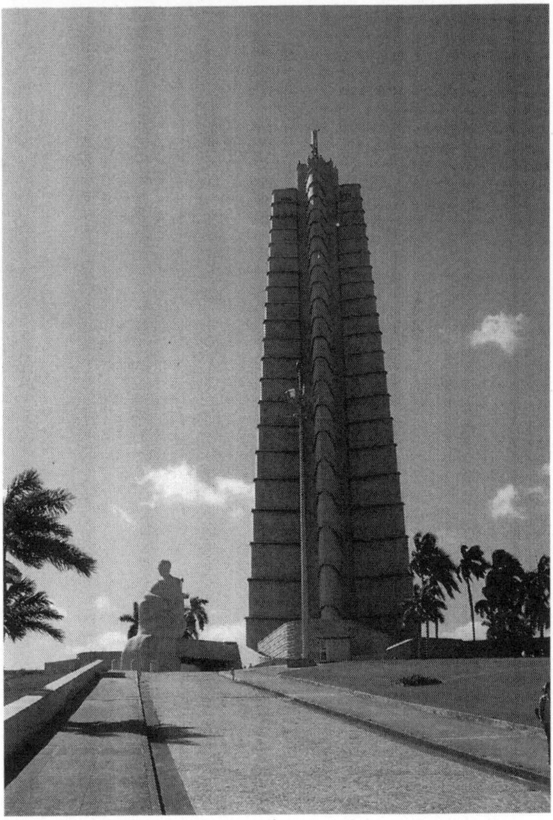

Figure 11.3 Martí statues at the José Martí Memorial (Monumento a José Martí), Havana, Cuba. Wikipedia.

torious 1898 war against Spain, there is also a matter of American military identification to be dealt with. To that end, revolutionary reinscription frequently finds its counterpart in erasure and effacement. At most of the sites still cherished by Americans as part of Spanish-American War legend—Daiquiri, Siboney, Las Guasimas, El Caney—there is virtually no documentation. On San Juan Hill, there is no celebration of Theodore Roosevelt or the Rough Riders. Where statues or memorials relating to American participation remain, some are partially dismantled; others have had their narrative plaques removed. Where historical text is supplied, the emphasis is on contemporary betrayal and humiliation by Americans, as in the refusal to allow Calixto García and his *Mambise* freedom fighters to enter Santiago. Nowhere mentioned on any day anywhere on the island of course is nearby Guantánamo, that perpetual finger in the eye of the Cuban nation.

Today, all of the more recent major sites of history and memory hew to that grand contextualizing narrative of reinscription of Cuban heroism and erasure of US power and presence. The one great monument to the defeat and humiliation of the military giant across the straits, of course, remains the Bahía de Cochinos, known to Americans as the site of the Bay of Pigs debacle, in US history hardly without equal as a shameful, inept combination of halfhearted policy commitment and military incompetence, to this day an ignominy everyone involved would just as soon forget save for those who had friends and family die or be taken prisoner. A favorite spot for Cubans and international tourists, two hours south of Havana and now a thriving recreational beach and tourist destination, it still announces its status in revolutionary lore on an array of fading billboards—marking the turns to an increasingly forlorn Playa Girón military park and museum—as the site of the "Pre-eminent Victory of Socialism in America"; of the "Destruction of Yanqui Imperialism of Latin America"; of the "Stand of the Comandante Fidel in Combat." Similarly, on the Atlantic coast devoted revolutionary pilgrims and others visit the tomb of Che Guevara at Santa Clara, the site of the Che's crucial 1958 victory over the retreating Batista army propelling the Revolution to triumph in the west, but now, as importantly, the burial place of the hero's body, itself rescued from US desecration through CIA murder and mutilation in Bolivia.

As might be suspected, nothing much remains in history or memory of the Cuban Missile Crisis. One sees the occasional photo of antiaircraft batteries on the Malecon. And there is that mangled turbojet spy plane engine on the ground outside the *Granma* building. Increasingly, the US, along with the Spanish and the British, seem just another failed military and political oppressor consigned to a place in the Museo de la Revolucíon.

Apace, it is also in Havana—ironically, the great capital of the Revolution, site of the Museo de la Revolucíon, the Parque de la Revolucíon, the Plaza de la Revolucíon—that the myth of the Revolution now finds itself increasingly threatened by absorption into the newest popular mythologizings of history and memory. This also seems in the nature of Cuban history and memory. If Santiago and Oriente are the traditional hotbeds of insurrection, Havana then and now remains the place where the earnest easterners—such as the brothers Castro themselves—have never felt at home, where they have always seemed out of step. Bound by tradition, romantic, steeped in island culture, they find Havana invested with a kind of cynical, corrupt opportunism. To borrow a European conceit: in Berlin, it is said, the situation is always serious but never hopeless; in Vienna, the situation is always hopeless but never serious. For the mass of Cubans, somewhere in between has always lain the true, great, indigenous, peasant and worker struggle for *la Independencia*.

Nowhere is this sense of narrative and ideological rupture more pronounced, even after decades of US attempts at restriction and isolation, than in today's tourist-dense metropolitan Havana, the place attracting the vast majority of visitors. Here, the archaeologies of culture have become so thoroughly interfused as to make the Revolution itself into a museum artifact, an important but increasingly integral element in the larger national narrative it increasingly struggles to contain. One may inventory alone the great citadels of historic power. At the old Spanish fortress La Punta, guarding the western entrance to the harbor, stands a monument to the medical student martyrs of 1871, executed by the Spanish, as memorably stated by Che Guevara, himself soon to join the great revolutionary roll, for the "crime of being Cuban." Just across at El Morro, the story is the assault and occupation by the British. Its companion fortification, Las Cabanas, contains the restored office of Che Guevara, the city's Revolutionary governor. Little mention is made of the execution wall, the site where political opponents were executed in the hundreds. At twilight, the daily sunset cannon-firing ceremony is a great tourist attraction, with balcony seats recommended as coming with a free drink. In the old city itself, in the Plaza de Armas, the old Spanish imperial headquarters, the Palacio de los Capitanes Generales features extensive historical exhibits centering first on artifacts from colonial European rule and then on the heroes of great nineteenth-century independence movement, including the famous Armando Menocal portrait of the Death of Maceo. A separate display preserves the office of General Leonard Wood, the commander of US forces during the 1898 war and military governor under the despised post-1898 American occupation. (Ironically, it is also only here, as noted below, that one may find any material relic of the legendary *USS Maine*.)

As to larger public symbologies of the Cuban independence struggle, in a walk along the Havana Malecon one may note that images of Che Guevara and Camilo Cienfuegos fade into the wall while great heroic statues again honor a triad of nineteenth-century revolutionary predecessors. At the eastern extreme of the long seawall walk is Calixto García. At the other is Máximo Gómez. In the middle, dominating a park for the children of Havana, is Antonio Maceo. Decorative panels on one the side of the pedestal supporting the huge equestrian statue in bronze depict Maceo's humble birth, his black father, and his revered mother, Mariana Grajales Coello, herself a national heroine. On the other side, other panels depict numerous figures with African features, emphasizing his liberation of the enslaved. A multitude of statuary figures attend Maceo on the ascendant pedestal. They are Cubans of all visible races, joined together in reverent pose.

Of the three statues, it seems significant that the Revolution left them standing, as it did not many others. One can only infer that they are part of Cuban memory that no one has ever thought to deny. The same might be said of the more recent initiative to preserve and memorialize many locales and buildings marked as places of earlier twentieth century resistance, anti-Machado, anti-Batista, anti-American. The effect is to engraft together a succession of independence episodes into a tissue of distinctly *Habanero* history and memory. At the beautiful, peaceful, almost idyllic University of Havana, with its central quadrangle modeled on its great urban counterpart on Washington Heights in New York City, Columbia University, an armored car sits at one corner, marking a general history of student revolt. At the bottom of the magnificent steps leading up to the main gain, a bar/restaurant offers tours of the upstairs rooming house where various plotters convened.

Here again, as in Santiago, attempts persist at the elimination of nearly all traces of US participation in the 1895–98 War of Independence. Most notable in this regard is the wreckage of the *USS Maine* monument on the Malecon, just below the Hotel Nacional. The military memorial was long ago totally dismantled. The space beyond, meanwhile, as if in fated conjunction with history itself, has been converted to an outdoor amphitheater concert facility, with huge lighting sponsons and stage frames permanently blocking an equally large, square, featureless building just to the west. The building is of course the US Interests Section, the only remaining official American government installation in the city. As to the few remaining relics of the battleship itself, as noted earlier, these were long ago removed to the Palacio de los Capitanes Generales. They too now occupy part of the corner office of Leonard Wood, US proconsul, together marking now one sordid, ignominious, last chapter in nineteenth century American military adventurism. So much for late nineteenth- and early twentieth-century Americans playing the liberator in Cuba, one might be tempted to say. That would be so, it turns out, were it not for one small, ad hoc footnote—the kind of thing one discovers repeatedly in Havana—roughly as far to the east of the aforementioned monument as the US Interests section now sits stolidly, intransigently to the west. It is a small monument and plaque, somehow strangely left behind, commemorating a figure described as an 1869 American general of the *Ejército Libertador Mambi* and commander of the Camagüey Cavalry Corps. Apparently a mysterious, solitary early volunteer, his name was Henry Reeve; and he seems to have been a fixture of the nineteenth-century revolution from the beginning to end. He joined de Céspedes in the original ten-year war; winning the respect of all the Cuban commanders, he later formed a comradeship with García. Known for his bravery and devotion to the cause, he was promoted to Brigadier General. He met his end heroically in 1876, as the story goes. With his unit overrun by Spanish forces, and rather than be taken prisoner, he killed himself with his own pistol.

Known at the time as *El joven legionario de la libertad*—the young legionary of liberty—he also managed to come down through memory somewhat conveniently as *El Inglesito*, the little Englishman. Further, on just those terms, would his history and memory be resuscitated by the Castro regime on yet another American centenary with the 1976 creation of the Henry Reeve medical brigade. A Cuban international mission of doctors and nurses—and traveling advertisement for Cuba's own rather impressive medical care system—it has won fame over the decades through its assistance to various groups of Caribbean hurricane victims. Its golden propaganda moment came surely in the humiliating offer to send Cuban medical teams to New Orleans to aid with the botched Bush administration handling of the Katrina disaster. To this degree, even anti-American history and memory have come a kind of absurd if intriguing full circle.

As to the harbor where the *Maine* went down, there now remains likewise not a sign of commemoration. But again, ingeniously, if opportunistically, something analogous—even better—has been substituted. Indeed, now highlighted as a major attraction, though as obscure to outsiders as the legend of Henry Reeve, is the memorial to the 1960 explosion of the French munitions ship *La Coubre*, which claimed between seventy-five and one hundred lives, with another two hundred wounded. The suspicion of course—now rendered into history and memory as revolutionary response, companion event, indeed mirror image of the "remember the *Maine*" legend—remains US sabotage. And so it will likely stand forever, recorded now as part of permanent revolutionary iconography, in perhaps the most famous photograph to come out of the Castro era, that of Che Guevara titled *El Guerillero Heroico*. It was taken by the great revolutionary photographer Alberto Korda at a memorial service for victims of the *Coubre* disaster.

Indeed, it is in a multitude of strangely miscellaneous and anachronistic Havana moments such as the one recorded, where revolutionary iconography intersects with commercial tourism, that old and new history and memory now take on an almost accordion-like quality. The latest twenty-first-century recontextualizations of la Revolucíon—images of black and white memory, stern, serious, armed, heroic, military struggle—are now integrated into multicolor efforts at traditional historical preservation, presided over by the powerful and well-connected city historian and revolutionary intellectual Dr. Eusebio Leal and emphasizing foregoing centuries of colorful, romantic history. (The interest of the Marxist literary intellectual Georgy Lukacz in the decadent form of historical romance as an allegory of class struggle proposes itself as an analogy here.) Vestigial local party headquarters remain on the cityscape, to be sure, along with peoples' courts, medical clinics, and homes for the aged, not to mention ubiquitous schools bursting with noisy, energetic children. Revolutionary paraphernalia, on the other hand, seem consigned to tourist shops—flags, scarves, T-shirts, posters, decorative pins, key chains, with the seemingly most plentiful and hottest selling items still centered on cult of Che Guevara. The Havana Vieja restoration, the colonial city infused with Spanish color and pageantry while cleansed of associations of Spanish tyranny, now extends into Havana Centro and Vedado and beyond to glamorous Miramar and Jaimanitas. Near the old Capitolio there now stand in restored nostalgic glow the grand old nineteenth-century hotels such as the Telegrafo and the Angleterre. From the early decades of the twentieth century, the age once known as the Dance of the Millions, now also seemingly resurrected in time are the bars, hotels, country clubs, shooting clubs, and yacht clubs. Fine collections of classic art are to be found at the Museo Nacional de Bellas Artes, with a separate Artes Cubana section featuring native twentieth-century modernists such as Eduardo Abela, Alberto Peña, Marcelo Pogolotti, Wilfredo Lam, Amelia Peláez, Leopold Romanasch, and Armando Menocal.

Everywhere, there seems the irresistible reassimilation of recent revolutionary history and memory, of stern, serious, armed, heroic, military struggle, of Fidel, Che, Camilo, and the rest, back into the corrupt, luxuriant, happy, decadent ambience of the prerevolutionary Machado and Batista eras. Further, it is a selling point promoted by the Revolution itself. Tourist lodgings include the Hotel Nacional, restored in thoroughgoing 1930s splendor; the Ambos Mundos, where Hemingway frequently stayed and wrote; the Seville, the Capri, the Meyer Lansky Las Vegas-style Riviera; even the old Havana Hilton, albeit restyled and renamed the Habana Libre, still sporting high-

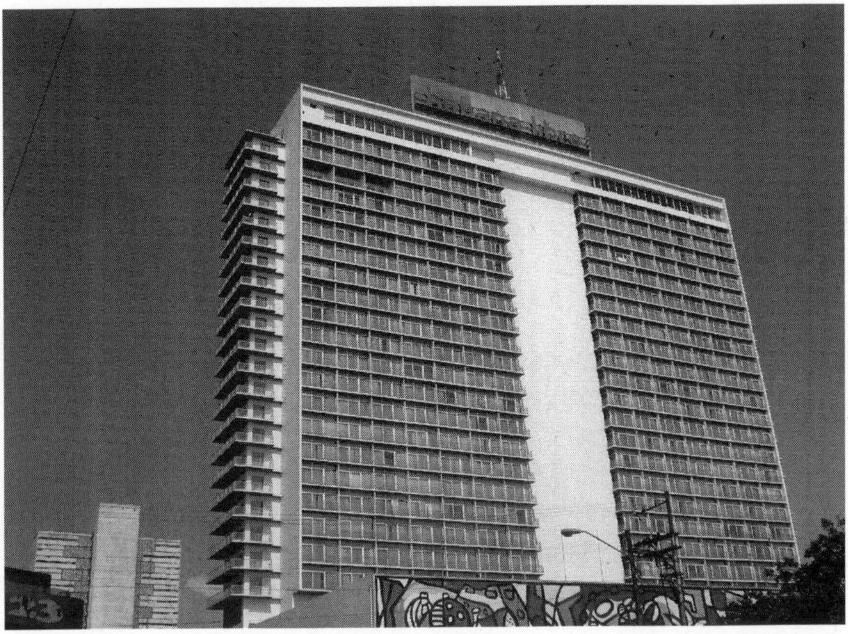

Figure 11.4 Habana Libre (previously Havana Hilton), Havana, Cuba.

1950s appeal while plastered with lobby photos of the *barbudos* in their grand moment of revolutionary glory. Nearly all market nostalgia with photographs of pre-revolutionary twentieth-century celebrities. At the Nacional, one finds Winston Churchill, David Niven, Eva Gabor, Erroll Flynn, and Fidel with various visiting heads of state. (One attempt at currency, on which the irony may or may not be lost, is Robert Redford, star of the revolutionary-era potboiler *Havana*.) The Seville features a vintage array, including Al Capone, Salvador Traficante, Graham Greene, Vincente Blanco Ibanez, Ted Williams, Joe Lewis, Prez Prado, and Josephine Baker. The Riviera—Ginger Rogers, Stewart Granger, William Holden, Cesar Romero, Johnny Weismuller, Leonardo de Caprio, Matt Dillon, and Danny Glover. The Habana Libre also lays claim to Matt Dillon, along with Dolores del Rio, Cantinflas, King Carlos and Queen Sophia of Spain, Salvador Allende, Conrad Hilton and then-wife actress Terry Moore, and of course, again, the Comandante himself, famously photographed there in his first great moment of victory celebration.

As if the old photo galleries have summoned the whole gaudy world of their backdrop into to life, post-Revolution Havana has become once again mainly the pre-Revolution city of restaurants, bars, supper clubs, and floor shows. In Vedado, the Tropicana flaunts its nostalgic glories. Yacht clubs have arisen again in Miramar. One is named the Marina Hemingway. The last famous American to have loved Cuba and to have been beloved of Cubans, Ernest Hemingway on his own has become a freestanding tourist industry, with his intermittent presence from the 1930s to 1950s playing into local legend of his appreciation of the spirit of *Cubanismo*. There is endless capitalization on the writer's presence in the city: at the Floridita, where he purportedly drank his *Papa Doble* daiquiris; at the Bodeguita, where he preferred his mojitos; at the old downtown hotel Ambos Mundos, where he sometimes wrote and where the visitor may now pay five tourist Cuban Currency Units (CUC) to see his room. Nearby, a taxi ride away, is the Finca Vigía, with his house, his car, his boat. Out at Cojimar where he fished, there is a bust and, of course, a bar. Frequently reproduced in the popular media are pictures of the aging author of *The Old Man and the Sea* at a fishing tournament with Fidel Castro, and transcriptions of a Nobel Prize interview suggesting that he dedicated his receipt of this honor to the Cuban people.

The time capsule dimension is everywhere. Beyond the hotels, clubs, marinas, surely the strangest of all residues of the prerevolutionary era lies in the nation's vast flotillas of 1950s classic American Cars. On the roads it is always the Revolution just on the eve of victory. In an ironic parallel, notable now as the communist regime moves toward its end is also how little attempt is made to restore postvictory representations of revolutionary devotion. Fading murals may be found of Fidel, Che, Camilo Cienfuegos, along with the odd silhouetted revolutionary profiles. The official party newspaper, distributed on the streets every day, is still called *Granma*. The US special interest section remains isolated, heavily secured, carefully disguised, and ignored. And it is now likewise with the departed Russians. The *Periodo Especial*, as it is called, the time of extreme economic disruption and poverty after the fall of the Soviet Union and the withdrawal of Russian aid, is a bitter memory, of which it is unusual even to hear someone speak. It as if the language has been cleansed of such forgettable Marxist history and memory. Oddly, the Russian era too seems mainly defined by its catastrophic automotive legacy: as with the great European "peoples' car" fiascos, the Trabi, the Yugo, the remnants of the Evil Empire here seem largely confined to a whole flotilla of smoking Fiat-like Ladas. To be sure, the nearly deserted Russian embassy still presides over the western city, sticking like a huge finger into the sky of Miramar. Children at school can be seen on special days dressed like communist Young Pioneers. But that's about it.

The old revolutionaries themselves, appearing at various commemorations, are increasingly feeble and few. As of this writing, Raul Castro has recently accepted what he says will be a final five-year term as *Presidente* before retirement. He is eighty-one. Making a rare public appearance at the same event

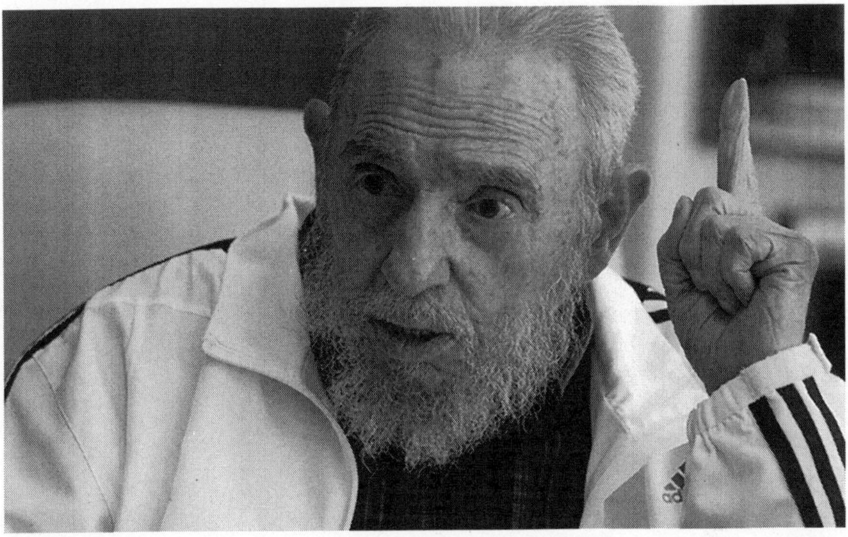

Figure 11.5 Fidel Castro, July 2014, Havana, Cuba.

was his brother, the retired eighty-six year-old Fidel Castro, the Comandante himself. Recent policy changes reveal an irresistible movement toward economic liberalization. Some years back, an enterprise niche was opened for private restaurants, operating out of personal residences called *Paladars*. Recently it has become legal in restricted ways to buy and sell cars and real estate. Private enterprise openings have been granted to small businesses. Liberalized passport and currency laws now allow Cuban citizens to leave the country and return, as they have for some time allowed American citizens of Cuban descent to visit relatives on the island and bring in money and consumer goods.

At home, even the old vestiges of a despised religion are enlisted for state revenue. Notably present everywhere in the capital are the old missions, convents, and cathedrals, preserved as tourist showplaces—the great central cathedral, the church of the Sacred Heart, the cathedral of the Hill of the Angel, the churches and convents of Saint Teresa, of Our Lady of Bethlehem, and of Santa Clara of Assisi. The greatest of the latter, the Church and Convent of St. Francis, has been converted to a performance space, with an extended back wall painted as a *trompe l'oeil*. When the stage is not in use, it features on an enormous easel what appears at first glance to be a painting of the eponymous saint. One looks at the face and finds the ideological joke. The Revolution gets maybe not the last laugh, but the next-to-the-last. The face is that of the Comandante. Most of the time, no one knows where he is. One recent photo shows him in a wheelchair sitting in a van having a conversation with a visiting Venezuelan dignitary. As to his brother, el Presidente, a recent speech against sloppy public behaviors was received as the grousing of a geriatric scold.

The fact is that the revolutionary dream of New World worker-peasant socialism is now a fading ideal with bad storyline. With appropriate irony for the last dialectical materialist regime on the planet save for North Korea, material relations could hardly be worse. There are at least three economies: a rickety, centralized, completely inefficient Marxist system, with a nearly worthless currency; a black market underground; and a tourist extravaganza. Together, they provide a material outcome at the level of daily life for most average Cubans that shows no hope of improvement beyond survival level. While Cubans focus on essential food, clothing, and shelter, Havana fills itself with fancy restaurants, designer stores, and luxury hotels. The latter provide lavish breakfast, lunch, and dinner buffets of cruise ship variety, of almost obscene abundance. Here is food that the average Cuban cannot imagine. A living anachronism, the worker's paradise gives subsistence feeding on thirty dollars a month. A new capitalist powerhouse, full of European, Latin American, and North American financiers, developers, and exporters, barely speaks to the US mainland or other continents on the telephone, let alone the Internet. Rigid information control has recently given way to Internet centers. At four dollars and fifty cents per hour, a single session would consume the weekly income of most Cubans. Meanwhile, desperate bloggers manage to crank out Internet journalism. In all these respects, all of Cuba, an entire system, has now become the type and image of the old *Granma*, hopelessly leaking at the seams. In every respect, the floodgates are about to open.

The fact is that not only are the last of the heroic old barbudos from Oriente getting ready to die, most of Cuba, tired of perpetual revolution, is waiting for them to do so. And so, one suspects, will die with them the myth of the revolution, absorbed back into the larger patterns of Cuban remembering. The famous words and numbers, *13 de Marzo*, *26 de Julio*, the final revolutionary roster of the dead, Che, Camilo, Raul, and, yes, Fidel, will be accordingly consigned to the strange blip on the radar screen of history and memory called the Cold War. The remaining question now would seem to be the manner in which it will all be entombed. As with Lenin in Moscow, Mao in Beijing (where two summers ago I saw people still lined up before daylight to get free government tickets), Ho Chi Minh in Hanoi, will the Plaza de la Revolucíon become Fidel's Tomb? Or will the shrine be out in Santiago where it all began? That would of course require sharing the marble mantle of revolutionary immortality with Martí. The hard fact is that this is pretty much already the case across the island. In town and country, Martí sculptures and domestic shrines decorate yards and fountains everywhere, not to mention the memorials in all major cities. Besides the mausoleum complex in Santiago, sites of memorial statuary are almost without number. In Havana alone one finds the shrine of the birthplace, la casa natal de Martí; the Parque Martí, or capital square; the Paseo de Martí, the city's grand avenue; the José Martí International Airport. Most lately, on the Malecon, the amphitheater masking the US Interests Section has been officially named the José Martí Anti-Imperialist Platform. The surrounding space is known as the Plaza de la Dignidad. Here, at a far corner, looking out to sea, a statue now commemorates the Elián González incident. A father holding his son—with whom he has been reunited after the boy's illegal abduction by his mother to the US—points accusingly toward the mainland. The face is clearly that of José Martí.

The capital joke may be something very like a last laugh. One suspects that any decision concerning the memorial disposition of the remains of el Comandante will be as much about tourist revenues and real estate as revolutionary consciousness. There will remain the great legend of Cuban resistance to the imperialist oppressor. Fidel will be put to rest with the other honored dead in the lineage of Hatuey, Placido, the Escalera Plotters, the Martyred Medical Students, Céspedes, Maceo, Gómez, García, Cienfuegos, Guevara, and all the rest. Rising above them all, one suspects, the ghost of José Martí will again become the face of Cuban Independence. The vision embodied in the old rallying cry "*Cuba Libre*!" will be restored to its grand echo over the centuries. "*Viva la Revolucíon*," the call of a once and forever presence, will take its place within the national narrative with the legend of Hatuey and the "Grito de Yara!" as another piece of history and memory.

12
By the Numbers

Americans, Vietnamese, and the Figures of Sacrifice

No matter how advanced the geopolitical explanation or sophisticated the military technology, when a culture elects to engage in a war it enacts a ritual as old as Abraham and Isaac or Agamemnon and Iphigenia. It prepares to sacrifice its sons and daughters on the altar of belief. Because of this ritual element, such belief still nearly always requires the elevation of what Frank Kermode calls fictions—the stories we tell ourselves to make sense of the world—to the status of myths: "total and adequate explanations of things as they are and were." Throughout history, such explanations throughout history have frequently required, and in many cases still do, some significant element of religion. This is where the term "sacrifice" originates. Verb: to make or do unto God; to perform a priestly function. Noun: a ritual offering; something precious, even holy, given to acquire divine favor or avoid divine anger; in adoration or perhaps propitiation. At the individual level such behavior can also be practiced in the form of self-sacrifice. This we call martyrdom. In a large part of the world, despite the rise of secular individuality and the concept of allegiance to the modern nation state—and with the latter, of the Clauzewitzian idea of war as "the extension of politics by other means"—these elements of sacralization have nonetheless often continued to prove necessary in one way or another to maintain. Even as the conduct of war by most modern industrialized nations has devolved to the raising and maintenance of mass armies of highly trained and indoctrinated individual soldiers commanded by military managers, some new mythos of ideology akin to religion has usually been required to manufacture an ethos of heroic voluntarism. "Making the supreme sacrifice," as the politicians are given to saying. We can think here also of the Lincolnian "last full measure of devotion"; of "giving one's life for a greater end," for God and Country, King and Country, Cause and Country. Whatever their provenance, the validities of all such explanations are historically measured by the congruity of the rhetoric of sacrifice with some acceptable public standard of the meaning of the term.

Historically, Americans at the beginnings of US military involvement in the Vietnam War remember the abstract discourse of sacrifice justifying the enterprise in John F. Kennedy's January 1961 inaugural address. "Let every nation know," went the stirring declaration, "whether it wishes us well or ill, that we shall pay any price, bear any burden, meet any hardship, support any friend, oppose any foe, in order to assure the survival and the success of liberty." As a matter of American Cold War plainspokenness, Kennedy's immediate successor, Lyndon B. Johnson, probably expressed it better: "Nail the coonskin to the wall." Even as the enterprise went irreparably wrong, Richard Nixon tried to dignify an exit as "Peace with Honor." For many Americans, the dismal wretchedness of the thing seemed to reach bottom with Gerald Ford and the 1975 fall of Saigon, followed by Jimmy Carter's presidential pardoning of draft evaders. As quickly, however, came a new spirit of revisionary uplift with Ronald Reagan's "Noble Cause," which in turn now seems to continue its projection into post-Desert Storm and post-9/11 triumphalism.

Meanwhile in popular culture remembering nearly a half century later, the nation has produced an immense body of work about the war in literature, film, music, and the visual arts, with multiple National Book Awards, Pulitzer Prizes, and Academy Awards. Print titles alone currently number around thirty thousand, totaling perhaps somewhere around three trillion words. With its words quite literally engraved in stone, there is also the National Vietnam War Memorial—reportedly now the most visited location in the nation's capital—with its 58,282 names of the American dead.

Still, in all this, there remains one signal matter of memorialization and quantification that we have still not come to terms with. It concerns the numbers of all the other nameless, faceless dead of the war nobody wants to remember. I speak of course of the Vietnamese—according to estimates, between two and four million of them.

To be sure, within even the earliest American contributions to the literature of the war one could find serious claims concerning the heedless infliction of death and destruction by US forces upon the Vietnamese. These were, for the most part, half-read or dismissed, even when they were meticulous in their research and documentation, in such distinguished early accounts such as Jonathan Schell's *The Village of Ben Suc* (1967) and *The Military Half* (1968). In more literarily rendered antiwar texts, poets such as Robert Bly, Denise Levertov, Allen Ginsberg, Galway Kinnell, and protest singers such as Joan Baez, Bob Dylan, and Phil Ochs dealt in recurrent images of genocidal violence. Across the cultural spectrum, "Counting Small-Boned Bodies" and "Wichita Vortex Sutra" merged with "Blowin' in the Wind" and "A Hard Rain is Gonna Fall." In other forms such as fiction and drama, Norman Mailer's virtuoso experimental novel *Why Are We in Vietnam?* and Arthur Kopit's now largely forgotten play *Indians* offered similar images, albeit through complex strategies of symbolic indirection. Eventually, as the war widened, what Alfred Kazin called "the manic plenitude of American destructiveness there" would become a major trope in popular culture representations of the war, ranging from journalism and reportage to memoir, novel, poem, play, and film. Indeed, in what came to be two of the most widely renowned works of literary journalism to emerge from the conflict, Michael Herr's *Dispatches* and Frances Fitzgerald's *Fire in the Lake*, it came to sound as the war's persistent mythic undertone.

"You'd stand there nailed in your tracks sometimes," writes Herr, "no bearings and none in sight, thinking *Where the fuck am I*, fallen into some unnatural East-West interface, a California corridor cut and burned deep into Asia, and once we'd done it, we couldn't remember what for. Anyhow," he goes on, "you couldn't use standard methods to date the doom; might as well say that Vietnam was where the Trail of Tears was headed all along . . . might as well just lay it on the proto-Gringos who found the New England woods too raw and empty for their peace and filled them up with their own imported devils." Meanwhile, "the best-armed patrols in history went out after services to feed smoke to people whose priests could let themselves burn down to consecrated ash on street corners. . . . Holy war, long-nose jihad like a face off between one god who would hold the coonskin to the wall while we nailed it up, and another whose detachment would see the blood run out of ten generations, it that was how long it took for the wheel to go around. There was such a dense concentration of American energy there," he writes, in telling appraisal, "American and essentially adolescent, if that energy could have been channeled into anything more than noise, waste and pain, it would have lighted up Indochina for a thousand years."

Fitzgerald, viewing the war through the contexts of Vietnamese life and culture, spoke of the US military presence on the Asian landscape in comparably surreal figurations:

> Young men from the small towns of America, the GIs who came to Vietnam found themselves in a place halfway round the earth among people with whom they could make no human contact. Like an Orwellian army, they knew everything about military tactics, but nothing about who they were or who the enemy was. And they found themselves not attacking fixed positions but walking through the jungle or through villages among small yellow people, as strange and exposed among them as if they were Martians. Their buddies were killed by land mines, sniper fire, and mortar attacks, but the enemy remained invisible, not only in the jungle but among the people of the villages—an almost metaphysical enemy who inflected upon them heat, boredom, terror, and death, and

gave them nothing to show for it—no territory taken, no visible sing of progress except the bodies of small yellow men.

Herr's text, here and elsewhere, remains the *locus classicus* marking the Vietnam War as the inevitable catastrophic end point of the American historical mission, the country's myths of historical innocence and geopolitical invincibility now fused with the endless capacity for dealing death. "America's heart of darkness trip," it would come to be called, playing itself out in tropes and figures of ungoverned violence and destruction; or, as aptly, in the title of the film still considered the great iconic Hollywood production of the era, *Apocalypse Now*. Yet for all the flashy metonymy, in the works of Herr, Coppola, and their contemporaries—*The Deer Hunter*, for instance, with its recurrent figure of Russian Roulette, or *Rambo/First Blood*, with its renegade Green Beret bringing the war back home in an orgy of heartland destruction—one still never quite gets to the actual Americans and the Vietnamese involved save as American popular culture conceit. Near the beginning of *Apocalypse Now*, bedecked with crossed sabres, napalm madness burning in his eyes, Wagner blaring from huge helicopter speakers, an American cavalry colonel stages an airmobile assault on an alleged Viet Cong village by the sea *because it is a prime surfing location*. At the end, the equally mad apostate Green Beret colonel Kurtz, dying in his jungle imperium—himself now both the master of war and the scapegoat blood-god—issues his great Conradian summons of death: "Exterminate the brutes." Meanwhile, as if to complete the apocalyptic design, the Marlow-like narrator-protagonist, Captain Willard, calls in the final visitation of fire and sword in an annihilating jet airstrike.

The second uncannily apposite figuration, in Fitzgerald's now classic text, speaks to Herr's across an abyss of culture and consciousness, although with much the same mythic implication. Appearing in a crucial chapter titled "States of Mind," the trope is that of catastrophically alien worlds of culture and consciousness. Remorseless, inhuman, near-robotic, American myrmidons move about on a landscape of endless threat and menace, soldiers of the empire lashing out endlessly in their pain and frustration, fear, and waste. Thus in combat memoirs, novels, poems, plays, and films, one finds a ubiquitous core of atrocity, a strain of bloody murder serving as the recurrent focus of national guilt, the image of the American soldier as conscript killer. In major print texts by Philip Caputo, Ron Kovic, Gustav Hasford, James Webb, Tim O'Brien, and Larry Heinemann; in movies such as *Apocalypse Now*, *The Deer Hunter*, *Platoon*, *Casualties of War*, and *Full Metal Jacket*, some dark act of horror involving a war crime or torture/murder atrocity is repeatedly committed by average soldiers against Vietnamese prisoners and other noncombatants, not to mention—in a notable number of instances—against each other. In text after text, it is the ultimate formulaic moment, the combat equivalent of the Freudian primal scene. It is as if the war has bred some guilty terrible thing; some awful, inexpiable curse for having been a part of it. Yet the primary focus of guilt and/or expiation remains American. Having survived the Manichean struggle of the sergeants Barnes and Elias, not to mention a near massacre at an overrun firebase near the Cambodian border, Chris Taylor (emphasis on ChrisT), the "reborn" narrator-protagonist of *Platoon*, lifts off in the helicopter that will begin both his geographical and his psychological journey home. The defiant boy marines at the end of *Full Metal Jacket* march back to barracks from the surreal inferno of Hue City singing the Mickey Mouse anthem. Here, two classic works by Tim O'Brien, considered the fictional laureate of the war, put a succinct point to the limits of the mythic conceit. In *The Things They Carried*, an aging Vietnam veteran, a literary author-narrator named "Tim O'Brien" attempts to keep faith with the redeeming power of fiction. He tries keep "the dead alive," he says, "with stories." In a subsequent, much darker novel, *In the Lake of the Woods*, the story of a Vietnam veteran protagonist named John "Sorcerer" Wade—who, in his aspiration to high political office has nearly managed to erase from all official record his participation in the My Lai massacre—testifies to the brute intransigence of fact. At the limits of writing itself, O'Brien tells us, a thing so immense in the evidentiary burden of countless Vietnamese bodies cannot and will not be airbrushed from history.

And it is just this that has remained missing for the most part from a body of literature and film frequently outdone by its own metaphorical inventiveness and virtuosity. On the one hand, the figure of horror has been that of stoned 1960s apocalypticism. On the other, it has been that of surreal, involuted, even insane metafiction. In either case, it becomes a literature of remorseless violence and destruction devoid of virtually any mention of larger purpose, let alone sacrifice, ironic or otherwise. Beyond the power even of the great tropes of twentieth century conflict—the familiar evocations of pointless mutual military slaughter or of the absurd omnipotence of the war-breeding system—it is a literature of sheer, unredeemed killing, with the Vietnamese awaiting only the dread enumerations. Now that work has been done. On the basis of new archival research and forensic study of Vietnamese casualties during the American war, we now have it by the numbers. And the numbers—where those of US sacrifice continue to be dwarfed by those of the Vietnamese—may at last be allowed to speak for themselves.

After so many years, one might ask, where have these harrowing statistics finally come from? Most prominent is a 2008 UK survey from the *British Medical Journal*, the most prestigious of all such British publications. There the death estimate for the period of the American war is 3.8 million Vietnamese. This is further divided into an estimated one million- plus military dead and a corresponding two million-plus civilian dead. Also projected as to Vietnamese families are figures of 1 million war widows and 800,000–1.3 million war orphans. Comparable overall results are postulated in a Harvard University-University of Washington study, with at least 2 million civilian deaths paired with 5.3 million wounded, and 11.7 million forced refugees. 4.8 million were further exposed to heavy doses of toxic herbicides. This is in a country with a 1965 population North and South—at the beginning of major U.S. military action—of thirty-eight million.

Indeed, once the doors of history and memory are opened to such statistical fact, everywhere one looks the numbers come flooding in. Accordingly, as an account of what has now come to be called "asymmetrical war" beyond literary tropes and figures, beyond even language itself, they now comprise a discourse of sheer overwhelming numeracy. Periodic campaigns of strategic bombing over North Vietnam are conservatively estimated to have resulted in sixty-five thousand civilian dead. Secret bombings of Cambodia killed forty thousand more. We will never know how many were killed and wounded by bombings in South Vietnam, where ordnance included high explosive, antipersonnel fragmentation, daisy cutter, flechette, and napalm. In total, over a land area comparable to Florida from roughly Orlando southward, through B-52 strikes and missions by US Navy, Air Force, and Marine fighter-bomber aircraft, American forces dropped approximately twice as many explosives as dropped in all theaters during World War II, with the usual figure given as 4 million tons, as opposed to the World War II total of 2.7. Altogether, total individual aircraft sorties are estimated at 3.4 million. Aerial spraying of toxic chemical defoliant, most notably Agent Orange, is estimated as having resulted in four hundred thousand maimed or killed by poisoning; and, in the years following, five hundred thousand more birth defects—figures of horror matched only by the insouciance with which the latter activity was designated by the Americans as "Operation Ranch Hand," with the motto "Only you can prevent forests."

Add to this the aerial violence delivered by flotillas of armed helicopters on a daily basis and one simply despairs of even estimating additional totals of Vietnamese killed by rockets, automatic cannons, and door-mounted machine guns. American representations of the helicopter war then and now have tended to focus on infantry airlift, supply, reconnaissance, and medical evacuation. Less known was the rampant killing from the air in helicopter assault and ground support missions, in aerial sweeps of larger open areas designated as free-fire zones, during forced evacuations of villages, and in wanton murder of peasants simply claimed as additions to the body count. Over the course of the war, helicopters of all types flew an estimated thirty-six million sorties.

Similarly, no one will ever know remotely the full number of deaths caused by the constant fall of artillery from the demilitarized zone southward. Fire missions and types of weaponry and ammunition alone were of a nearly inexhaustible variety and plenitude. Artillery units fired 105-, 155-, 175-millimeter and 8-inch rounds from howitzers and self-propelled tracked vehicles. Mortars included 81-millimeter and 4.2-inch types. Units in the field fired preplotted defensive concentrations, referred to as Defcons. Random targets were selected for Harassment and Interdiction, otherwise known as H&I. Nearly any enemy contact could warrant a fire support mission. Altogether, an estimate of total munitions fired comes to somewhere around fifteen million tons, again largely on the most populous half of the country. When US troops were hit by errant artillery, the result was termed Friendly Fire—surely one of the better Orwellianisms of the war. But again it now seems surely to have been the innumerable Vietnamese on the landscape who took the brunt of it.

There remains close combat on the ground—rightly noted by Philip Caputo as the worst kind for indiscriminate killing, combining civil war with guerrilla warfare. In their initial actions, US major-unit forces began the campaign with the worst way to fight the war with respect to finding the communist forces while distinguishing the military enemy from the country's civilian inhabitants. Massive, World War II-style big-unit operations included Attleboro, Junction City, Cedar Falls, and White Wing (with the latter, at the behest of a nervous Lyndon Johnson, renamed from the original "Masher.") After initial large-unit clashes in the Ia Drang with the First Air Cavalry revealed enormous American advantages in firepower and mobility, communist forces reverted to small-unit, hit-and-run tactics. The Americans continued their big sweeps, cordon and control, and evacuation of villagers to strategic hamlets. The main mission became Search and Destroy. Victory on the battlefield devolved to a single standard of measurement. Body count. As recorded in literature and film, the war became a set of variations on one ubiquitous killer joke with a Vietnamese laugh line. Question: "How can you shoot women and children?" Answer: "It's easy, you just don't have to lead 'em so much." American soldiers, given to their boyish sports metaphors, quickly learned the name of the game. "Bag 'em and tag 'em." "If they're dead, they're VC." Any doubts were resolved by the TOG rule. TOG: "They're only gooks." For ranking officers in the field, "managers of violence" given a chance to prove their professional talents in revolving six-month command tours, the metaphors of success were predictably industrial. Good officers were producers of enemy bodies, meeting weekly and monthly quotas. At the operational level, with unbelievably advanced weaponry leveled against an almost impossibly poor and wretched people, in James William Gibson's phrase, it became Technowar on a scale never dreamed. The country became a destruction and death factory, even down to the very ground on which human beings walked. Across the landscape—the rice fields of the Delta, the forests of the midsection Annamese Cordillera, the populous coastal lowlands, the barren DMZ—were sowed a murderous crop of chemical toxins, booby traps, land mines, and unexploded munitions that extended also into Laos and Cambodia. Behind the pretense of what Michael Herr calls the American mission's "overripe bullshit . . . 'Hearts and Minds, Peoples of the Republic, tumbling dominoes, maintaining the equilibrium of the Dingdong by containing the ever encroaching Doodah,' everyone knew what only the occasional young soldier might be willing to say. 'All that's just a *load*, man. We're here to kill gooks. Period.'"

As a result, during roughly five years of large-scale American military involvement, we practiced wanton killing and destruction against a supposedly allied people on a scale that by any analogy would have been unthinkable in occupied France or Italy during World War II. By the end of the third year, in early 1969, when I served as an armored cavalry platoon leader, my own topographical maps in the III Corps region centered on Saigon—extending from the South China Sea to the Parrot's Beak region on the Cambodian border—were dense with names and locations of villages in Long Khanh and Binh Thuy province. The last US units had been in there during Tet 1968. Not a single village remained standing. It was like the surface of the moon. I do not exaggerate to say that once we moved off the roads, not a single civilian habitation could be found on the landscape. It was that kind of war. As tragically, the expectation of such wanton American over expenditure of violence came to be fundamental to the National Liberation Front/North Vietnamese Army (NLF/NVA) battle doctrine. In the early big-unit encounters and later in the small-unit engagements, the American tactic was to withdraw and call in massive firepower: artillery—attack helicopter—tactical jet airstrike—repeat as needed. The enemy stayed close. Hugging the belt, they called it. Meanwhile, the firepower could be counted on to cause maximum civilian casualties. A sniper bullet or a rocket propelled grenade from a village, a few mortar or rocket rounds, led to a complete breakdown of what was called fire discipline. Most notably in the Tet Offensive, it worked to even more devastating effect in major population centers, Saigon, Can Tho, and Hue. In the latter case, the massively violent recapture of the city took three weeks. Especially toward the end, as US military discipline broke under the strain, an increasingly depopulated country became a vast de facto free-fire zone. Rules of engagement went out the window, and common infantry tactics crossed the line into military atrocities, most infamously in 1968 at My Lai. As ruefully noted by Colonel Oran Henderson, the commander of the three-battalion brigade that included the Medina company and the Calley platoon, "Every unit of brigade size has its My Lai hidden someplace." To this end, on several occasions when protocols might have required an "incident report," body counts were actually scaled down so as not to invite inquiry. Whatever the jiggling of the figures, this fact remains: overall, for the entire war, by simple mathematics, with fifty-eight thousand Americans ultimately killed versus 3.8 million Vietnamese, on any day one US death was matched by the deaths of sixty-five Vietnamese. A chapter in a book by a recent researcher on the subject is titled "A My Lai a Month." According to raw numbers, if not similarly sized incidents of mass murder, it should probably have been more like "A My Lai a Week." To borrow another's phrasing: My Lai was not aberrational, My Lai was operational.

As noted earlier, something of this was at least portended at the time, as reflected in the work of early Anglo-European writers such as Graham Greene and Bernard Fall; pioneering American journalists such as David Halberstam, Malcolm Browne, and Jonathan Schell; and early American novelists of the war such as James Crumley, Martin Russ, and William Eastlake. "They laid the bodies out in front of the spotting tower and everyone had to come see them," writes a character in Crumley's *One to Count Cadence*, "to gape at the guts hanging out of the one like an atrophied paper-mâché bag, to slap me on the shoulder, to point out my brilliant shooting." Another, in Martin Russ's *Happy Hunting Ground*, reports of a fellow soldier, after a confirmed "kill": "When I asked him to what part of the body he hit the man, he smirked and looked at me unblinking eyes, and said 'Blew the fucker's head off. Turned it to jelly.'" The tenor of Eastlake's *The Bamboo Bed* is evident in the original title of the short story out of which it grew: "The Greatest Thing since Custer." The work of reporters Ron Ridenour and Seymour Hersh led to the My Lai investigations. The subsequent years have seen revelations about the secret bombings of Laos and Cambodia; the civilian-targeted Phoenix assassination program, reportedly resulting in twenty-six thousand civilian killings with eighty-two thousand others "neutralized"; and the killing sprees conducted by units such as the Americal, 101st Airborne, 1st Air Cavalry, and 9th Infantry Divisions. Across the records of all major American formations, it is as if the war has finally uncovered its guilty secrets, frequently under the eyes of those who believed that they and their unit comrades had somehow been exempted from the ghastly inculpation. In the literature, accordingly, where once we might have accused some of the most eminent and astringent of antiwar writers—poets especially—of polemical excess, we now see that they probably did not go far enough. "This is what it's like for a rich country to make war," writes Robert Bly in "The Tooth Mother Naked at Last." "This is what it's like to bomb huts (afterward described as 'structures')/this is what it's like to kill marginal farmers (afterwards described as 'Communists')." In Galway Kinnell's "Vapor Trail Reflected in the Frog Pond," we read, "The old look on their/thick eyes/puff and foreclose by the moon. The young, heads/trailed by the beginnings of necks/shiver,/in the guarantee they shall be bodies." "What Were They Like?" asks Denise Levertov in the poem so titled. "Remember," she concludes,

most were peasants; their life
was in rice and bamboo.
When peaceful clouds were reflected in the paddies
and the water buffalo stepped surely along terraces,
maybe fathers told their sons old tales.
When bombs smashed those mirrors
there was time only to scream.

Now, after all these years, and beyond all the amassing of a vast body of text rich in National Book Awards, Pulitzer Prizes and other emblems of cultural prestige, we now have it both *on the literary record* and *by the numbers,* with full results definitively compiled and committed to the record in three major texts. From a German scholar, Bernd Greiner, we have *War without Fronts*; from US investigative journalist Deborah Nelson, *The War Behind Me*; and from forensic researcher Nick Turse, *Kill Anything That Moves.* All are based on a little-known (until the end of the century) and now no longer available source maintained in the National Archives with the title *Vietnam War Crimes Working Group.* Compiled in the wake of My Lai on orders from Secretary of Defense Melvin Laird, it contains nine thousand pages of incident reports and testimony. Its purpose seems to have had nothing to do with instructional or preventative purposes, but rather with avoiding being caught flat-footed should more war crime information be publically reported. If this was the case, the mission failed miserably.

The three resulting texts are almost unbearable to read, with their sheer weight and density of documentation. Overwhelming, appalling, numbing, are some of the words that come to mind. Any American reader, veteran or nonveteran, will be simply plunged into depression to know that the nation's military forces had been part of *that.* Report follows upon report of the torture, abuse, wounding, and killing of unarmed civilians, in the case of women with rape frequently followed by murder. Driving incidents abound with accounts of hit and run, intentional collision and injury, throwing C-ration cans, knocking people off bicycles, killing water buffalos, pigs, ducks, chickens, pet dogs and cats, shouting racial epithets and sexual slurs.

The books come at a crucial time. Back in the world, as we used to call it, nearly five decades later current popular culture remembering of the war for the most part continues a long slide into self-comforting accommodation. In high school or college, students may read a chapter or so of Tim O'Brien's *The Things They Carried*, with emphasis on the redemptory power of stories and perhaps the occasional sidelong tear for American boys in the age of My Lai; *Forrest Gump* now stands as the twentieth most watched US movie of all time, with the nearest other Vietnam War entry, *Platoon*, at two hundred. (In the former, the hero, an inspired idiot, decidedly a lover not a fighter, wins the Congressional Medal of Honor not for killing Vietnamese but for rescuing Americans; in the process he becomes an icon of the antiwar movement.) Musical remembering runs to oldies soundtracks, the Rolling Stones, the Animals, Jim Morrison and the Doors. Actually, the hit most likely to be associated by today's Americans with the war is Bruce Springsteen's "Born in the USA," with its celebration of the once-despised vet rising to a new anthem of national pride. The Vietnam Wall, initially decried as a shameful gash in the earth, has had its starkness buffered by two additional, more-affirming statues, one for the infantrymen and one for the nurses.

Amid current wars and rumors of wars, still, why this new dredging up of horrors a half-century old? Here I can only speak for myself—although I would honestly like to think that, beyond the Vietnamese, I also honor the memory of the vast preponderance of my fellow combatant generation of the war. The fact of the matter is that we are old men, starting to die. We may have once been, according to Michael Herr's memorable phrasing, a bunch of rock and roll kids with one foot in the grave. Now we are in every sense the Winter Soldiers. To paraphrase James Webb, in an epigraph to his novel *Fields of Fire*, we were not Bundy's kids, or McNamara's; we were at the end of the line and we knew it; and we knew also that we were alone. Here too, nobody ever said it better than the ubiquitous Michael Herr:

> Was it possible that they were there and not haunted? No, not possible, not a chance, I know I wasn't the only one. Where are they now? (Where am I now?) I stood as close to them as I could without actually being one of them, and then I stood as far back as I could without leaving the planet. Disgust doesn't begin to describe what they made me feel, they threw people out of helicopters, tied people up and put the dogs on them. Brutality was just a word in my mouth before that. But disgust was only one color in the whole mandala, gentleness and pity were other colors, there wasn't a color left out. I think that those people who used to say that they only wept for the Vietnamese never really wept for anyone at all if they couldn't squeeze out at least one for these men and boys where they died or had their lives cracked open for them . . .

For what it would also cost us over the years, I cite a passage from Larry Heinemann's *Close Quarters*, a novel of heavy-weapons, mechanized unit war-

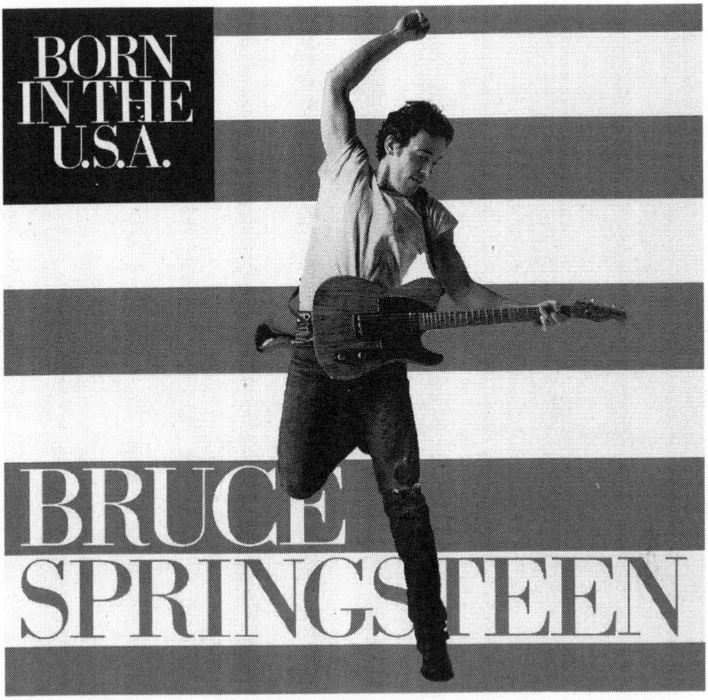

Figure 12.1 "Born in the USA" album cover, Bruce Springsteen, 1984. Columbia Records, 1984.

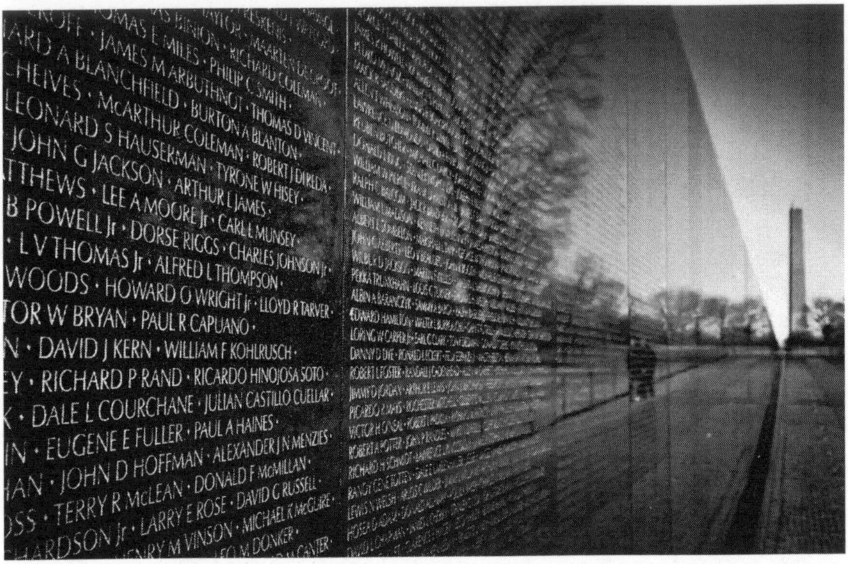

Figure 12.2 Vietnam War Memorial, Washington, DC.

fare I associate closely with my own service. "I have traveled to a place where the dead lie above the ground in rows and bunches," he writes. "Time has gone somewhere without me. This is not my country, not my time. . . . I hear voices, I have seen a wraith, Ma. He wore black boots and britches and strange livery. He talked to me, he whispered, he laughed. He touched my stomach with the back of his hand, like people will put an arm on your shoulder when they speak, and it burns."

And it burns. Anyone who went there, fifty years later, feels the dread complicity in the thing. This is what we now have to say one last time for younger people. This is what they need to know. This is how it turned out. We continue to be a nation of moral narcissists, debating the protocols of other people's genocides. Meanwhile, the grimness of our own record continues to echo down the corridors of history.

For the US military engaged in the latest wars of American empire, the emphasis has been on public relations: "Learning the Lessons"; "Correcting the Mistakes." As to the politics of military sacrifice, the draft has been replaced by a volunteer army. Deployment is by unit rather than by individual replacement. Heavy commitments have been made to PTSD counseling and educational benefits. What really sells best in our recent military adventures are happy numbers: extremely low US casualties—in more than ten years, four thousand-plus fatalities in Iraq and slightly more than two thousand in Afghanistan. Almost no mention is made of dead Iraqis and Afghans. And certainly no one even gets near such phrasings as "Body Count" or "Kill Ratio." Most lately the emphasis has been on drone attacks, making the business of military killing nearly as sanitary as one can get.

To many of us, this only compounds the urgency with which we need to enter a new phase of remembering before it is too late, of remembering the costs to countless others of an American way of thinking about the world, our obstinate, incorrigible belief in ourselves as the Redeemer Nation. As we get better and better with the numbers, especially where American bodies are concerned, we simultaneously reinforce our bloodstained myths of historical innocence and geopolitical invincibility. Fifty years after the first US units went into Vietnam, we still persist as heedlessly as ever in the assumption that millennia-old non-Western cultures really deep down inside want to be a two hundred-year-old Western democracy.

This, then, is the service done by Greiner, Nelson, and Turse to the American and Vietnamese dead of the Vietnam War at least, and in some degree to those who have followed in the latest American wars. In their new archival studies, coupled with follow-up investigations on hundreds of reports and interviews with thousands of US veterans and Vietnamese survivors, they make the numbers speak. The show us in the most dreadful detail that Michael

Herr was right when he wrote, "Vietnam was where all the mythic tracks intersected." When it was over, we knew it was as we were warned in the dread phrasings of the beloved English Bible on which most of us grew up. We became a curse unto the nations, a horror and a byword.

The Vietnamese have an old saying: "that's true and there's a poem to prove it." If such is the case, no one, I would propose, has fulfilled the bargain with the burden of the Vietnam War in American remembering better than W.D. Ehrhart, the dean of a generation of Vietnam soldier-poets, in a small masterpiece titled "Making the Children Behave:"

Do they think of me now
in those strange Asian villages
where nothing ever seemed
quite human
but myself
and my few grim friends
moving through them
hunched
in lines?
When they tell stories to their children
of the evil
that awaits misbehavior
is it me they conjure?

"You'd better listen to your parents or the Americans will come and get you." You can almost hear it now in Bagdad, Kabul, maybe Damascus. To borrow a chapter heading from a recent text on veterans' witness, soldiers frequently come out of wars with things that stain the soul. Sometimes those things are so large that they stain the soul of a nation. Until Americans are willing to face those things about the Vietnam War in the full weight of their hideous enumerations, all the words we have expended to date over this epochal passage in our history will have amounted to nothing.

Conclusion

The Forever Wars

In 1972, an American Vietnam War veteran named Joe Haldeman published a novelistic memoir about his 1968–69 tour of duty as a combat engineer. He called it *War Year*. It largely came and went. Nobody wanted to read about it. In 1974 he tried a new, more adventurous synthesis of experience and art. He published a second novel of combat, this time in the guise of futuristic science fiction. It detailed the experiences of a protagonist similar to the narrator of *War Year* projected forward thirty years, now drafted into the army through the Elite Conscription Act of 1996. His mission, as a member of what we would now call a Special Operations unit, is to defeat a strange, remorselessly violent enemy from outer space called the Taurans. Soldier experience involves multiple tours, including frequent interstellar goings and returns, coping with time warps and other forms of psychological and historical alienation, and ending for most combatants in inevitable extinction. The units deployed are composed of both male and female combatants. Their relationships include battlefield comradeship and sexual fraternization. The military characters are death soldiers at death's door, after all. Their choices are to kill or to die. If they do not stop killing, the war will go on. The longer the war goes on, the more likely it is that they will be killed. The war, it turns out, is pointless. Its causes were bogus to begin with. Its results resolve nothing. Haldeman called the novel *The Forever War*. Today, it continues to be regarded as a science fiction classic.

In 2008 award-winning journalist Dexter Filkins published a book now regarded as one of the indispensable chronicles on the American wars in the Middle East. Its first scenes are set in Afghanistan in 1998, three full years before the 9/11 al-Qaeda attacks on the World Trade Center. Its reaches its conclusion in Baghdad, as the civil and religious war provoked by the 2003 American invasion still rages. In between a journalistic history unfolds, not unlike that of Michael Herr's *Dispatches*, of both the ongoing Afghanistan and Iraq Wars. As with Herr's Vietnam, from the policymakers in Washington to the civilian and military war managers, not to mention the American soldiers and marines on the ground, the experience depicted is essentially a war without history and a war without memory. It has begun for reasons that nearly no one can remember, let alone explain. It goes on because nobody can stop the killing. Without a trace of irony, Filkins titled the book *The Forever War*. It is considered a classic of military journalism and reportage.

Thus the latest forever wars. And thus some of the ways in which they are already in the process of being mythologized into the latest genealogies of art, history, and memory. Filkins is now regarded—not without reason—as the Michael Herr of the Desert Wars. A novel by an infantry combat veteran Kevin Powers, *The Yellow Birds* is now considered the Iraq War equivalent of Tim O'Brien's *The Things They Carried*. *Billy Lynn's Long Halftime Walk*, by another veteran, Ben Fountain, is now considered the era's *Catch-22*. Eloquent nonfiction titles include Craig Mullaney's *The Unforgiving Minute*, Nathaniel Fick's *One Bullet Away*, David Finkel's *The Good Soldiers*, Jake Tapper's *The Outpost*, and Sebastian Junger's *War*. The urge of art, history, and memory toward popular-culture representations likewise continues. The Vietnam War, with its dark notoriety, produced a bumper crop of Long Range Reconnaissance Patrol (LRRP), Special Forces, Navy SEAL, and Marine Recon books; the mass-market adventure chronicles of Afghanistan and Iraq now outnumber such productions. It is fair to say that movie equivalents for *Saving Private Ryan*, *Apocalypse Now*, or *Platoon* may emerge from among such offerings as *Stop Loss*, *The Hurt Locker*, or *Zero Dark Thirty*.

Even here we test the limits of traditional genre in what is now a world of war increasingly beyond traditional definition or representation. In a new age of global terror and random upheaval, what does one now make of twenty-first-century war-writing such as Jonathan Safran Foer's *Extremely Loud and Incredibly Close*, Khalid Hosseini's *Kite Runner*, Ha Jin's *War Trash*, or Ishmael Beah's *A Long Way Gone*? Or of postapocalyptic films such as *Oblivion*, *Elysium*, *After Earth*, and *World War Z*? And these are just examples of print and film, already endlessly outpaced by new forms and technologies of representation and dissemination. For instance, the spectacular tale of the Chechen bombers of the Boston Marathon was in every sense a production of the new electronic media, from an Internet video onward. In our evolving visions of war in art, history, and memory, the materials of human experience and imagination will continue to be passed through this new matrix of technological consciousness.

Whatever the newest technologies of representation, they will further continue to be stretched by the very global expanse of the subject. Somalia, Yemen, Syria, Egypt, Sudan, Congo, Central African Republic, Darfur, Mali, Nigeria, Mauretania, Korea, Afghanistan, Myanmar, Colombia, Mexico, Pakistan, Chechnya, Dagestan, Israel, the Palestinian territories: these are all names on a map. They are also names comprising a current cartography of global war. Call it what one will: the extension "of political intercourse with the intermixing of other means" (the actual German is "*des politischen Verkehrs mit Einmischung underer Mittel*"); or the primal curse of human nature, the taking in armed combat of a human life by another human, the oldest ritual slaying, the propitiation of the beast. And then still find it over all the endless millennia perpetually committed to history and memory, by combatant and noncombatant alike, in the mysterious rites of symbolic representation we call art.

Thus the ongoing dreadful fascination, in all its forms, of the deadly business we call war. In this context, we may return to my opening questions. Why do people make art out of war? What is the human fascination with war as a subject of popular culture myth? What strange imperatives of instinct and/or imagination provoke us to keep going back to it in history or memory? In addition, other questions emerge from the preceding chapters. How do we as readers, viewers, listeners, museum goers, and visitors to historical and memorial sites respond to such constructions of art, history, and memory in their appeals to our own mythic consciousness? What do such activities demonstrate to us about the power of myths of individual and collective heroism, of military nationhood, of victory and/or defeat? How do we differentiate myth in its conventional sense as traditional story or cultural archetype from its darker totalizing forms of religion or ideology? Is there such a thing as good war art as opposed to bad war art, real as opposed to phony, honest as opposed to dishonest, worthy versus unworthy? Does the participant or the survivor enjoy any particular authority of vision or experience? Is a spectator entitled to such authority of representation? Where does personal witness or authorial imagining slide over from moral or historical purpose to prurient sensationalism? When does it attempt to tell the whole insane truth of the thing and when does it become a pornography of violence?

These are all questions long at the heart of what Samuel Hynes has called "the soldier's tale." "Do dreams offer lessons?" writes Tim O'Brien. Do nightmares have themes, do we awaken and analyze them and live our lives and advise others as a result? Can the foot soldier teach anything important about war, merely for having been there? I think not. He can tell war stories. Wilfred Owen, writing shortly before his own death in battle, is even more succinct on the matter. "All the poet can do today," he says, "is warn."

But they are also questions, I would propose, familiar to a Homer, a Beethoven, a Tolstoy, a Shakespeare or a Stephen Crane, a Ralph Vaughan Williams, a John Singer Sargent, a John Huston, a Kurt Vonnegut, a Virginia Woolf, or a Maya Lin. All great artists, some of them ex-combatants, some of them imaginative creators, inhabiting in one way or another what I have called death's gray landscape, they are part of the long roster of those have tried to come to terms with the dreadful fascination of war. They will be joined in our own time in what is already a global community of creative witness by others who will achieve their visions through new forms, technologists, and media representations as yet undreamed. They will be creative technologies, science fictionists in every sense. Yet as surely as the first oral poets, dramatists, and storytellers, creators of music, painting, sculpture, and dance, and their inheritors who successively discovered writing, print, photography, movies, radio, TV, music and video recording, and the new electronic media, many of them will also succeed in making art. At its most highly achieved, they will remind us of how we are incessantly born and reborn of war as the creations of our own history and memory; and that will be to the good.

In the same moment, as I move toward the end of a decades-long encounter, both personal and professional, with such artists and their texts—intertwined as it is with my own telling of the soldier's tale—I find that it is time for me to leave those questions to someone else. To put it simply, I must confess that in surveying the vast cultural record of the latest wars of American empire, I no longer have the heart for it, for the ongoing journey of chronicling, as Tim O'Brien has called it, the lives of the dead. The latest crop of maimed, bleeding, dying civilians somewhere amid the rubble, victims of a car bomb, an air strike, a gas attack; another American infantry unit getting blown or shot to pieces out on the end of nowhere for next to nothing: the stories all begin to blend together. For one who has been granted the gift of survival all these years, it all becomes part of a vast, irredeemable sadness. Accordingly, I now find myself at least aspiring to the path laid out for me by an earlier writer-critic, like myself an ex-combatant from a modern war who spent most of his literary life trying to come to terms with it both personally and professionally.

That figure, now largely forgotten, is Sir Herbert Read, a British veteran of the 1914–1918 fighting in Flanders and Picardy and in his own time a widely published aesthetic theorist and critical spokesman for art between the wars. Here I find my own new marching orders, so to speak, in an astonishing letter written by Lieutenant Read to his family from the western front. The letter is not about fighting or writing, but about reading and living. It is, that is to say, about art. "I have started *Walden*," he says matter-of-factly, "and find it full of wisdom, especially in the use to be made of life." As with more famous contemporaries such as Robert Graves, Siegfried Sassoon, Edmund Blunden, and others, Read went on briefly to become a memoirist; but his real fame will always be that of a writer-critic productively engaged over a subsequent lifetime with the theory and practice of aesthetics. This now seems a good turn for me to make as well. Seventy seems a good time to be moving on. The subject might even be Thoreau. Or Gustav Mahler. Or Mark Twain. It will be something like that, in the time I may yet be allowed, having to do with the use to be made of life.

Notes on Sources and Further Reading

Introduction: A Dreadful Fascination

The late Paul Fussell's *The Great War and Modern Memory* (New York: Oxford UP, 1975) remains the definitive text on representations of modern war. Relating to my own experience as a combatant and as a writer about the American war in Vietnam, Tim O'Brien's novel-critique *The Things They Carried* (New York: Houghton-Mifflin, 1990) has now achieved a similar classic status.

1. Arms and the Bard: Soldiering in Shakespeare

Jonathan Bates's engaging biography of Shakespeare is *Soul of the Age: the Life, Mind and World of William Shakespeare* (New York: Penguin, 2009). Harold Bloom's well-known claim for the author's unique genius is inscribed in the title of his 1998 *Shakespeare and the Invention of the Human* (New York: Riverhead Books, 1998). Coppelia Kahn's "Remembering Shakespeare Imperially," a review of Israel Gollancz's *Homage to Shakespeare*, appeared in *Shakespeare Quarterly*, Volume 52, Number 4, Winter 2001. Film versions and adaptations abound of Shakespeare's plays, including *Hamlet, Othello, Macbeth, Lear, Henry IV, Henry V, Romeo and Juliet, As You Like It, The Taming of the Shrew, A Midsummer Night's Dream*, and others. For the general reader, a substantial literature exists as well on Shakespeare and film, including *The Cambridge Companion to Shakespeare and Film*, edited by Russell Jackson (Cambridge, 2007), and *Shakespeare and Film: A Norton Guide*, edited by Samuel Crowl (New York, 2007). All Shakespeare text citations are taken from Stanley Wells and Gary Taylor's *The Complete Works, Compact Edition* (Oxford: Oxford UP, 1988).

2. Bury Their Hearts at Horseshoe Bend

As noted in the text, the Battle of Horseshoe Bend been has been locally and regionally mythologized in various forms over the years, including as a classic nineteenth-century history, a novel, and an epic poem. The US Park Service has also done an immaculate job of historical preservation and documentation at the battlefield site in east central Alabama. In the twenty-first century, accurate, readable scholarship has finally caught up with legend in *Tohopeka: Rethinking the Creek War and the War of 1812*, edited by Kathryn H. Braund (Tuscaloosa: University of Alabama Press, 2012).

3. Ted Turner et al. at Gettysburg; or, Reenactors in the Attic

For all the impingements of popular commercialism, the US National Military Park at Gettysburg remains an exemplar of battlefield historical preservation still renowned for its military "readability" as a model of modern warfare. In the early part of the twentieth century, it was the object of a field trip by every graduating class of West Point cadets. In the middle and later decades, it came under threat from various attempts at for-profit encroachment, including a car dealership and a viewing tower, but somehow not only survived the threats but finally outlived them. The latest feature of park stewardship has been the restoration of the actual topography—forest, field, plant species, etc.—to contemporary depictions of the landscape. A recent study, *Gettysburg: The Last Invasion* by Alan Guelzo (New York: Vintage, 2013), provides a fresh, fast-moving, and newly informative view of persons and events.

4. What Lady Butler Knew

Remnants of an Army was shown at the 1879 Royal Academy Exhibition and eventually purchased by the Tate Britain. It furthered Butler's reputation for military realism gained in *The Roll Call* (1874) and lead to perhaps her most famous battle painting, *Scotland Forever!* (1881). A notable antiwar painting of the same period was the 1879 *Listed for the Connaught Rangers*. Major/Brevet Lieutenant Colonel Patrick Butler not only survived the war but also published a memoir, *A Galloper at Ypres* (London: Fisher Unwin, 1920), with a frontispiece by his mother.

5. Qingdao and the Archaeologies of War

I discovered the history of the Battle of Qingdao, the only combat engagement in Asia between major World War I powers, during a guest professorship at Ocean University. The battle is memorialized through a military museum and the preserved fortifications on Qingdao Hill. The city, directly across the Yellow Sea from Inchon, Korea, remains a true archeological text of its histories. A fifteenth-century temple is a tourist site on the seafront. Buildings connected with German, Japanese, and American occupiers are marked as historical preservation sites. The new city is a modern commercial metropolis. As a resort, it features a twenty-six mile beachfront promenade lined by vacation high rises. Far beyond the financial reach of most Chinese, these locals are said to be attractive especially to very rich Koreans.

6. Ralph Vaughan Williams's Long Journey Out of War

Peter Ackroyd's trenchant assessment of the "Englishness" of Ralph Vaughan Williams's body of music appears in *Albion: The Origins of the English Imagination* (London: Chatto, 2002). For Alain Frogley, see "Constructing English in Music," the opening essay in his edited volume *Vaughan Williams Studies* (Cambridge: Cambridge UP, 1996). Biographical studies cited include Simon Heffer's *Vaughan Williams* (Boston: Northeastern UP, 2001) and that of the composer's wife, Ursula Vaughan Williams's *R.V.W.* (Oxford: Oxford UP, 1964). The 2010 documentary DVD *O Thou Transcendent* provides a splendid overview of Vaughan Williams's life and career.

7. History and Memory in the Great War Paintings of John Singer Sargent

Sargent's horrifying depiction of British wounded in *Gassed* was nonetheless voted 1919 Picture of the Year by the Royal Academy of Arts. *General Officers of the Great War* is now displayed at the National Portrait Gallery with two other commissioned companion pieces, *Statesmen of World War I* by Sir James Guthrie and *Naval Officers of World War* I by Sir Arthur Stockdale Cope.

8. The Great Party Crasher: *Mrs. Dalloway*, *The Great Gatsby*, and the Cultures of World War I Remembering

It is not often remarked how frequently war appears in the works of Virginia Woolf. The titular protagonist of Woolf's third novel, *Jacob's Room* (1922), is killed in World War I, as is Andrew Ramsay in *To the Lighthouse* (1927). Woolf's posthumously published final novel, *Between the Acts* (1941), is set ominously just before the outbreak of World War II. At the time of her suicide, the new war had begun and Woolf's London home was destroyed in a German air raid. As has been noted, Ernest Hemingway's *The Sun Also Rises*, roughly contemporary with *Mrs. Dalloway* and *The Great Gatsby*, centers on war-damaged characters from the 1914–18 conflict. It should be noted that nearly ten years later in Fitzgerald's *Tender Is the Night* (1934), the culture of World War I remembering dominates the novel in both form and theme in quite similar ways.

9. What Kurt Vonnegut Saw in World War II That Made Him Insane (Along with Billy Pilgrim, Rabo Karabekian, Eliot Rosewater, and Others)

All references to Kurt Vonnegut fiction titles are taken from the uniform Dell paperback editions. References to *Fates Worse than Death* come from the 1992 Berkeley edition. For readers interested in a memoir of the Dresden firebombing prisoner-survivors as a group, see *Shadows of Slaughterhouse Five: Recollections and Reflections of the Ex-POWs of Schlachthof Fünf, Dresden, Germany* by Ervin E. Szpek Jr., Frank J. Idakowski, and Heidi M. Szpek (iUniverse, 2008).

10. Script by Stephen Crane, Novel by John Huston, Movie by MGM

Lillian Ross's 1952 book on the making of the film version of *The Red Badge of Courage* titled *Picture* (New York: Rinehart) remains the definitive text on the subject; on the crucial roles played in the process by producer David O. Selznick, director John Huston, and costars Audie Murphy and Bill Mauldin; and on the revisions resulting in the final film text as it is known to twentieth-century audiences. Quoted material concerning on-set conflicts comes from Lawrence Grobel's *The Hustons: the Life and Times of a Dynasty* (New York: Scribners, 1989). Bill Mauldin's classic GI cartoon collection *Up Front* (New York: Henry Holt) was published just as the war ended in 1945. A movie version appeared in 1951. Audie Murphy's autobiography *To Hell and Back* (New York: Henry Holt) appeared in 1949, followed by the Technicolor movie starring Audie Murphy in 1955.

11. In the Museo de la Revolucíon; or, The Ghost of José Martí

The on-site research for this chapter was facilitated by the University of Alabama–Cuba initiative, whereby I was able to travel twice to the island for extended periods. Out of this period of work came the narrative for a photographic volume by Chip Cooper and Nestor Marti, *Old Havana/La Habana Vieja* (Tuscaloosa: University of Alabama Press, 2012), and my previous book, *The Island Called Paradise: Cuba in History, Literature, and the Arts* (Tuscaloosa: University of Alabama Press, 2014).

12. By the Numbers: Americans, Vietnamese, and the Figures of Sacrifice

No one who cares to read about the American war in Vietnam can be without two masterpieces of cultural journalism, Michael Herr's *Dispatches* (New York: Knopf, 1977) or Frances Fitzgerald's *Fire in the Lake* (New York: Little Brown and Company, 1972). Tim O'Brien's cycle of Vietnam War writings include, most notably, a memoir, *If I Die in a Combat Zone* (New York: Delacorte, 1973), and novels such as *Going After Cacciato* (New York: Delacorte/Seymour Lawrence, 1978), *The Things They Carried* (New York: Houghton Mifflin/Seymour Lawrence, 1990), and *In the Lake of the Woods* (Houghton Mifflin/Seymour Lawrence, 1994). He is surely the fictional laureate of the war. Poems cited by Robert Bly, Denise Levertov, and Galway Kinnell were included in a ground breaking anthology by Walter Lowenfels, *Where is Vietnam?* (Garden City, NJ: Doubleday/Anchor, 1967). I make reference to the Bernd Greiner text *War without Fronts* (New York: Random House, 2010), Debra Nelson's *The War Behind Me* (New York: Basic Books, 2008), and Nick Turses's *Kill Anything That Moves* (New York: Picador, 2013). Larry Heinemann, author of *Close Quarters*, cited in the text (New York: Farrar, Straus and Giroux, 1974), followed that powerful novel of combat with another, *Paco's Story* (New York: Farrar, Straus and Giroux), which won the 1986 National Book Award. W. D. Ehrhart, author of "Making the Children Behave," is the dean of American soldier-poets of the Vietnam War, an advocate of early writers, and arguably the single person responsible for the emergence of the literature of the war.

Conclusion: The Forever Wars

Joe Haldeman's *War Year* (New York: Holt, Rinehart and Winston, 1972) and *The Forever War* (New York: St. Martin's, 1974), have both become cult classics among literature on the Vietnam War. Dexter Filkins has acquired similar status as, in many people's opinions, the Michael Herr of the desert wars. Samuel Hynes's *The Soldier's Tale* (New York: Penguin, 1994) offers a study of war narrative by combatants, and Herbert Read provides his insights on war in a memoir of his experiences as an infantry officer on the Western Front, *The Contrary Experience* (London: Haskell House, 1946).

Index